CICERO'S *Catilinarians*

T0355267

OXFORD APPROACHES TO

CLASSICAL LITERATURE

SERIES EDITORS
Kathleen Coleman and Richard Rutherford

OVID's *Metamorphoses*
ELAINE FANTHAM

PLATO's *Symposium*
RICHARD HUNTER

CAESAR's *Civil War*
WILLIAM W. BATSTONE
CYNTHIA DAMON

POLYBIUS' *Histories*
BRIAN C. MCGING

TACITUS' *Annals*
RONALD MELLOR

XENOPHON's *Anabasis, OR The Expedition of Cyrus*
MICHAEL A. FLOWER

ARISTOPHANES' *Frogs*
MARK GRIFFITH

CICERO's *Catilinarians*
D. H. BERRY

CICERO'S
Catilinarians

D. H. BERRY

OXFORD
UNIVERSITY PRESS

OXFORD
UNIVERSITY PRESS

Oxford University Press is a department of the University of Oxford. It furthers
the University's objective of excellence in research, scholarship, and education
by publishing worldwide. Oxford is a registered trade mark of Oxford University
Press in the UK and certain other countries.

Published in the United States of America by Oxford University Press
198 Madison Avenue, New York, NY 10016, United States of America.

Library of Congress Cataloging-in-Publication Data
Names: Berry, D. H., author.
Title: Cicero's Catilinarians / D. H. Berry.
Other titles: Oxford approaches to classical literature.
Description: New York, NY, United States of America : Oxford University Press, 2020. |
Series: Oxford approaches to classical literature |
Includes bibliographical references and index. | In English; some text in
Latin with English translation.
Identifiers: LCCN 2019048911 (print) | LCCN 2019048912 (ebook) |
ISBN 9780195326468 (hardback) | ISBN 9780195326475 (paperback) |
ISBN 9780197510827 (epub) | ISBN 9780197510834
Subjects: LCSH: Cicero, Marcus Tullius. In Catilinam. | Catiline,
approximately 108 B.C.-62 B.C.—In literature. |
Cicero, Marcus Tullius—Influence. | Speeches, addresses, etc.,
Latin—History and criticism. | Literature and history—Rome. |
Rome—History—Conspiracy of Catiline, 65-62 B.C.
Classification: LCC PA6279.C5 B47 2020 (print) | LCC PA6279.C5 (ebook) |
DDC 875/.01—dc23
LC record available at https://lccn.loc.gov/2019048911
LC ebook record available at https://lccn.loc.gov/2019048912

1 3 5 7 9 8 6 4 2

Paperback printed by LSC Communications, United States of America
Hardback printed by Bridgeport National Bindery, Inc., United States of America

Contents

List of Figures   *vii*

Editors' Foreword   *ix*

Preface   *xiii*

Preliminary Note   *xvii*

Introduction   *xix*

1
The Patrician and the New Man   *1*

2
What Are the *Catilinarians*?   *56*

3
Denouncing the Living/Dead Catiline:
The *First Catilinarian*   *83*

4
Persuading the People: The *Second* and *Third Catilinarians*   *117*

5

Pro Cicerone: The *Fourth Catilinarian*   164

6

Catiline in the Underworld and Afterwards   *194*

APPENDIX 1. A Catilinarian Chronology, 108–57 BC   *225*

APPENDIX 2. Catiline's Surviving Words   *232*

APPENDIX 3. Two Bowls Inscribed with the Names of Catiline and Cato   *240*

Maps   *246*

Bibliography   *249*

Index   *267*

List of Figures

1.1 Bowl with inscription recording the endorsement by Lucius Cassius Longinus of Catiline's candidature for the consulship. Museo Nazionale Romano alle Terme di Diocleziano, Inv. 441423. Photographer: Géza Alföldy. Photo courtesy of the Corpus Inscriptionum Latinarum, Berlin: Foto-Archiv CIL, Inv.-Nr. PH0007670. By permission of the Soprintendenza Speciale per i Beni Archeologici di Roma.   22

1.2 Drawing of the inscription inside the Catiline bowl (Fig. 1.1). Artist: Silvio Panciera. Photo courtesy of the Corpus Inscriptionum Latinarum, Berlin: Foto-Archiv CIL, Inv.-Nr. PH0007672.   22

1.3 Bowl with inscription announcing Cato's candidature for the tribunate of the plebs. Museo Nazionale Romano alle Terme di Diocleziano, Inv. 441422. Photographer: Géza Alföldy. Photo courtesy of the Corpus Inscriptionum Latinarum, Berlin: Foto-Archiv CIL, Inv.-Nr. PH0007677. By permission of the Soprintendenza Speciale per i Beni Archeologici di Roma.   24

1.4 Drawing of the inscription inside the Cato bowl (Fig. 1.3). Artist: Silvio Panciera. Photo courtesy of the Corpus Inscriptionum Latinarum, Berlin: Foto-Archiv CIL, Inv.-Nr. PH0007678.   24

1.5 Silver denarius of Scribonius Libo commemorating the defeat of Catiline, 62 BC. Crawford 1974: 1.441–2 (no. 416/1c). ANS 1950.103.47. Photo courtesy of the American Numismatic Society.   53

1.6 Silver denarius of Lucius Aemilius Paullus commemorating the defeat of Catiline, 62 BC. Crawford 1974: 1.441 (no. 415/1). ANS 1896.7.90. Photo courtesy of the American Numismatic Society.   54

2.1 Bronze statuette of a grammarian teaching Cicero's *First Catilinarian*, from Fendeille. Owner unknown. Photographer: Michel Passelac. Photo courtesy of Michel Passelac.   64

2.2 Drawing of the inscription on the base of the statuette from Fendeille (Fig. 2.1). Artist: Michel Passelac. Photo courtesy of Michel Passelac.   65

6.1 William Caslon, specimen sheet of typefaces. From E. Chambers, *Cyclopaedia: Or, an Universal Dictionary of Arts and Sciences*, 2nd ed. (London, 1738). Photo: Wikimedia Commons.   214

Editors' Foreword

The late twentieth and early twenty-first centuries have seen a massive expansion in courses dealing with ancient civilization and the culture and literature of the Greek and Roman world. Never has there been such a flood of good translations available: Oxford's own World Classics, the Penguin Classics, the Hackett Library, and other series offer the English-speaking reader access to the masterpieces of classical literature from Homer to Augustine. The reader may, however, need more guidance in the interpretation and understanding of these works than can usually be provided in the relatively short introduction that prefaces a work in translation. There is a need for studies of individual works that will provide a clear, lively, and reliable account based on the most up-to-date scholarship without dwelling on the minutiae that are likely to distract or confuse the reader.

It is to meet this need that the present series has been devised. The title *Oxford Approaches to Classical Literature* deliberately puts the emphasis on the literary works themselves. The volumes in this series will each be concerned with a single work (apart from cases where a "book" or larger collection of poems is treated as one work). These are neither biographies nor accounts of literary movements or schools. Nor are they books devoted to the total oeuvre of one author: our first volumes consider Ovid's

Metamorphoses and Plato's *Symposium*, not the works of Ovid or Plato as a whole. This is, however, a question of emphasis, and not a straitjacket: biographical issues, literary and cultural background, and related works by the same author are discussed where they are obviously relevant. Series authors have also been encouraged to consider the influence and legacy of the works in question. As the editors of this series, we intend these volumes to be accessible to the reader who is encountering the relevant work for the first time; but we also intend that each volume should do more than simply provide the basic facts, dates, and summaries that handbooks generally supply. We would like these books to be essays in criticism and interpretation that will do justice to the subtlety and complexity of the works under discussion. With this in mind, we have invited leading scholars to offer personal assessments and appreciations of their chosen works, anchored within the mainstream of classical scholarship. We have thought it particularly important that our authors be allowed to set their own agendas and to speak in their own voices rather than repeating the *idées reçues* of conventional wisdom in neutral tones.

The title *Oxford Approaches to Classical Literature* has been chosen simply because the series is published by Oxford University Press, USA; it in no way implies a party line, either Oxonian or any other. We believe that different approaches are suited to different texts, and we expect each volume to have its own distinctive character. Advanced critical theory is neither compulsory nor excluded; what matters is whether it can be made to illuminate the text in question. The authors have been encouraged to avoid obscurity and jargon, bearing in mind the needs of the general reader; but, when important critical or narratological issues arise, they are presented to the reader as lucidly as possible.

This series was originally conceived by Professor Charles Segal, an inspiring scholar and teacher whose intellectual energy and range of interests were matched by a humility and generosity of spirit. Although he was involved in the commissioning of a number of volumes, he did not—alas—live to see any of them published. The series is intended to convey something of the excitement and pleasure to be derived from reading the extraordinarily rich and varied literature of Greco-Roman antiquity. We hope that these volumes will form a worthy monument to a dedicated classical scholar who was committed to enabling the ancient texts to speak to the widest possible audience in the contemporary world.

Kathleen Coleman, Harvard University
Richard Rutherford, Christ Church, Oxford

Preface

The aim of this book is to give readers of Cicero's *Catilinarians* an account of what I think it is that they are reading (chapter 2) and how I think it should be understood (chapters 3–5). Further chapters provide the historical context (chapter 1) and an outline of how other readers have made use of the figure and story of Catiline in their own creative work (chapter 6). The historical chapter takes into account two pieces of potential epigraphic evidence, discovered in 1969 and published in 1980, which have never been cited before in any publication on Cicero or Catiline (see pp. 20–25 and Appendix 3), and also little-known numismatic evidence, three series of coins from 62 BC commemorating the defeat of Catiline (see pp. 52–54). The core of the book (chapters 2–5) expounds my own personal approach (in fact two approaches, designated A and B) to the *Catilinarians*, an approach elucidated through a comparison of the *Catilinarians* with the *Private Diaries* of Piers Morgan, published in 2005 (see pp. 83–87). This approach is the only one, I believe, that fully takes into account what the *Catilinarians* are and the different audiences to which they are addressed. The book includes an attempt to identify the specific individuals who prompted Cicero to publish the speeches of his consulship (pp. 100–103) and also contains a discussion of his epic *Consulatus suus*, in which the poem's most famous fragment, *o fortunatam natam me consule Romam*, is reassigned to a new context (see pp. 158–162). An appendix provides the first complete collection of the surviving words of Catiline (Appendix 2). To my knowledge, this is the first book-length discussion of the *Catilinarians* in any language.

The book has been long in the writing, having been researched and written only during those short and widely separated periods when I have been free from other academic duties. I hesitate to admit the length of time that passed between the signing of the contract and the submission of the completed typescript, but it was the same as that from Cicero's election to the quaestorship to his election to the consulship. During all these years, the series editors, Kathleen Coleman and Richard Rutherford, have been unfailingly kind and supportive, never showing frustration at my snail-like progress and always providing me with much-needed encouragement, together with valuable feedback on the chapters as I wrote them. They also gave help with practical matters, particularly with obtaining the illustrations. I am more grateful to them than I can say.

I have many other debts to record. My good friend John Ramsey read chapter 1, the appendices, and about a dozen drafts of my paragraphs on the Catiline and Cato bowls and improved them considerably. He also advised me on a number of points in Sallust and shared with me his views, which are about to be published, on the date of the consular elections in 63 BC. Gavin Kelly read the first five chapters in draft, made useful suggestions, and drew my attention to the Torre di Catilina in Pistoia. Andreas Fassbender of the Corpus Inscriptionum Latinarum kindly provided me with photographs of the Catiline and Cato bowls and drawings of the inscriptions on them. Michel Passelac, with great generosity, provided me with a photograph of the Fendeille bronze that he had taken in the 1960s (he is, as far as is known, the only person to have photographed this important antiquity in the brief period between its discovery and its sale and disappearance), and he also redrew the inscription on it especially for this book. Scott Walker made the maps and, in Map 1, used the resources of Digital Augustan Rome for the surface topography. Stephen Milner drew my attention to the literature on Catiline from medieval and Renaissance Florence, and Roland Mayer to William Caslon's quotations from the *First Catilinarian* on his specimen sheet of typefaces. My former pupil William Norman educated me on Ibsen. Virginia Campbell, Christina Kuhn, Alison Rosenblitt, and Cristina Rosillo-López provided bibliographic help. Margot Krebs Neale and Giacomo Peru kindly helped me with foreign correspondence. To all these colleagues and friends I offer my heartfelt thanks. This book is much the better for their contributions.

Preliminary Note

Cicero's *Catilinarians* are quoted from the Teubner text of Tadeusz Maslowski (Maslowski 2003). This is an important edition because it is the first to incorporate substantial papyrus evidence dating from the fourth to fifth centuries AD, more than four hundred years before the earliest medieval manuscript of the speeches. However, two further papyri, not included by Maslowski, have since been identified and edited by Dario Internullo (Internullo 2011–12 and 2016). Maslowski's edition is also valuable for its listing of all the ancient quotations from the speeches. Translations of the *Catilinarians* are taken from my Oxford World's Classics edition, *Cicero: Political Speeches* (Berry 2006), with occasional departures where I have had second thoughts. Translations of Sallust's *Bellum Catilinae* are taken from Woodman 2007, with modifications. Unless otherwise acknowledged, all other translations are my own. Abbreviations of ancient authors and their works mostly follow the conventions of the *Oxford Latin Dictionary* for Roman and the *Oxford Classical Dictionary* for Greek authors, except that *In Catilinam* is abbreviated as "*Cat.*". In references, "Cic." and "*Cat.*" are omitted wherever possible; thus "4.7," for example, denotes Cic. *Cat.* 4.7. References in any Cicero speech to, for example, "10a" or "10b" mean "the first part of § 10" or "the second part of § 10" respectively, where the second part is indicated in the text by the start of a new paragraph. References to Plutarch follow the numeration currently used in the Loeb editions.

Those wishing to read the *Catilinarians* and Sallust's *Bellum Catilinae* in translation are directed toward Berry 2006 in the former case and Woodman 2007, Batstone 2010b, or Rolfe 2013 (which is a revision by John T. Ramsey) in the latter. The standard commentary on the *Catilinarians* is Dyck 2008.

Introduction

In 63 BC, Rome's greatest and most influential prose author, the foremost orator of antiquity, and the creator of a model Latin prose style, Marcus Tullius Cicero, held the chief magistracy at Rome, the consulship. His year of office could easily have been an uneventful one; after all, nothing too exciting happened to disturb either the consulship of Lucius Julius Caesar and Gaius Marcius Figulus (64 BC) or that of Decimus Junius Silanus and Lucius Licinius Murena (62 BC). But as good luck would have it, 63 BC provided the raw material for great literature, in the form of the Catilinarian conspiracy, an armed rising that it fell to Cicero to suppress. And—doubly fortunate—the consul's actions in suppressing it proved deeply controversial and required sustained retrospective justification. The result was a set of four speeches, published in 60 BC, called *In Catilinam* ("Against Catiline"). From then till now, the *Catilinarians*, as they are known in English, have been among Cicero's most read and most admired orations, their opening words *Quo usque tandem . . . ?* ("How far, I ask you . . . ?"), together with, ten lines further in, *o tempora, o mores!* (translated by the playwright Ben Jonson as "O age and manners!"; more loosely, "What a decadent age we live in!"), being the best known quotations from Cicero's voluminous works and among the most familiar Latin tags. As one of the characters in Tacitus' *Dialogus de oratoribus* is made to declare a century and a half later, "Cicero is not a great orator

Cicero's Catilinarians. D. H. Berry, Oxford University Press (2020). © Oxford University Press.
DOI: 10.1093/oso/9780195326468.001.0001

because he defended Publius Quinctius or Licinius Archias; it was Catiline and Milo and Verres and Antony who covered him with this glory" (*Dial.* 37.6).

The Catilinarian conspiracy was an attempted coup d'état, a plot against the state, an act of high treason. Something terrifying and evil, which threatened the existence and even the name of Rome—that was how Cicero presented it. "A plot has been formed to ensure that, following a universal massacre, there should not be a single person left even to mourn the name of the Roman people or to lament the destruction of so great an empire" (*Cat.* 4.4; cf. 4.7, 12). The villain who conceived this plot was Lucius Sergius Catilina ("Catiline"), a blue-blooded patrician (unlike Cicero) and a man with a correspondingly high opinion of himself (Cicero too had a high opinion of himself). Catiline had stood against Cicero in the election for the consulship of 63 and lost. After losing again for 62, he turned to violence, together with a little band of electorally unsuccessful and bankrupt politicians at Rome, and a large number of impoverished Italian farmers, men who were unlucky in many respects, but not least in their notion that Catiline could improve their lot. Pitched against Cicero, whose oratorical brilliance was matched by an extraordinary ability to gather information and to use it effectively, he had no chance of success. First, he attempted to assassinate Cicero, and failed. Cicero denounced him before the senate in a speech later published as the *First Catilinarian*, and then allowed him to leave Rome, justifying himself before the people in a speech later published as the *Second Catilinarian*. While Catiline built up an army in Etruria, Cicero tricked the conspirators in the city into writing letters incriminating themselves and then had four of the men arrested. The letters were opened and read out in the senate, and the conspirators, in each case, either admitted their guilt or failed to deny it. Cicero reported these events to the people in a speech later published as the *Third Catilinarian*. Two days later he held a debate in the senate, making comments himself that were later included in a speech published as the *Fourth Catilinarian*. The senate voted that the arrested men (there were five of them by this time) be put to death, and accordingly Cicero, on his own authority as consul, had them immediately executed by strangulation. These executions were illegal, since the men were Roman citizens and were therefore entitled to a trial (the senate was not at this date a court of law). But the executions had the desired effect. No outbreak occurred within the city, and when the news of the executions reached Etruria, most of Catiline's army (seven thousand men out of ten thousand) melted away. The remainder, including Catiline himself, were defeated and killed at the start of 62 by Cicero's fellow consul, Gaius Antonius Hybrida.

Cicero was wildly popular for having prevented a civil war from breaking out within the city. But two tribunes of the plebs repeatedly attacked his violation of the law. His position was vulnerable, and would continue to be so indefinitely. In 60, he took steps to defend his reputation by publishing accounts of his consulship in Greek prose and Latin verse, along with a collection of twelve political speeches that he had made as consul. Eight of these speeches survive, including the four *Catilinarians*, which are the subject of this book. In 58, his enemy Publius Clodius Pulcher used his execution of the conspirators as a means of bringing about his exile. Cicero was able to secure his recall the following year. But he never recovered from the blow to his pride at having been exiled, as he saw it, for saving Rome.

Around 42 BC, the historian Sallust wrote a monograph on the Catilinarian conspiracy. By that time, Cicero was dead, as were Caesar and Cato, the two men who had made the most influential speeches in the debate on the punishment of the conspirators (Caesar had argued against execution, Cato for). Sallust's *Bellum Catilinae* ("The war against Catiline") is, together with Cicero's speeches, the most important source for the conspiracy. Other Cicero speeches that deal with it include *Pro Murena* (63), *Pro Sulla* (62), and *Pro Caelio* (56): Murena was the consul of 62 who would have had to take on Catiline if he had not already been defeated by Antonius, Sulla was an alleged Catilinarian conspirator, and Caelius had been a friend of Catiline's before he began his conspiracy. So rich are these various sources—the speeches of the man who personally exposed and crushed the conspiracy and the monograph of the historian who recorded and analyzed it two decades later—that the Catilinarian conspiracy is now the most fully attested single event in Roman history (at least until late antiquity). Sallust's account complements rather than duplicates Cicero's evidence, providing much information about which Cicero is silent, such as on his detection and entrapment of the conspirators (cf. Sal. *Cat.* 41.5, 44.1, and 45.1 with Cic. *Cat.* 3.4). Sallust's grasp of chronology is surprisingly poor, but the chronology is clear enough from Cicero. Instead, Sallust's main concern is with character. While the *Catilinarians* present Catiline in almost unremittingly negative terms (only at 3.16–17, a passage clearly written after Catiline's death, does the tone change), Sallust gives his readers a more nuanced portrait, allowing Catiline sufficient redeeming features to explain how it was that he was able to attract a following—something that Cicero does not explain, except by painting the other conspirators in the same lurid colors in which he paints Catiline himself. Sallust also provides his own versions of the speeches of Caesar and Cato, in order to throw light on the characters of the men who would go on to lead the opposing sides in the civil war of the 40s. He does not provide versions of Cicero's speeches, since Cicero had already published his own versions, and those would have been thoroughly familiar to his readership (they were also in a style out of keeping with that employed by Sallust). In fact, only one of Cicero's speeches is alluded to in Sallust's account, the *First Catilinarian* (although Sallust does not give it that title). But any notion that Sallust was hostile to Cicero is dispelled by his remark that the *First Catilinarian* was "brilliant, and of service to the state" (*luculentam atque utilem rei publicae, Cat.* 31.6). Sallust gives the consul his due, calling him at one point "the best of consuls" (*optumo consuli, Cat.* 43.1), but avoids making him the primary focus of his work.[1] The reason for this is that Cicero was irrelevant to Sallust's central theme of moral decline: he was obviously not an example of moral decline himself, but neither did he possess, in Sallust's view,

---

[1] Broughton 1936 provides a detailed refutation of the view that Sallust was hostile to Cicero and makes the interesting suggestion that he was cautious in his depiction of him because he was writing under the second triumvirate. See also Syme 1964: 105–11.

the "enormous prowess" (*ingenti virtute, Cat.* 53.6) of Caesar or Cato. Sallust was not interested in contrasting the aristocratic conspirators who sought to attack Rome with the equestrian incomer who protected and saved it: that was a theme of a different moralist one and a half centuries later, the satirist Juvenal (8.231–44).

Cicero would like posterity to believe that his suppression of the Catilinarian conspiracy was the most important event in Roman history, since by it Rome was saved from total destruction. In other words, he would like his oratorical exaggerations to be accepted at face value. In reality, the conspiracy was a genuine emergency that did result in substantial loss of life: three thousand men died with Catiline, and there were casualties on the government side too. It affected many regions of Italy, not just Etruria, and attracted the support of many people of different classes and backgrounds: debtors, bankrupts, failed politicians, former supporters of Marius who had been dispossessed by the dictator Sulla, and former soldiers of Sulla who had been rewarded with land but had run into financial difficulty. It was, therefore, an event of some significance. Militarily, however, Catiline was never a serious threat to Rome. He did not manage to raise the force he needed, and only about a quarter of his men were properly equipped, many of the others being armed only with sharpened sticks (Sal. *Cat.* 56.3). His army in Etruria was trapped and then annihilated by the government forces. As for the conspirators in the city, they could have done considerable damage by starting fires, but it was never their intention to do this until such time as Catiline was at hand with his army. Once that army had been defeated by Antonius, the remaining conspirators at Rome— the ones who had not been executed—thought only of avoiding detection and capture. Even if by some miracle Catiline's little army had won a victory, it would have been only temporary (the point is made in different ways by both Cicero, *Cat.* 2.19, and Sallust, *Cat.* 39.4). Pompey was on the point of bringing his legions home from the east, where they had recently won a long and hard-fought war against Mithradates VI Eupator, the king of Pontus. The conspirators intended to counter this threat to their scheme by kidnapping Pompey's children and using them as hostages (Plut. *Cic.* 18.1). The fact that the conspiracy's chances of success depended entirely on the conspirators' ability to kidnap Pompey's children and so coerce the great conqueror into meeting their demands shows just what a reckless and foolhardy project the conspiracy was. It was a project that was doomed from the start.

The Catilinarian conspiracy, then, did not pose the danger to the state that Cicero claimed it did, and it would therefore be a misjudgment to treat it as one of the most important events—and still less, as Cicero represents it, the defining event—of the late republic. It was, without doubt, an event of huge significance for Cicero: it led, five years later, to his exile and colored his view of Roman politics for the rest of his life (in his speeches he repeatedly compares his later enemies Clodius and then Mark Antony to Catiline). It also gave him a greatly enhanced standing in the senate: in the coming years, he expected to be asked for his opinion before the other senators were asked for theirs (Cic. *Att.* 1.13.2). But as an event in Roman history the conspiracy ranks merely as an unsuccessful rising, alongside the risings of Lepidus (78–77 BC) and Sertorius (76–72 BC) in the previous decade—both of them, significantly, put down by Pompey.

The importance of the conspiracy in literature, on the other hand, is considerable. Unlike the risings of Lepidus and Sertorius, it happened to be suppressed by one of Rome's greatest writers, a man who felt impelled to record and justify what he had done. In the *Catilinarians*, Cicero produced his own authoritative verdict on the conspiracy and its members, delivered with overwhelming rhetorical force. The speeches were clearly intended to become classics, and it is likely that they did so quickly. About eighteen years after their publication, Sallust penned his own classic account of the conspiracy, the *Bellum Catilinae*. The conspiracy thus provided the material for Cicero's speeches and for Sallust's monograph, literary works that bestowed on it an unwarranted celebrity. It was, in truth, a minor event in history, and an event without long-term repercussions. But in the literature of the late republic it makes an impression as great as, or greater than, Pompey's victory against

Mithradates, Caesar's conquest of Gaul, or the Civil War, events that changed the course of world history.

The reason why the Catilinarian conspiracy makes such an impression is in part because of the atmosphere of crisis, danger, crime, and immorality that both Cicero and Sallust convey. But what gives the *Catilinarians* and the *Bellum Catilinae* their particular fascination is, above all, the character of Catiline himself. Cicero's Catiline is an extraordinary and compelling literary creation. Through his speeches, Cicero was not content to destroy his adversary; he also wanted to damn his memory for ever. He succeeded to an extent that might have surprised him. Forty-one years after the publication of the *Catilinarians*, Virgil's *Aeneid*, Rome's national epic, was revealed to the world. Catiline appears twice in that poem, as a character from Roman history embodying supreme wickedness (*Aen.* 6.623, 8.668–69). In the second passage, he is contrasted with Cato, the man who persuaded the senate to vote for the illegal execution of the conspirators. Virgil pointedly depicts Cato dispensing justice to the virtuous: Cato's actions, and by implication those of Cicero, are endorsed, and Catiline's condemned. But, surprisingly perhaps, Cicero's voice has not entirely drowned out that of Catiline (see Appendix 2). In chapter 1, the historical Catiline will now be recovered, so far as is possible.

CICERO'S *Catilinarians*

· 1 ·

The Patrician and the New Man

What ancestry more exalted than yours, Catiline, or that of
Cethegus can be found? Yet you plotted to attack homes and
temples at night and set them on fire, like the sons of trousered
Gauls and descendants of the Senones, committing an outrage
which could lawfully be punished by the "uncomfortable shirt."[1]
But the consul is alert: he halts your banners. He—a "new man"
from Arpinum, of humble origin, a municipal equestrian new to
Rome—posts helmeted troops all around to protect the terrified
people, and is busy on every hill. So, without stepping outside
the walls, his peacetime toga brought him as much titled distinction as Octavius grabbed for himself at Leucas and on the fields
of Thessaly with his sword wet from ceaseless slaughter—though
Rome was still free when she called Cicero the parent and father
of his country.

Juvenal 8.231–44, tr. Susanna Morton Braund, with modifications

The personalities of the late republic came in pairs. Marius and Sulla.
Clodius and Milo. Pompey and Caesar. Antony and Octavian.
And, of course, Cicero and Catiline. In the case of the first, third, and
fourth of these pairs, each politician wanted to obtain a dominating position in Roman politics without a rival, and because there was a rival,
civil war ensued. Clodius and Milo were locked in a violent political
struggle that persisted for a number of years and ended only when one
of them murdered the other. But Cicero and Catiline are different. It
was not inevitable that they should become enemies, and they initially

---

[1] The *tunica molesta*, a shirt coated in pitch in which criminals convicted of arson were
burned alive.

Cicero's Catilinarians. D. H. Berry, Oxford University Press (2020). © Oxford University Press.
DOI: 10.1093/oso/9780195326468.001.0001

fell out only because they both happened to be competing for the consulship in the same year. And Catiline did not start his conspiracy because he was defeated by Cicero in the elections for 63 BC; he started it because he was defeated by Decimus Junius Silanus and Lucius Licinius Murena in the elections for 62. If he had been successful in that election, there would have been no reason for him and Cicero to maintain their opposition to each other. After all, neither aimed, as Caesar did, at dominating the state in perpetuity.

Nevertheless, posterity has tended to view Cicero and Catiline as polar opposites, almost as irreconcilable forces of nature. Over the centuries, Cicero has typically been seen as the *novus homo*, or "new man" (the first of a family to enter the senate), who saved Rome and was hailed as the "parent" and "father of his country" (*parens patriae, pater patriae*), while Catiline has been seen, by contrast, as the patrician who sought to destroy Rome and, with it, the Roman empire (the passage from Juvenal quoted at the beginning of this chapter encapsulates this polarity). Catiline has also gone down in history as a model of every kind of vice and criminality. This is how, in 1878, Edward Spencer Beesly described the prevailing image of him:[2]

> Of all the characters in history Catiline has been painted blackest. He is to the historians what Judas Iscariot is to the divines. The name itself has a wicked sound to us. The very syllables of it seem to connote a monstrous depravity. We cannot hear it but there rings in our ears a confused hurtle of *incendia, caedes, latrocinium, audacia, furor, scelus, parricida, sicarius* [arson, slaughter, banditry, violence, frenzy, crime, parricide, cutthroat], and other choice missiles from the Ciceronian armoury. We think of him not as a man, but as a demon breathing murder, rapine, and conflagration, with bloodshot eyes and pallid face, luring on weak and depraved young men to the damnation prepared for himself; a horrid portent rising from below, without visible cause or warning, like some earthquake or volcano, to scorch the fair face of civilisation and convert order into chaos.

---

[2] Beesly 1878: 3. On Beesly, see Wiseman 1998.

That characterization, and the persistence of it, is the achievement of the *Catilinarians*. Cicero's four speeches succeeded totally in determining the common perception of Catiline for the next two millennia. It was a perception that Beesly set out to counteract. He too saw Cicero and Catiline as polar opposites, but with Catiline as the better man:[3]

> Catiline and Cicero were not merely political opponents. The natures of the two men were thoroughly antipathetic. Cicero thought that society existed for the glory of clever writers and eloquent speakers. . . . Catiline, on the contrary, was the man of action, who would rather see a thing done than hear it talked about.

However, Beesly's attempt to rewrite history in Catiline's favor proved unsuccessful, because the evidence did not support his case.[4] Cicero, the victor, had ensured that it would be his presentation that would shape the historical record. The posthumous reputation of Catiline shows that "it is not good to make a literary man your enemy."[5]

There exist three character sketches of Catiline from the end of the republic, two by Cicero and one by the historian Sallust. The first is at Cicero, *In Catilinam* 3.16–17:

> When I was driving him [Catiline] out of the city, I foresaw, citizens, that once he was out of the way I would have nothing to fear from the lazy Publius Lentulus, or the obese

---

[3] Beesly 1878: 35.

[4] For more recent defenses of Catiline, see Waters 1970 and Seager 1973, answered by E. J. Phillips 1976. For book-length defenses, see Kaplan 1968 (Catiline as a precursor of Caesar); Fini 1996 (Catiline as the opponent of senatorial corruption); Galassi 2014 (too full of errors to make an effective case).

[5] Beesly 1878: 35. See also Syme's remarks on the period, in his famous chapter on political catchwords (1939: 149): "Crime, vice and corruption in the last age of the Republic are embodied in types as perfect of their kind as are the civic and moral paragons of early days; which is fitting, for the evil and the good are both the fabrication of skilled literary artists. Catilina is the perfect monster—murder and debauchery of every degree."

Lucius Cassius, or the reckless, insane Gaius Cethegus. Out of all of them, he was the only one to be afraid of—and only for so long as he remained inside the city walls. He knew everything; he could get through to anybody. He had the ability and the nerve to accost anyone, to sound them out, to push them to revolt. His mind was predisposed to crime—and in whatever direction his mind went, his tongue and hand would be sure to follow. He had particular people selected and assigned for particular tasks. But when he delegated something, he did not suppose it already done: there was nothing that he did not personally attend to, take in hand, watch over, toil over. He could endure cold, thirst, hunger. He was so keen, so bold, so well prepared, so clever, so vigilant in committing crime, and so thorough in depravity that if I had not succeeded in driving him away from his plots inside the city and towards armed rebellion— I give you my real opinion, citizens—then it would have been no easy task for me to remove so great an evil from over your heads.

In this brief portrait, Cicero presents Catiline as a man who is above all else supremely qualified to initiate a coup d'état. In the first place, he is a bad man, someone whose mind is predisposed to crime and who is prepared to act on that predisposition. Secondly, in marked contrast to his leading supporters, who lack his qualities, he is dangerous: he has the ability to make contact with any person he chooses and persuade them to follow him. There is a hint here of Catiline's social position: doors that are closed to others are open to him ("he could get through to anybody"). Thirdly, he is able to delegate, but he knows that his followers, being less able than he is, need close supervision; this attentiveness is a quality of a good general.[6] Next, he has outstanding powers of physical endurance; again, he resembles a good general. Finally, he is keen, bold, well

---

[6] Cf. Cic. *Phil.* 4.15, where Cicero contrasts Catiline's diligence (*industria*), in a military context, with Antony's lack of it.

prepared, clever—but it is all in a bad cause. Catiline is a formidable general, but an enemy general, and someone whom the Roman people will underestimate at their peril.

What is most striking about this portrait is that it does not, like the rest of the *Catilinarians*, consist exclusively of denigration and abuse. Elsewhere in the four speeches, Cicero has nothing good to say about Catiline. Here, he attributes to him knowledge, influence, qualities of leadership, attentiveness, endurance, and intelligence. Courage is not mentioned explicitly, but it is perhaps implied in the references to "nerve," "keenness," and "boldness" (even though those terms are all used in a negative sense: an enemy general can still possess courage). Another striking feature of this portrait is that it is put in the past (imperfect) tense. Although Catiline was very much alive when Cicero delivered the *Third Catilinarian*, this passage reads as if it is Cicero's obituary of him.[7] While Catiline was alive, he was a target for Cicero's invective; once he was dead, there was no need of invective (Cicero had other enemies to abuse), and in the published version of his speech the orator could give a more balanced, more believable, and no doubt more truthful picture of his erstwhile foe—a foe who was by no means to be despised.

Cicero's second portrait of Catiline dates from 56, the year after his return from exile, and appears in *Pro Caelio*. Catiline had been dead for six years by this point, and Cicero found himself defending a client, Marcus Caelius Rufus, who was accused of having been a friend of the conspirator. Unable to deny the allegation outright, Cicero admits that Caelius was a friend of Catiline, but only during the election campaign of 63, that is, in the period immediately before Catiline started his conspiracy (he then uses arguments from probability to deny that Caelius became a conspirator). To explain this friendship, he presents a picture of Catiline that is far removed from the invective of the *Catilinarians*, but which instead develops the picture given in the "obituary." Catiline's good qualities are again described, and Cicero claims that these were qualities that

---

[7] Cf. Dyck 2008: 165 ("quasi-obituary"), 190 ("like an obituary").

caused other loyal and patriotic citizens, not merely Caelius, to give Catiline their support (*Cael.* 12–14):

> Yes, he did support Catiline, after he had spent a number of years in the forum, Caelius that is—just as many others did, from every class and of every age. For Catiline had, as I am sure you remember, a great many indications of the highest qualities—not fully developed, mind you, but sketched in outline. He mixed with numerous individuals of bad character; yet he pretended to be devoted to the best of men. He drove people, by numerous means, to depravity; yet he could also stimulate them to effort and hard work. The fires of passion burned within him; yet he was a keen student of military affairs. For my part I do not think the world has ever seen a creature made up of such contrary, divergent, and mutually incompatible interests and appetites.
>
> Who was more agreeable, at one particular time, to men of high rank, and who more intimate with scoundrels? Who at one time a more patriotic citizen, and who a more loathsome enemy of this country? Who more corrupt in his pleasures, and who more able to endure hard work? Who more avaricious in rapacity, and who more lavish in generosity? That man, gentlemen, had many features that were paradoxical. He had a wide circle of friends, and he looked after them well. What he had, he shared with everyone. He helped all his friends in times of need with money, influence, physical exertion, even, if necessary, with violence and crime. He could adapt and control the way he was to suit the occasion, and twist and turn his nature this way and that. He could be stern with the serious, relaxed with the free-and-easy, grave with the old, affable with the young, daring with criminals, and dissolute with the depraved. And so this complex, ever-changing character, even when he had collected all the wicked traitors from far and wide, still held many loyal, brave men in his grasp by a sort of pretended semblance of virtue. Indeed, that heinous attempt to destroy

this empire could never have come into being had not that monstrous concentration of so many vices been rooted in certain qualities of skill and endurance.

In this passage, Cicero does not retract the invective of the *Catilinarians*: as in those speeches, Catiline is still a bad man, bent on the destruction of the Roman empire (cf. *Cat.* 4.4, 7, 12). But what he does is to add more information to the picture. As in the "obituary," Catiline is a good motivator and a knowledgeable general, and he is well connected and sociable, and physically strong. But here the quality of generosity is added, and also, crucially, the ability to simulate virtue. It is this last quality that enables Cicero to explain how so many good men, including, he argues, his client Caelius, were taken in by Catiline. But, whether Catiline's virtue was real or simulated, the picture that emerges from the "obituary" and from *Pro Caelio* does convincingly explain the attraction he evidently had. Catiline was a man, as Cicero himself testifies, who made a powerful impact on his contemporaries; a man of considerable talent, energy, and charisma; and a man who felt confident and at ease when mixing with others at every level of society. It is not at all surprising that such a man should have considered himself deserving of the consulship, and should also have considered himself unjustly treated after that office had twice been denied to him.

There is nothing inherently unconvincing or incredible, incidentally, about Cicero's picture of a paradoxical personality. It need not be a mere rhetorical trick, designed to explain away Caelius' connection with Catiline. Such personalities do exist. Here, for example, is a character sketch of a politician from modern times, written by one of his closest associates three months after his death:

> His personality, to me at least, is a puzzle full of contradictions and opposites. . . . There were certainly a combination of great opposites in him. He could be kind and make his circle enthusiastic about himself; in spite of that, however, he was merciless and unjust. And that not only towards his political and ideological enemies, but also towards his immediate circle. He could be loyal and honest and yet was amoral

in his basic conceptions. He was extraordinarily generous to his artists and co-operators, tolerant towards their human weaknesses. . . . He was neither stable and balanced nor detached; on the contrary he was in constant inner agitation, and always ready to rush into decisions. On the other hand, important decisions would hang over his head for months without his being able to make up his mind, even if it was imperative that he should do so.

Such, in the words of Albert Speer, was Adolf Hitler.[8] As Juvenal predicted, "You may find a Catiline among any people, under any sky, but nowhere will there be a Brutus, or an uncle of Brutus" (Juv. 14.41–43).[9]

The third extant portrait of Catiline is that of Sallust (*Cat.* 5.1–8):

Lucius Catiline, born of a noble line, had great strength of both mind and body, but a wicked and crooked disposition. From adolescence internal wars, slaughter, seizures, and civil disharmony were welcome to him, and there he spent his young manhood. His body was tolerant of hunger, cold, and wakefulness beyond the point which anyone finds credible; his mind was daring, cunning, and versatile, capable of any simulation and dissimulation; acquisitive of another's property, prodigal with his own; burning in desires; his eloquence was adequate, scant his wisdom. His ravaged mind[10] always desired the unrestrained, the incredible, the heights beyond reach. After the dominion of Lucius Sulla, he had been assailed by his greatest urge, to capture the commonwealth; and he attached no weight to the methods by which he might achieve it, provided he acquired kingship for himself. His defiant spirit was exercised increasingly each day by his lack of private assets and a consciousness of his crimes,

---

8   Quoted from Overy 2001: 237–38.
9   Marcus Junius Brutus was the tyrannicide, the assassin of Caesar; his uncle Marcus Porcius Cato committed suicide rather than submit to Caesar's tyranny.
10 This translation of *vastus animus* is proposed and argued for by Krebs 2008.

both of which he had augmented by the qualities which I recalled above. He was incited, too, by the community's corrupt morals, which were afflicted by those worst and mutually different maladies, luxury and avarice.

In this passage, Sallust presents Catiline as a bad man, as Cicero does, and as a danger and a menace. The emphasis that Sallust places on Catiline's powers of physical endurance (the mark of a good general) and his daring and cunning echo the passage from the *Third Catilinarian* more than they do the one from *Pro Caelio*, but Sallust has clearly taken from *Pro Caelio* Catiline's generosity and his talent for simulation. Since Sallust (unlike Cicero) is concerned with the causes of the conspiracy, particular emphasis is placed on the financial aspect: Catiline seized property in times past, he is acquisitive of it, and yet he is also prodigal; but he has no assets left and is incited by the contemporary vices of luxury and avarice. In the passage from *Pro Caelio*, Cicero presents Catiline's character as paradoxical. Sallust does not take up that idea, although he does follow *Pro Caelio* in calling Catiline *varius* ("versatile," "ever-changing")[11] and in describing him as acquisitive and yet prodigal. What Sallust adds to Cicero's characterization is Catiline's desire for kingship (*regnum*). That is an allegation not found in Cicero: Cicero attributes a desire for kingship to Catiline's associate Publius Cornelius Lentulus Sura (3.9, 4.12) and, loosely, to some of Catiline's other followers (2.19), but never to Catiline himself. It is safe to infer from this that, in Cicero's eyes, all Catiline wanted was the consulship. It is instructive to see, in this instance, the historian exaggerating and the orator refraining from doing so.[12]

Sallust states that Catiline was "born of a noble line."[13] Catiline was a patrician; that is, he belonged to one of a select group of Roman clans (*gentes*) dating back to the regal period, in his case the

---

[11] Plutarch (*Cic.* 10.2) describes Catiline's character as *poikilos*, which means the same as *varius*.

[12] For an extended discussion of Sallust's portrayal of Catiline throughout the *Bellum Catilinae*, see Wilkins 1994. Appian also claims that Catiline aimed at tyranny (*B. Civ.* 2.2). On the figure of the tyrant in Roman historiography, see Dunkle 1971–72.

[13] The historical account given in the rest of this chapter supersedes Berry 2006: 134–56.

gens Sergia (Sergian clan). By the first century BC, most members of the Roman nobility were plebeians (non-patricians); some plebeians, such as the Caecilii Metelli, were very grand indeed, and although patrician birth placed Catiline in the highest social rank, it did not lead automatically to high office. Discrimination against patricians was enshrined in law: since 367 BC it had been illegal for two patricians to hold the consulship together, although there was no bar preventing two plebeians from doing so. Patricians were also ineligible for the offices of tribune of the plebs—necessitating adoption into a plebeian family for those patricians such as Publius Clodius Pulcher and Publius Cornelius Dolabella who desired the tribunate—and plebeian aedile. But one advantage that patricians may have enjoyed (although the evidence for it is slender) was the right to hold senior magistracies two years earlier than plebeians.[14] If so, then Catiline, whose year of birth is not attested, would have been born in the same year as Cicero, 106 BC, since he and Cicero held the praetorship in 68 and 66, respectively. But if patricians did not enjoy this advantage, then Catiline would have been born two years before Cicero, in 108.

The patrician Sergii claimed descent from Sergestus, the Trojan hero and follower of Aeneas ("Sergestus, from whom the Sergian house has its name," Virg. *Aen.* 5.121).[15] Despite this impressive, if fictitious, lineage, and despite his patrician ancestry, the name of no consular ancestor of Catiline is recorded; presumably there was such an ancestor, in view of Sallust's comment about his noble line. Catiline did have a famous forebear, however, in his great-grandfather, Marcus Sergius Silus, praetor in 197 BC, whose exploits and relationship to Catiline are attested by Pliny the Elder (*Nat.* 7.104–6). Silus was a great fighter during the period of the Second Punic War. In two campaigns he was wounded twenty-three times and permanently disabled in both hands and both feet. Despite this,

---

[14] For Badian's theory of a two-year advantage for patricians in the minimum ages required for senior magistracies, see Badian 1959.

[15] On the fashion in the late republic for legendary ancestors, see Wiseman 1974, with mention of Sergestus at 154.

he continued to perform military service, later suffering the loss of his right hand. After having an iron prosthesis fitted, he took up fighting once more, with considerable success, taking twenty enemy camps in Gaul. Two of his horses were killed under him. He was captured twice by Hannibal and kept permanently shackled, but both times he escaped and returned to the fighting. Pliny remarks that "others have conquered men, but Sergius conquered fortune too" (*Nat.* 7.106). His verdict is that "no one could justly rate any man above Marcus Sergius, even though his great-grandson Catiline detracts from the honor of his name" (*Nat.* 7.104).[16]

The Ciceros, by contrast, had never produced a Roman senator, and did not even come from Rome; instead, they were local aristocracy at Arpinum, a town about seventy miles southeast of Rome that had possessed Roman citizenship since 188 BC. Other families comprising the Arpinate aristocracy were the Marii and the Gratidii. Cicero's paternal grandmother, Gratidia, had a brother called Marcus Gratidius (a noted orator) who was married to Maria, the sister of Gaius Marius, the *novus homo* and seven-time consul. The son of Gratidius and Maria was called, after his adoption by Marius' brother Marcus, Marcus Marius Gratidianus. This man was a popular hero and held the praetorship twice, during the period of Cinna's domination in the 80s. Nothing is known about Cicero's father. A hostile tradition, not to be believed, claimed that he was born and bred in a fuller's workshop, a lowly establishment: fullers cleaned cloth by trampling on it in tubs of urine. The Ciceros were said to be descended from a Volscian king called "Tullus Attius" (more properly, Attius Tullius) who fought against the Romans (Plut. *Cic.* 1.1; Arpinum was in Volscian territory). Cicero, however, never makes this claim himself, although at *Tusculan Disputations* 1.38 he jokingly refers to the Roman king Servius Tullius as a fellow clansman. Cicero's mother, Helvia, had distant senatorial ancestors; one of them was praetor in 197 BC, the same year as Marcus Sergius

---

[16] In 116 or 115 BC, another of Silus' descendants, a quaestor also called Marcus Sergius Silus, minted a denarius showing the famous warrior on horseback, carrying a sword and a severed head in his left hand. See Crawford 1974: 1.302, 2.pl.39.24 (no. 286).

Silus. But the Ciceros belonged squarely within Rome's equestrian class (i.e., the division of the Roman upper class that often equaled or surpassed the senatorial in wealth but was distinguished from it by holding no political offices).

Cicero performed military service during the Social War in 89, first under Pompey's father, the consul Gnaeus Pompeius Strabo (Cic. *Phil.* 12.27), and later under the general Sulla (Cic. *Div.* 1.72; Plut. *Cic.* 3.1). An inscription (*CIL* 6.37045) records the names of those who served on Strabo's staff; they do not include Cicero but do include Pompey (who was also born in 106) and a certain L(VCIVS) SERGI(VS) L(VCI) F(ILIVS) TRO(MENTINA) ("Lucius Sergius, son of Lucius, of the Tromentine tribe"), who is presumably Catiline. Cicero is therefore likely to have become acquainted with both men at that time. At *Pro Caelio* 12, he describes Catiline as "a keen student of military affairs"; perhaps he was thinking back to the Social War and remembering that Catiline was a more enthusiastic soldier than he himself was.

Catiline, but not Cicero, went on to serve as one of Sulla's officers in the civil war of 83–82.[17] He was put in charge of a siege (Sal. *Hist.* 1.46 M), but the details of where and when are not known. His acts of brutality during this period are better attested.[18] He is said to have murdered his brother, and then to have persuaded Sulla to have the man's name entered posthumously onto the proscription lists (official lists of people to be outlawed and their property confiscated), in order to make the killing appear legal. He murdered his sister's husband, Quintus Caucilius, and also four others, named as Marcus Volumnius, Lucius Tanusius, Titinius, and Nanneius (in the case of these last three, the killings were carried out by some Gauls whom Sulla had put under Catiline's command). A further murder may have been falsely credited to Catiline by Cicero during the consular campaign of 64. Cicero's cousin Marcus Marius Gratidianus was killed in the proscriptions in a particularly brutal way. In a speech delivered to the senate shortly before the

---

[17] Broughton 1951–52: 2.72; Broughton 1986: 192.
[18] The sources are listed at Berry 1996: 277–78.

consular elections of 64, *In toga candida* ("In a whitened toga," a whitened toga being the dress worn by candidates for election; this is the origin of the word "candidate"), Cicero accused Catiline of having been the killer and of having carried Gratidianus' head, still breathing, through the streets of Rome to Sulla (*Tog. Cand.* ap. Asc. 90 C). But there are good reasons for thinking that Catiline was not the man responsible for the execution and that Gratidianus was actually killed by Catiline's friend Quintus Lutatius Catulus (another supporter of Sulla's who was soon thereafter to become consul in 78).[19] Besides committing murders, Catiline turned himself into a rich man at this time, by buying up the confiscated estates of Sulla's proscribed Marian enemies, presumably for a fraction of their true value. The profits he made would finance his political career and provide him with the means to be generous to his friends. Sallust sums up this period of Catiline's life succinctly: "From adolescence civil wars, slaughter, pillage, and political discord were agreeable to him" (*Cat.* 5.2).

Cicero, meanwhile, was beginning his career as a forensic orator; two of his early cases concerned injustices committed by Sulla and his supporters. In 80 he undertook his first criminal case, a defense of an Italian, Sextus Roscius of Ameria. Roscius' father had been murdered; his name, like that of Catiline's brother, had been entered posthumously onto the proscription lists, and his estates had then been sold for a derisory sum to a freedman of Sulla's, Chrysogonus. To stop him laying claim to his father's property, Roscius was accused of having murdered his father himself. Cicero secured his acquittal, and then went on to defend many other clients, one of whom was a woman from Arretium, a town disenfranchised by Sulla. In defending the woman's freedom, Cicero argued that all disenfranchisement was invalid. He won his case, even though Sulla was still alive.

At around this time, Cicero married Terentia. Little is known of her background, but she was wealthy and may have had a consular

---

[19] See Marshall 1985.

ancestor. From 79 to 77 Cicero studied in Greece, Rhodes, and Asia Minor; Terentia probably accompanied him, and their daughter Tullia was born in c. 78. In 76 Cicero was elected quaestor at Rome; he served his year of office (75 BC) in Sicily, and on his return entered the senate as a *novus homo*. Catiline must also have held the quaestorship and entered the senate during this period.

In 73 Catiline was prosecuted for having had sexual relations with one of the Vestal virgins, a priestess of the goddess Vesta whose name was Fabia and who was a half-sister of Terentia.[20] Fabia was also prosecuted. Had they been convicted, Catiline would have been scourged to death with rods, and Fabia would have been buried alive as punishment for having broken her vow of chastity. Public opinion seems to have held that the pair were guilty. However, Catiline had friends in high places: former consuls rallied to his defense, and his friend Catulus, who was probably the president of the court, managed somehow to engineer an acquittal. Catiline and Cicero must have both been relieved. Catiline regarded himself as forever in Catulus' debt (Sal. *Cat.* 35.1), while later in 64 Cicero alluded to the trial in *In toga candida* in a way that ingeniously implied both Fabia's innocence and Catiline's guilt (ap. Asc. 91 C).[21]

In 70 Cicero secured a notable success in his prosecution of Gaius Verres, a corrupt former governor of Sicily (73–71 BC), the province Cicero knew well from his year as quaestor. Verres, defended unsuccessfully by Quintus Hortensius Hortalus, withdrew into exile, and Cicero was considered to have taken Hortensius' place as the leading advocate at Rome. The next year, Hortensius was consul, and Cicero was plebeian aedile. Catiline's career was progressing too: in 68 he held the praetorship, and then in 67–66 he served as governor of Africa.[22] In that province, however, he proved to be another Verres. Even while he was still governor, embassies came to Rome to complain to the senate about his rapacity, and

---

[20] See Alexander 1990: 83 (no. 167); Syme 2016: 158–61 (cf. 358–59).
[21] This account of the trial follows Cadoux 2005; see also Lewis 2001. On Fabia, see Treggiari 2007: 30–31.
[22] Broughton 1951–52: 2.138, 147, 155; Broughton 1986: 192.

many senators expressed their disapproval of his behavior. A trial for extortion on his return was inevitable.

Catiline returned from his province in the summer of 66. Cicero was by that time praetor and, as it happened, president of the extortion court; but no charge was brought against Catiline for the time being. A political scandal had just occurred, and Catiline hoped to turn it to his advantage. In the recent consular elections, Publius Cornelius Sulla (the nephew of the dictator)[23] and Publius Autronius Paetus had been elected consuls for 65, but they had then both been prosecuted for electoral malpractice and had both been convicted, expelled from the senate, and permanently debarred from public office.[24] A supplementary election was required to fill the vacant consulships. Catiline calculated that if he were elected himself at that election, he would be able to avoid being put on trial, since magistrates holding a senior public office were immune from prosecution. He therefore put his name forward. But his plan failed. The presiding consul, Lucius Volcacius Tullus, refused to accept his candidature on the grounds that he had not submitted his nomination within the specified period (meaning, presumably, that he had not been a candidate in the original election). So Lucius Manlius Torquatus and Lucius Aurelius Cotta, candidates in the original election and the prosecutors, respectively, of Sulla and Autronius (although the prosecutor of Sulla may have been Torquatus' son of the same name),[25] were elected to the consulships of 65.

The events of the following months (late 66 to early 65) are uncertain and confusing, and gave rise to the myth of a "first Catilinarian conspiracy." There was speculation that Sulla and Autronius would try to recover their forfeited consulships by violence against the new consuls. There were also disturbances over the

---

[23] My argument that this Sulla was, as stated by Dio (36.44.3), the dictator's nephew (Berry 1996: 320–21), is accepted by Santangelo as "a conclusive demonstration" (Syme 2016: 362). It is now known that Syme also saw no reason to doubt Dio's statement (Syme 2016: 169).

[24] See Alexander 1990: 100–101 (nos. 200, 201); Berry 1996: 4–5.

[25] See Alexander 1999.

impending trial for extortion of Gaius Manilius, the tribune of 66 who ceased to hold office on 10 December of that year. Manilius had proposed the *lex Manilia* (Manilian law) that gave Pompey command of the war against Mithradates, a law Cicero had supported in an extant speech, *De imperio Cn. Pompei* ("On the command of Gnaeus Pompeius"). As praetor in charge of the extortion court in which Manilius would be tried, Cicero initially scheduled the trial for the last day of the year (29 December), but was then forced by a popular demonstration to postpone it until 65 and agree to serve as defense counsel.[26] Apparently that trial (for extortion) was disrupted by violence, resulting in Manilius being reindicted for violence or treason.[27] When that trial eventually took place, the senate asked the consuls to attend and keep order, causing Manilius to abandon his defense and suffer conviction. What role Catiline played in these events is unclear. He is said to have appeared in the forum, armed with a weapon, on the last day of 66 (Cic. *Cat.* 1.15),[28] the day on which Manilius was to have appeared in Cicero's court, and also to have put off his plans for murder until 5 February 65 (Sal. *Cat.* 18.6). These incidents could conceivably be explained as having some connection with the demonstrations at the trial or trials of Manilius. If so, then Catiline is more likely to have been acting against Manilius, not for him.[29] In other accounts by Cicero, however, as well as in the accounts of Sallust and later historians, Catiline is implicated in sinister plotting by Sulla and Autronius, and his involvement is blown up into a "first conspiracy," a plot to murder the consuls of 65 (Torquatus and Cotta) and leading senators with the aim of seizing power. One convincing argument that can be made against Catiline's involvement in such a plot is the known fact that one of his alleged victims, the consul Torquatus, appeared at Catiline's extortion trial in 65 to give him his support (Cic. *Sul.* 81). In any case, no one made any physical attempt to murder anyone or seize power,

---

[26] See Ramsey 1980; Alexander 1990: 103 (no. 205).
[27] See Ramsey 1985; Alexander 1990: 105–6 (no. 210).
[28] This is the only reference in the *Catilinarians* to the "first conspiracy."
[29] See Gruen 1969; Marshall 1977b.

and no one was prosecuted for any such crime. But eighteen months later Cicero began to make vague allegations against Catiline in his *In toga candida* speech of around June 64 (ap. Asc. 92, 93 C). Later still, in 62 when Cicero found himself defending Sulla on a charge of violence laid against him by the son of the consul Torquatus, he was only too happy to defend his client by attributing as many of the alleged incidents of violence as possible to Catiline, who by that time was dead. This, in turn, influenced Sallust, who tries and fails to make sense of what he calls the "earlier conspiracy" (*superiore coniuratione, Cat.* 19.6). Writing just over twenty years after the alleged conspiracy of 66–65, Sallust links every rumor from the mid-60s to his protagonist (*Cat.* 18–19). Henceforth, the "first Catilinarian conspiracy" was accepted at face value by ancient and modern historians alike until the myth was exploded by Robin Seager and Ronald Syme (independently) in 1964.[30]

In the summer of 65, Catiline was finally brought to trial for extortion in Africa.[31] The trial prevented him from standing for the consulship in that year, so instead he would stand in 64, the year in which Cicero would also be a candidate. In a letter to his friend Atticus, Cicero considered Catiline's guilt to be as clear as day (*Att.* 1.1.1), but nevertheless he contemplated taking on his defense— another sign that Catiline could not yet have been regarded as a participant in a conspiracy. In another letter to Atticus (*Att.* 1.2.1), which he opens with the news of the birth of his son, Marcus, Cicero says that he hopes that Catiline, if acquitted, will cooperate with him in the campaign for the consulship. Evidently Cicero's plan was that, in return for being defended by him, Catiline would agree not to oppose him in the campaign and that they would both be elected together. On the other hand, if Catiline were convicted, Cicero says, he would bear it philosophically—by which he means that he would be pleased to be rid of a competitor. He adds that they have the jury they want, and he hints at collusion with the prosecution (the prosecutor was Publius Clodius, his future enemy).

---

[30] Seager 1964; Syme 1964: 86–102.
[31] See Alexander 1990: 106–7 (no. 212).

But, in the event, Cicero did not defend Catiline.[32] Catiline stood trial, was supported by the consul Torquatus, and was acquitted. At *Pro Caelio* 14, Cicero looks back on his near defense and cites it as evidence of Catiline's ability to simulate virtue:

> I, I myself, I tell you, was almost taken in by him on one occasion, when I took him to be a loyal citizen, eager to be on good terms with all the best people, and a dependable and faithful friend. I did not believe his crimes until I came upon them with my eyes, or suspect them until I had laid my hands on them. If Caelius was also among his wide circle of friends, it is better that he should be angry with himself at his own mistake (just as I sometimes am about my own misjudgment of Catiline) than that he should have to fear a charge of having been a friend of his.

At some point in the mid-60s, Catiline married a woman called Aurelia Orestilla (he had been married at least once before).[33] She was rich, and she already had a daughter, who was also rich (Sal. *Cat.* 35.3). Sallust memorably remarks that no good man ever praised anything in Orestilla except her looks (*Cat.* 15.2), and he makes it clear that Catiline married her out of passion (which in Roman eyes was discreditable, unlike marrying for money, which was not).[34] Cicero claims that Catiline murdered his previous wife in order to clear the way for marrying Orestilla, and he hints at a further crime too horrible to mention (*Cat.* 1.14). Sallust reveals what it was (*Cat.* 15.2): initially, Orestilla was unwilling to marry Catiline because he had a grown-up son, so Catiline murdered the son and thereby removed the obstacle to their marriage. If these stories are true, Catiline murdered his wife and son in order to persuade

---

[32] E. J. Phillips 1970 argues that Catiline, confident of acquittal and considering Cicero unworthy of the consulship, rejected his offer.

[33] On the date, see Marshall 1977a; on Orestilla's family, which was consular, Evans 1987; and on Catiline's marriages, Syme 2016: 154–57 (cf. 356–57).

[34] When Cicero, aged sixty or sixty-one (in 46 or 45 BC), married Publilia, a girl of perhaps fourteen or fifteen, he was accused of marrying out of passion; but Tiro recorded that he had married her for her money (Plut. *Cic.* 41.3).

Orestilla to accept him. No wonder, then, that good men did not praise her. Cicero, in *In toga candida*, made the further claim that one of Catiline's wives was his own (Catiline's) illegitimate daughter (ap. Asc. 91 C). If Orestilla was the woman alluded to, then the son whom Catiline murdered would have been her half-brother. However, these allegations cannot be taken at face value and reveal more about typical themes and slanders found in Roman invective than they do about Catiline's domestic history.

It was in the election of 64, then, that Catiline first stood for the consulship, in competition with Cicero. Of the five other candidates, there was only one serious contender, Gaius Antonius Hybrida, the son of Marcus Antonius the orator (the consul of 99 BC) and uncle of Mark Antony. Among the lesser candidates was Lucius Cassius Longinus, the future Catilinarian conspirator, who had been a praetor with Cicero in 66. Antonius was about as disreputable as Catiline. He too had been an officer under Sulla (he had used squadrons of Sulla's cavalry to commit robberies in Greece) and had been involved in the proscriptions. Later, in 70, he had been expelled from the senate for his crimes in Greece, for escaping a judicial verdict by an appeal to the tribunes, and for falling below the property qualification on account of his debts, but he had quickly secured readmission, becoming tribune in c. 68 and praetor in 66. In the praetorian elections for 66, Cicero had been the first of the candidates to be elected; he then gave his support to Antonius, with the result that Antonius rose from last place to third. In 64, despite the fact that Antonius owed Cicero a debt of gratitude for his earlier support, he and Catiline made a pact (*coitio*, Asc. 83 C) in order to defeat him. They were supported by Crassus and Caesar and engaged in massive bribery. The senate met and agreed that there should be a stricter law on electoral malpractice, but its decree was vetoed by a tribune. This caused anger, and it was in this context that Cicero rose and delivered a virulent attack on the respective characters and records of Catiline and Antonius in his *In toga candida*.[35] The two men responded by attacking his status as a

---

[35] On this speech, which exists only in fragments, see Lintott 2008: 133–35.

novus homo: "Catiline and Antonius each made an insulting reply to this speech of Cicero's in the only way they could, by attacking his newness" (Asc. 93–94 C = Appendix 2, no. 1; cf. App. *B. Civ.* 2.2; *Scholia Bobiensia* 80.13–16 Stangl).When the elections came, the nobility and the equestrians both backed Cicero, who was once again elected first.[36] Antonius, helped by the good reputation of his father, narrowly defeated Catiline and secured the second place.

Just before the elections, Catiline's uncle, Lucius Bellienus, was prosecuted for a murder committed during Sulla's dictatorship and was convicted.[37] After the elections had taken place, Catiline was prosecuted by a friend of Cicero's, Lucius Lucceius, for the murder of men proscribed by Sulla.[38] In his speech, Lucceius repeated Cicero's allegation that Catiline had married his own daughter (Asc. 91–92 C). As in 73, Catiline found former consuls to support him (although this time Torquatus did not do so), and he was acquitted. His unsuccessful campaign and at least his extortion trial (Q. Cic. *Pet.* 10) must have done serious damage to his finances.

Cicero, then, had a former ally of Catiline for his colleague as consul. Early in 63, he struck a deal with Antonius. In the allocation of provinces for the consuls of 63, Cicero had received Macedonia, which offered an unscrupulous governor great opportunities for self-enrichment, while Antonius had been allotted the much less lucrative Cisalpine Gaul. Cicero had no wish to govern a province and be absent from Rome, and so he bought Antonius' cooperation, or at least his neutrality, by exchanging provinces with him. Later in the year, he publicly renounced Cisalpine Gaul, and so, unusually, did not proceed to a province when his year as consul was at an end. (Cisalpine Gaul was assigned instead to the praetor Quintus Caecilius Metellus Celer, the future consul of 60.)[39]

In the summer of 63, Catiline was standing for the consulship for the second time. It would be his final attempt. The other candidates

[36] On Cicero's relationship with the equestrians, see Berry 2003.
[37] See Alexander 1990: 108 (no. 215).
[38] See Alexander 1990: 108 9 (no. 217).
[39] On Cicero's exchange of provinces, see Ramsey 2007b: 135.

were Decimus Junius Silanus, who had sought that office unsuccessfully in 65,[40] Lucius Licinius Murena, and Servius Sulpicius Rufus, who was a leading jurist and a friend of Cicero. Sulpicius was a patrician, and therefore legally he and Catiline could not both be elected (since two patricians could not hold the consulship together). Cicero backed the candidature of Sulpicius, thereby damaging Catiline's chances (Cic. *Mur.* 7–8). Catiline was supported in his campaign by Gaius Manlius, a Sullan veteran from Etruria who in October would raise the army that Catiline joined as its commander in mid-November (Plut. *Cic.* 14.2). He would also seem to have been supported by Cassius, who had stood against him the previous year but in 63 joined his conspiracy (Asc. 82 C).[41] Cassius, who is described by Cicero as "obese" (*L. Cassi adipes,* "the obesity of Lucius Cassius," *Cat.* 3.16), appears to have helped Catiline by providing food to the voters in his own name (either at a banquet or on the street): an earthenware bowl in the possession of the Museo Nazionale Romano alle Terme di Diocleziano in Rome (Inv. 441423) bears the inscription, roughly and somewhat carelessly scratched onto its inside, CASIVS LONGINV QVEI CATILINAE {SV} / SVFRAGATVR ("Cassius Longinus who is {su} supporting Catiline"; see Figs. 1.1 and 1.2).[42] If authentic, this bowl would have been one of the bowls in which the food was served. After eating its contents, the voter would have seen the message endorsing Catiline's candidature (but not explicitly telling him to vote for Catiline). This would have helped him to remember the name of the candidate, so that he could write it down, as he was required to do, at the election.[43] The bowl is small (10.2 cm wide, 4.4 cm high) and could have held only a modest amount of food, which is what would be

---

[40] Broughton 1991: 11–12.

[41] Broughton 1991: 10.

[42] *CIL* 6.40897; *A. Epig.* 1979 (1982): no. 63; Friggeri, Cecere, and Gregori 2012: 204. After the relative clause, the reader is left to complete the sense of the inscription by supplying words meaning "is providing this" or similar. The election must be that of 63, not 64, because Cassius stood himself in 64. For a discussion of the authenticity of this bowl and that of Cato (below), see Appendix 3.

[43] Rosillo-López 2018: 77 (mentioning both bowls, 76–77).

FIGURE 1.1 Bowl with inscription recording the endorsement by Lucius Cassius Longinus of Catiline's candidature for the consulship of 62 BC. Museo Nazionale Romano alle Terme di Diocleziano, Inv. 441423.

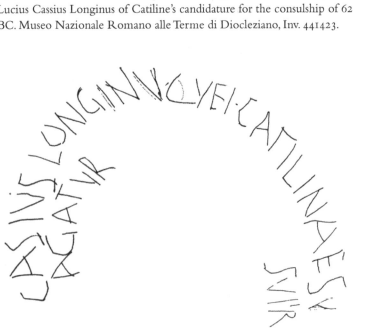

FIGURE 1.2 The inscription inside the Catiline bowl (Fig. 1.1).

expected if a large number of voters were to be fed. It is possible, however, that it was filled more than once.

The provision of food to voters was a common practice (Q. Cic. *Pet.* 44) and was not considered illegal, unless the distribution was "wholesale" (*volgo*, Cic. *Mur.* 67, 72, 73). It was more acceptable, however, if the food was provided not by the candidate himself but instead by a friend (*Mur.* 72), such as Cassius, or by a relative, such as Murena's stepson Lucius Pinarius Natta, who courted equestrian voters (*Mur.* 73). In *Pro Murena*, Cicero claims that it is only Marcus Porcius Cato, one of the prosecutors and a man with impossibly high moral standards, who objects to the custom: "Cato disputes with me coldly, like a Stoic. He says that it is wrong to purchase goodwill with food; he says that in choosing magistrates, men's judgment should not be perverted by pleasure" (*Mur.* 74). Four months before Murena's trial, Cato had himself stood for public office and had been elected to the tribunate. In view of the remarks that Cicero attributes to him in *Pro Murena*, it is ironic that the only other bowl resembling the one endorsing Catiline's consular candidature bears the inscription M CATO QVEI PETIT TRIBVNV PLEBEI ("Marcus Cato who is standing for tribune of the plebs"; see Figs. 1.3 and 1.4).[44]

It is worth noting that the wording of the two inscriptions is revealing of each man's character and situation; and this, in turn, constitutes an argument for the authenticity of the bowls. Catiline's bowl shows him taking care not to expose himself to the risk of prosecution for violating the law on electoral malpractice: the message is issued, and the food supplied, by Cassius, not Catiline. Catiline had suffered prosecution three times already and was trying hard to avoid a fourth trial. If taken to court, he could disown Cassius' liberality. Cato, on the other hand, boldly declares his candidature and distributes the food in his own name, without hiding behind a third party, confident that no one will dare to prosecute

---

[44] *CIL* 6.40904; *A. Epig.* 1979 (1982): no. 64; Friggeri, Cecere, and Gregori 2012: 203. This bowl is also in the Terme di Diocleziano (Inv. 441422). It is 9.8 cm wide and 3.6 cm high. The inscription is in a different hand from the one on the Catiline bowl (Panciera 1980: 1650).

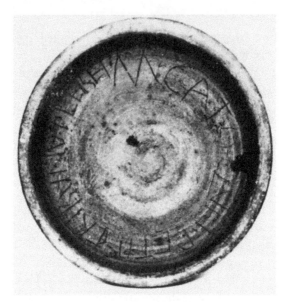

FIGURE 1.3 Bowl with inscription announcing Cato's candidature for the tribunate of the plebs of 62 BC. Photographed when wet to enhance the inscription. Museo Nazionale Romano alle Terme di Diocleziano, Inv. 441422.

FIGURE 1.4 The inscription inside the Cato bowl (Fig. 1.3).

him, because of his reputation for moral rectitude. His refusal to rely upon supporters is entirely consistent with his position just over a decade later when, as a candidate for the consulship in 52, he persuaded the senate to pass a decree forbidding candidates to allow others to canvass on their behalf (Plut. *Cat. Min.* 49.3). It strains credibility that a forger would have indulged in such subtlety of presentation on bowls promoting two different candidates standing for election in the same year. Nevertheless, the possibility that the bowls, or at least the inscriptions on them, are fakes cannot altogether be discounted.

Bribery in its more blatant forms was widely resorted to during the campaign, and once again the senate attempted to suppress it. First, following Cicero's proposal, a senatorial decree was passed clarifying the terms of the law on electoral malpractice, the *lex Calpurnia* (Calpurnian law) of 67 (*Mur.* 67–68); this was the law under which Sulla and Autronius had been convicted. Afterwards, on Sulpicius' insistence, Cicero and Antonius together carried a new law, the *lex Tullia* (Tullian law), which regulated electoral practices, defined malpractices more specifically, and added a ten-year exile to the earlier penalties (*Mur.* 3, 5, 45–47, 67, 89).[45] The passage of the *lex Tullia* is likely to have delayed the consular elections until September, since it was not normally possible to carry legislation in the run-up to elections.[46] During this period, Cato threatened to prosecute any candidate for the consulship who engaged in bribery, although he would, he added, make an exception for his brother-in-law Silanus—who can probably therefore be assumed to have been guilty (Plut. *Cat. Min.* 21.2). In the senate a few days before the elections were finally held, he specifically threatened Catiline with prosecution (*Mur.* 51).[47] Catiline made a defiant reply to the effect that "if his own fortunes should be set on fire, he would put out the

---

[45] Lintott 1990: 8–9; Berry 1996: 167–68.

[46] Lintott 2013: 152 (cf. Wiseman 1994: 354; Lintott 2008: 142; *contra*, Stockton 1971: 336–37; Benson 1986). July was the normal month for consular elections, although postponements were common: Taylor 1966: 63, 141 n. 12. The vexed question of the date of the consular elections of 63 is to be fully discussed by Ramsey 2019.

[47] See Alexander 1990: 111 (no. 222).

flames not with water but by demolition" (*Mur.* 51 = Appendix 2, no. 2); at Rome, fires were sometimes contained by demolition of the buildings in their path, as for example by Nero at Tacitus, *Annals* 15.40.1. (Sallust at *Bellum Catilinae* 31.9 turns this into direct speech and inserts it into the wrong context, as Catiline's response to Cicero's *First Catilinarian*: "Since I have been surrounded . . . and am being driven headlong by my enemies, I shall put out the fire besetting me by demolition.") Catiline's words, as reported in *Pro Murena*, are vivid and menacing but reveal the desperation of his situation.

It looks as if Catiline had run out of money. Shortly before the elections were due to take place, he gave an inflammatory address at his house, recommending himself as someone who was prepared to go to any lengths on behalf of the poor and desperate, among whom he included himself. Cicero claims to report his words at *Pro Murena* 50 (= Appendix 2, no. 3):

> You will recall what that unspeakable gladiator was widely reported to have said at a meeting held at his house—that there could be no loyal defender of the poor who was not also poor himself; that people who were poor and in trouble should not trust the promises of the rich and trouble-free; that those who wished to recoup what they had spent and recover what they had forfeited should look at the size of his debts, the limits of his possessions, and the lengths to which he was prepared to go; and that the man who was going to be the leader and standard-bearer of the desperate should be the one who was the least afraid and most desperate himself.

Of course, it is impossible to know to what extent these words are Catiline's and to what extent they are Cicero's. "The leader and standard-bearer of the desperate" (*dux et signifer calamitosorum*) sounds Ciceronian and so is more likely to be Cicero's formulation than Catiline's. Cicero's intention is to portray Catiline as a wicked and reckless demagogue. But the way in which Catiline is made to draw a distinction between himself and the richest members of the aristocracy, and to claim that his own lack of means is a point in his favor, perhaps rings true.

Catiline is represented in the sources as having depended for his support on three groups of people: those from all levels of society, in Rome and Italy, who were suffering as a result of debt, Sullan veterans in various parts of Italy who had been rewarded with land in colonies but had fallen on hard times, and country dwellers, especially in Etruria, who had been dispossessed in Sulla's confiscations (such people had typically been supporters of Marius). The first group partly overlapped with the other two; the second and third groups were originally sharply distinct but by 63 BC may have come together to some extent to comprise the rural poor. In the passage just quoted, "those who wished to recoup what they had spent" applies primarily to unsuccessful politicians but could also apply to impoverished Sullan colonists, while "those who wished to . . . recover what they had forfeited" describes the dispossessed Marians. The fact that Catiline later rallied his supporters under a silver eagle used by Marius in the war against the Cimbri (Cic. *Cat.* 1.24, 2.13; Sal. *Cat.* 59.3) would suggest that he found more support at that point among the dispossessed Marians than among the former Sullans, and Sallust indicates that the insurgents in Etruria who Catiline was to join in mid-November consisted essentially of the dispossessed but also contained some brigands and a sprinkling of Sullan colonists (*Cat.* 28.4). On the other hand, Catiline had himself been an officer of Sulla's, and his supporter Manlius had been a Sullan centurion. In the list of the six types of conspirator at *In Catilinam* 2.18–24, where the Sullan colonists are given prominence (§ 20) but the dispossessed are not specifically mentioned, Cicero exaggerates the extent to which Catiline's support was drawn from the colonists, in order to turn his audience against him. The colonists, who had been given the property of others but had nevertheless fallen into debt, were unpopular, while there may well have been sympathy for the dispossessed. Cicero also maintains that in the campaign itself Catiline was accompanied by colonists from

Arretium and Faesulae (in Etruria), but with an admixture of the dispossessed (*Mur.* 49):

> People . . . could see Catiline, lively and enthusiastic, escorted by a crowd of young men, guarded by informers and cutthroats, buoyed up by the hopes of his soldiers and the promises he claimed my colleague [Antonius] had made to him, and borne along by an army of colonists from Arretium and Faesulae—a uniform rabble, but distinguished by the inclusion of men of a very different sort, those ruined in the time of Sulla. The rage in his face, the criminality in his eyes, and the insolence in his speech gave the impression that the consulship was already confirmed as his and laid down for him at his house.

It is possible that while he was campaigning, Catiline was indeed accompanied more by colonists than by the dispossessed (it may have been easier for the colonists to travel to Rome) but that, in the later stages of his rising, it was the dispossessed, who were the more desperate, who stayed with him, having nowhere else to go.[48]

Rome and Italy were suffering at this time from an array of social problems which the senate, as was usual under the republic, showed little interest in addressing.[49] The main one was debt, and it affected a wide range of people, from the urban and rural poor to senators who had borrowed money to finance their political careers (and were unable to pay it back unless those careers culminated in the governorship of a rich province or the holding of a military command). With the end of the Third Mithradatic War (73–63 BC), Rome's eastern provinces, which had suffered a decade of devastation, were in need of investment and reconstruction. Interest rates

---

[48] On the composition of Catiline's rural followers, see Harris 1971: 289–94. He concludes that "Catiline's support was variegated, but the bulk of his supporters in Etruria were probably Etruscans who had suffered from the Sullan confiscations" (292).

[49] See Yavetz 1958 on the difficulties faced by the urban plebs; Yavetz 1963 on debt as a factor in the Catilinarian conspiracy; and Frederiksen 1966 on debt more generally. Wiseman 1994 is a good concise account of the conspiracy in its social context.

in the provinces were higher than at Rome, and the result was a calling in of debts and a shortage of cash in Italy, and a rush to lend money overseas. Italian agriculture, meanwhile, was still suffering from the effects of Sulla's civil war, his settlements and confiscations, and, only eight years previously, the slave revolt of Spartacus (73–71 BC). Sulla had settled at least thirty thousand of his veterans, mostly in Italy (there was one colony in Corsica), and the new colonists were prohibited by law from selling their allotments.[50] Some of these men had failed at farming and looked to a fresh proscription to restore their fortunes. Life for those dispossessed by Sulla, on the other hand, must have been a wretched existence. Many would be unemployed, or employed in bad conditions. Dangerous work, for example, tended to be performed by hired labor rather than slaves, because slaves were an investment on the part of their owner and had a monetary value, at least while they were young. As for Rome itself, the city was grossly overcrowded and suffered repeatedly from fire, famine, disease, and unemployment. An attempt by the tribune Publius Servilius Rullus to assign large amounts of public land in Campania and elsewhere to the urban poor was defeated by Cicero in January 63 on behalf of the aristocracy, who were ideologically opposed to the redistribution of land and distrusted the motives of the promoters of the scheme.[51]

To many people, the most attractive solution to these problems was "new accounts" (*tabulae novae*), that is, a one-off cancellation of debts or some other type of debt relief. Two decades later, in 44, Cicero observed that pressure for this type of reform had never been greater than during his consulship (*Off.* 2.84). But it was a solution that was unacceptable to the property-owning classes, and particularly to the equestrians, whose representative and spokesman Cicero was. Catiline, however, saw cancellation of debts as his means of gaining the support of the bankrupt senators on the one hand and the urban and rural plebs on the other. This was, therefore, the

---

[50] Thirty thousand is the recent, low estimate of Thein (2010: 87–89, 93–96). Appian gives a figure of 120,000 for those rewarded by Sulla with land or gifts (*B. Civ.* 1.104).

[51] See further pp. 118–119.

platform on which he stood for the consulship.[52] But, according to Sallust, he also promised his supporters a proscription of the rich, confiscations, and the magistracies and priesthoods that, owing to the pressure of political competition, they had previously failed to obtain (*Cat.* 21.2, although the promise is made in the context of an unhistorical meeting on or around 1 June 64). Most of the senate, including Crassus and Caesar (Crassus was one of Rome's biggest creditors), and all of the equestrians (if they had ever supported him in the first place) must have abandoned him at this point.

Once the content of Catiline's election address at his house had been reported to Cicero, Cicero persuaded the senate (presumably, in a "Catilinarian" speech, not now surviving) to call off the elections so that they could discuss the speech Catiline had made. So the senate met, and Catiline, on being invited by Cicero to justify himself, did not deny what he had said but gave a further speech in the same vein (Cic. *Mur.* 51 = Appendix 2, no. 4):[53]

> But he, forthright as ever, instead of attempting to clear his name, incriminated and trapped himself. He said that the state had two bodies, one feeble with a weak head, and the other one strong but with no head at all, and that this latter body, provided that it showed itself deserving of him, would never be without a head so long as he lived.

(Plutarch turns this into direct speech at *Life of Cicero* 14.4: "What . . . am I doing that is so terrible, if, when there are two bodies, one thin and wasted, but possessing a head, and the other headless, but big and strong, I myself put a head on the latter?") To Cicero's dismay, the senate then failed to pass a decree of sufficient

---

[52] Giovannini 1995 argues that Catiline must have proposed something less drastic than outright cancellation, such as a reduction of the rates of interest payable or a change to the conditions of repayment. But there is no hint of this in the sources, and Catiline's other promises to his supporters were extreme in character.

[53] The date of this meeting will be 23 September, the day on which Gaius Octavius, the future emperor Augustus, was born, if the meeting is the same as the one "about the conspiracy of Catiline" described by Suetonius at *Aug.* 94.5 (cf. 5.1). See Holmes 1923: 1.458–59.

severity, and the elections therefore went ahead without further delay. Catiline attended with a gang of armed men. Cicero, who was presiding, came with a bodyguard, and ostentatiously wore a large cuirass under his toga. He did this partly to register his disagreement with the senate about the nature of the threat posed by Catiline and partly to bring home to the people the danger that Catiline represented. The voting took place, and Silanus and Murena, the two plebeians, were elected.

Neither of the defeated candidates, however, abandoned their hopes of obtaining the consulship. Sulpicius and Cato launched a prosecution of Murena under the *lex Tullia*. Catiline, on the other hand, decided to seize the consulship in an armed rising.

On 19 (or perhaps 18) October,[54] at midnight, Crassus came to Cicero's house (in the Carinae district on the Oppian Hill, immediately to the north of where the Colosseum now stands), accompanied by Marcus Claudius Marcellus (the future consul of 51) and Quintus Caecilius Metellus Pius Scipio Nasica (the future consul of 52), and handed him a set of letters that had been delivered to his house.[55] Crassus had opened only the one addressed to himself. It was anonymous, and warned him of an impending massacre by Catiline and advised him to leave Rome in secret. The next morning, Cicero convened the senate and had the rest of the letters read aloud by their addressees (it is not known who they were). All the letters carried the same message as the letter to Crassus. After this, on 20 October (and therefore either at this same

---

[54] On the problems of dating referred to in this paragraph, see Moles 1988: 164–65 (on Plut. *Cic.* 15).

[55] Plutarch (*Cic.* 15.1–3), the source for this event, does not give a reason why Crassus brought Marcellus and Metellus Scipio with him to Cicero's house. But he says that the letters had been handed to Crassus after dinner, and that Crassus had come "immediately" to Cicero: presumably, therefore, the two men had been his dinner guests. He also says that Crassus was concerned to free himself from the suspicion of being in collusion with Catiline. Marcellus and Metellus Scipio would therefore have been brought along in order to assure Cicero that Crassus had indeed obtained the letters in the way that he said he had, that he had been shocked by the contents of the letter addressed to him, and so on.

meeting of the senate or at another a day later), or alternatively on 21 or 22 October, Quintus Arrius, a former praetor, reported that news had come from Etruria that Manlius, the former centurion who had supported Catiline during his election campaign, was moving around the cities there with a large military force (Plut. *Cic.* 15.3). The senate therefore passed the emergency decree (*senatus consultum ultimum*, or "ultimate decree of the senate," often abbreviated to SCU), first used against Gaius Gracchus in 121 BC, urging the consuls to take whatever action they considered necessary for the security of the state. (The date of the decree, usually assigned to 21 October,[56] is very uncertain: it was either eighteen or seventeen days before the date of the delivery of the *First Catilinarian*, which is itself subject to dispute.)

On 27 October, Manlius, having received news of the passing of the emergency decree, had set up a military camp in the territory of Faesulae (Cic. *Cat.* 2.14), and was in open rebellion (Cic. *Cat.* 1.7; Sal. *Cat.* 30.1). Some modern scholars have suggested that his rising was at its inception independent of Catiline.[57] But there is no suggestion of this in the ancient sources, apart from an ironic rejection of the idea by Cicero at *In Catilinam* 2.14. Moreover, we know that Manlius supported Catiline during the election campaign. The arrangement between Manlius and Catiline seems to have been that Manlius would help Catiline achieve his ambition of being elected consul, in return for which Catiline would redress the grievances of Manlius' followers and give them relief from their debts. Once Catiline had decided, after his defeat in the election, that he would continue to seek his ends by other means, namely, the overthrow of the government, Manlius must have made a decision that it was in his best interest to continue the alliance.[58]

---

[56] 21 October is a day on which a meeting of the senate is known to have taken place (Cic. *Cat.* 1.7).

[57] Waters 1970: 201; Seager 1973: 240–41.

[58] On Manlius' connection with Catiline, see E. J. Phillips 1976: 443–44; Dyck 2008: 75–76.

Cicero now took a number of security measures, as he had been urged to do by the senate's decree. He made arrangements for the defense of Rome, and also of Praeneste, a Sullan colony only twenty-three miles from the city, which he believed the conspirators were planning to seize on 1 November. Around the end of October, the news of Manlius' rebellion arrived from Faesulae, and there were reports of slave revolts at Capua and in Apulia. To meet these threats, two generals who were outside the city waiting to be awarded triumphs, Quintus Marcius Rex (the consul of 68) and Quintus Caecilius Metellus Creticus (the consul of 69), were sent to Faesulae and Apulia respectively. In addition, two praetors, Quintus Pompeius Rufus and Metellus Celer, were sent, respectively, to Capua and Picenum. Rewards were offered to anyone who came forward with information about the conspiracy. No one did so.

All this time Catiline remained in Rome. There was as yet no evidence to incriminate him: the letters sent to Crassus had been anonymous, and so proved nothing. However, Lucius Aemilius Paullus (son of Lepidus the consul of 78, elder brother of the triumvir Lepidus, and the future consul of 50) gave notice that he intended to prosecute both Catiline and Gaius Cornelius Cethegus, a patrician senator, for violence.[59] Catiline responded by offering to place himself in the custody first of Manius Aemilius Lepidus (the consul of 66), then of Cicero, then of Metellus Celer (who evidently had not yet left for Picenum), then of a Marcus Metellus (possibly the praetor of 69). But, of these, the first three refused to accept him, and the fourth presumably refused also, since Catiline remained a free man. Neither case ever came to trial.

Quintus Marcius Rex, meanwhile, had arrived in Etruria. Manlius sent him a message stating his supporters' grievances, to which Marcius replied that the men should lay down their arms and put their trust in the senate's mercy. Understandably, they declined to take this advice. It is interesting that Manlius attempted to make

---

[59] For Paullus' action against Catiline, see Alexander 1990: 111 (no. 223). On his name (Paullus, not Lepidus), see Shackleton Bailey 1992: 11–12. For his action against Cethegus (not noted by Alexander 1990), see Cic. *Vat.* 25 with *Schol. Bob.* 149 Stangl.

terms with Marcius: this suggests that his support for Catiline was merely the means to an end, and that Catiline's consulship was in itself a matter of indifference to him.

On the night of 6 November, Catiline held a secret meeting in Rome with his chief supporters at the house of one of them, the senator Marcus Porcius Laeca, in the scythe makers' quarter. The location of this quarter is not known, but it was obviously not an aristocratic neighborhood (it must have been particularly noisy); perhaps it was out of the way, and chosen for this reason as the venue for the meeting. At the meeting, arrangements were made for Catiline to go to Manlius' army, and for other conspirators to go and take charge of the risings elsewhere in Italy (see Appendix 2, no. 5). Those who remained would organize murders and the firing of the city, which was divided into sectors for the purpose. Finally, two conspirators, Gaius Cornelius (an equestrian) and Lucius Vargunteius (a man who had been tried for electoral malpractice and probably expelled from the senate) would call on Cicero at his house early the next morning, taking a band of armed men with them, and stab him to death (Sal. *Cat.* 28.1).

Cicero makes much of the Catilinarians' alleged intention to burn Rome,[60] and it was this claim that enabled him to turn the urban plebs against the conspiracy (Sal. *Cat.* 48.2). Sallust mentions that twelve fires were planned: he says that the resulting confusion would make it easier for the conspirators in the city to attack Cicero and their other victims and then to rush out of the city and join Catiline (*Cat.* 43.2; cf. 32.2). Plutarch reports in detail a scheme involving a hundred men to set the whole city alight and to block up the aqueducts and kill anyone who fetched water (*Cic.* 18.2; cf. *Cat. Min.* 22.2). It is not credible that Catiline really intended to destroy Rome. Perhaps the true purpose of the fires was to ensure that the city gates would be opened and the city quickly vacated, allowing Catiline and his army to enter Rome unopposed and seize control.

---

[60] See Dyck 2008: 70.

Cicero gives the impression of being well provided with spies and informers throughout the course of the conspiracy, and he was usually one step ahead of Catiline. One of his informers was Fulvia, the mistress of one of the conspirators, Quintus Curius (an ex-senator, expelled in 70, and probably the famous dicer mentioned by Asconius at 93 C). She told him of the meeting at Laeca's house and the plot to assassinate Cicero. As a result, when Cornelius and Vargunteius arrived at the consul's house on the morning of 7 November, they found themselves shut out and the house more strongly defended than usual (Cic. *Cat.* 1.10).

Cicero immediately called a meeting of the senate, in the Temple of Jupiter Stator ("Jupiter the Stayer," i.e., of troops in battle).[61] The temple was probably chosen largely because it was easy to guard;[62] that would explain Cicero's reference to "these strongly

---

[61] The date of this meeting is a notorious problem. Many scholars, most recently Dyck (2008: 243–44), place it twenty-four hours later, on 8 November, because *quid proxima, quid superiore nocte egeris* (lit. "what you were up to last night, what you were up to the night before") at *Cat.* 1.1 seems to imply two nocturnal meetings, first the meeting at Laeca's house on 6–7 November (a fixed point: Cic. *Sul.* 52) and then a second meeting on 7–8 November. I have opted for 7 November because "where you were, whom you collected together, and what plan of action you decided upon" (*Cat.* 1.1) seems to me to imply a single meeting, and also because, if there was a second meeting, I think that Cicero would unquestionably have said something about it (whether or not he had precise information): a paragraph would have been added at the correct place in the chronological sequence, namely, halfway through *Cat.* 1.10. Moreover, Plutarch has the would-be assassins shouting outside Cicero's door (a detail not reported elsewhere) and Cicero then coming out of his house and summoning the senate (*Cic.* 16.2–3; the source will presumably be the lost account of his consulship in Greek that Cicero published in 60, for which see pp. 66–67). There is no room there for Dyck's speculation that "possibly the shaken consul took a day to compose himself and to confer with his advisors" (2008: 243–44). See further Berry 2006: 302–3 (partly now corrected by Dyck). Dyck lists other advocates of 7 November (2008: 242 n. 2), to which add Todd 1952. I wonder whether Cicero himself, writing up his speeches two and a half years after the event (see pp. 59–62), did not confuse, or adjust, the chronology; he says at *Cat.* 3.3 that Catiline had left Rome "a few days ago" (*paucis ante diebus*—in reality twenty-five or twenty-six days).

[62] Taylor and Scott 1969: 569; Dyck 2008: 65. The legendary associations of the temple, exploited by Cicero at *Cat.* 1.11 and 33, may also have played a part in his choice: see Vasaly 1993: 59. For the latest thinking on the location of the temple, see Wiseman 2013: 245–47.

defended premises in which this meeting is being held" (*Cat.* 1.1). It was surrounded by Roman equestrians and other "men of great courage," all armed and ready to attack Catiline (Cic. *Cat.* 1.21). The meeting began without Catiline, and Cicero gave a speech informing the senate of everything that had happened ("But yesterday, citizens, when I had narrowly escaped being assassinated in my own home, I summoned the senate to the Temple of Jupiter Stator and put the entire matter before the conscript fathers," *Cat.* 2.12). At that point, Catiline entered the building. No senator, not even any of his friends, greeted or spoke to him, and the leading senators moved away from the benches near him, leaving the area deserted (Cic. *Cat.* 1.16, 2.12). Cicero then turned to him and made a second speech, denouncing him and urging him to leave Rome.[63] This was the speech later published as the *First Catilinarian* ("How far, I ask you, Catiline, do you mean to stretch our patience?," *Cat.* 1.1). It is described by Sallust as "brilliant, and of service to the state" (*Cat.* 31.6), although in fact, as Cicero admits (*Cat.* 1.9, 13, 24, 27, 30; cf. 2.13), Catiline was planning to leave the city in any case. (The scene is well imagined in a fresco from the 1880s by Cesare Maccari in the Palazzo Madama, the seat of the Italian senate, in Rome; the fresco is familiar from the covers of numerous books on Cicero. The cover of the present book shows an earlier and less familiar depiction of the same scene by John Leech, published in 1852. Catiline is portrayed as physically powerful and somewhat bestial; his fellow conspirators can be seen acting suspiciously on the far right.) At some point during the meeting Catiline seems to have offered to go into voluntary exile, if the senate would pass a decree to that effect; but Cicero would have none of it (see Appendix 2, no. 6). When Cicero had finished, Catiline gave a reply on the same lines as his response to Cicero's speech *In toga candida* the previous year. He protested his innocence and pointed out that he was a patrician, whereas Cicero (being from Arpinum) was a mere squatter (Sal. *Cat.* 31.7–8 = Appendix 2, no. 7; cf. App. *B. Civ.* 2.2):

---

[63] This account of the meeting of the senate follows the reconstruction of Stroh (2000: 69–70). See also Dyck 2008: 60, 63.

But when he [Cicero] sat down, Catiline, prepared as he was to dissemble everything, with face downcast and suppliant voice began to demand of the fathers that they not believe rashly anything concerning him: he was sprung from such a family, and he had regulated his life from adolescence in such a way that he had good prospects in every respect; they should not reckon that, as a patrician whose own and whose ancestors' benefits to the Roman plebs were very numerous, he needed the destruction of the state—when it was being safeguarded by Marcus Tullius, a squatter citizen of the city of Rome. When he began to add other insults in addition, everyone heckled him and called him "public enemy" and "parricide."

At *Orator* 129, however, Cicero claims, less convincingly, that Catiline said nothing ("The criminal Catiline, accused in the senate by me, was struck dumb"). After making his reply, Catiline rushed out of the temple.

That night Catiline slipped out of Rome, with only a handful of followers—among them Tongilius, a sexual partner of his from Tongilius' boyhood onward, and two gluttons, Publicius and Minucius (Cic. *Cat.* 2.4).[64] He left behind letters for several former consuls in which he again protested his innocence and claimed that he had left for exile in Massilia in order to spare his country a civil war (Cic. *Cat.* 2.14, 16; Sal. *Cat.* 34.2). The road he took, the Via Aurelia (Cic. *Cat.* 2.6), was indeed the road to Massilia, not the one to Faesulae. But on the other hand he had already sent ahead a military force and a consignment of arms to wait for him at Forum

---

[64] Cicero says that Catiline took only a few companions with him (*parum comitatus, Cat.* 2.4), and Sallust says that he left Rome "with a few men" (*cum paucis, Cat.* 32.1). Plutarch, on the other hand, reports that he left Rome "with three hundred armed men" (*Cic.* 16.6), a figure accepted by Levick (2015: 59, 68). But it is hard to see why Cicero, who was desperate to convince everyone that Catiline was guilty of starting an armed insurrection, would have downplayed his following. Perhaps Plutarch was thinking of the "more than three hundred armed slaves" that Milo took with him when he left Rome on the day he killed Clodius in January 52 BC (Asc. 35 C).

Aurelium on the Via Aurelia (Cic. *Cat.* 1.24, 2.13), and from there he would be able to cut across to the Via Cassia and follow it through Arretium to Faesulae (as in the event he did, since he spent several days distributing the consignment of arms at Arretium before he joined Manlius at Faesulae: see Sal. *Cat.* 36.1, and Map 2). In view of this, it is unrealistic to suppose that he had any intention of going into exile. Instead, his choice of the Via Aurelia, and the letters he left behind, must have been intended to mislead public opinion, in order to minimize the chances of a force being sent after him. He also sent a letter to Catulus—quite different, Sallust says, from his other letters—which Catulus proceeded to read out in the senate. In that letter, Catiline made no mention of going into exile; hence he cannot have decided firmly on that course of action.

Sallust quotes Catiline's letter to Catulus in full (*Cat.* 35 = Appendix 2, no. 8). It is, he says, a "copy" (*exemplum*) of the actual letter. There is no reason to dispute the claim: the style and language of the letter are not Sallustian (words and phrases that do not occur elsewhere in Sallust's extant writings are underlined in the following quotation). It is not impossible, however, that Sallust has altered some of the phrasing, since he rephrased the letter of Lentulus to Catiline that he quotes later, and which he also describes as an *exemplum* (Sal. *Cat.* 44.4–45; cf. Cic. *Cat.* 3.12). Even so, this letter is the only text to give the actual words of Catiline, or possibly a lightly edited version of them, rather than a report of them. It reads as follows:

> L. Catilina Q. Catulo. Egregia tua fides, re cognita, grata mihi magnis in meis periculis, fiduciam <u>commendationi</u> meae tribuit. quam ob rem <u>defensionem</u> in novo consilio non statui parare: <u>satisfactionem</u> ex nulla <u>conscientia de culpa</u> proponere decrevi, quam <u>me dius fidius</u> veram licet cognoscas.
>
> Iniuriis contumeliisque concitatus, quod fructu laboris industriaeque meae privatus <u>statum dignitatis non obtinebam</u>, publicam miserorum causam pro mea consuetudine suscepi, non quin <u>aes alienum meis nominibus</u>

ex possessionibus solvere non possem—et alienis nominibus liberalitas Orestillae suis filiaeque copiis persolveret—sed quod non dignos homines honore honestatos videbam meque falsa suspicione alienatum esse sentiebam. hoc nomine satis honestas pro meo casu spes relicuae dignitatis conservandae sum secutus.

Plura quom scribere vellem, nuntiatum est vim mihi parari. nunc Orestillam commendo tuaeque fidei trado; eam ab iniuria defendas, per liberos tuos rogatus. haveto.

Lucius Catilina to Quintus Catulus. Your exceptional fidelity, known to me by experience and welcome to me in my great dangers, gives confidence to this commission of mine. For that reason I have decided not to prepare a defense of my novel course of action; but I have determined to put forward, though from no consciousness of guilt, an explanation which, as heaven is my witness, you can recognize as true.

Goaded by wrongs and aspersions, and because after being deprived of the fruit of my toil and industry I was unable to keep up the position of my rank, I publicly undertook the cause of the wretched, as is my custom; it was not that I could not pay off the debts against my name from my own possessions (or that the generosity of Orestilla could not pay off those against others' names from her own and her daughter's funds), but because I kept seeing unworthy men honored by the honor of office and I came to realize that I had been disqualified because of a false suspicion. On this account I have followed the hope—quite honorable, given my situation—of preserving what rank I have left.

Though I would like to write more, I am told that force is being prepared against me. As it is, I commit Orestilla to you and entrust her to your fidelity: keep her from harm, asked as you are in the name of your children. Farewell.

This letter, Catiline's justification of his conspiracy in his own words, is an extraordinary survival. Apparently written in a hurry[65] and in dramatic circumstances, it is highly revealing of Catiline's character and psychology, and also adds to our picture of his friendship with Catulus, the former consul who had saved him at his trial for sexual misconduct ten years earlier (cf. "your exceptional fidelity, known to me by experience"). It conveys a strong sense of Catiline as the injured party: he has been wronged and insulted, and he believes that he is entitled to the consulship because of his hard work and his patrician birth (his hard work is attested by Cicero at *Cael.* 13: "Who more corrupt in his pleasures, and who more able to endure hard work?"). Given that he had been on the receiving end of the full force of Cicero's oratory only hours earlier, it is perhaps surprising that he was able to make these points with such dignity and restraint (Napoleon III remarked on the contrast between the calmness of Catiline's letter and the vehemence of Cicero's speech).[66] Surprising also to modern readers, in view of his disreputable past, is Catiline's view of himself as a man with a history of helping the less fortunate: "I publicly undertook the cause of the wretched, as is my custom." He had just said the same thing in the senate, when he described himself as "a patrician whose own and whose ancestors' benefits to the Roman plebs were very numerous" (Sal. *Cat.* 31.7). He saw himself, therefore, as a patron with a long family tradition—in contrast with Cicero, a man without a client base (except for those clients he had acquired through his advocacy). In the letter, Cicero is alluded to not just in the phrase "goaded by wrongs and aspersions" but also in "I kept seeing unworthy men honored by the honor of office" (a reference that would additionally include Catiline's recent competitor Murena, who, although not a *novus homo*, was not a patrician and

---

[65] Haste is betrayed by the words *satisfactionem ex nulla conscientia de culpa proponere decrevi* ("I have determined to put forward, though from no consciousness of guilt, an explanation"), which Syme calls "a very clumsy expression" (1964: 72 n. 53).

[66] Napoleon III 1865: 322.

had no consular ancestors).[67] Such is Catiline's hatred for Cicero and his sense of social superiority that he declines to refer to him by name.[68] He places considerable emphasis on the matter of personal debt, denying that this is the reason why he has taken the action that he has (and implicitly denying as well that he no longer satisfies the property qualification for senatorial rank). This may be intended as an answer to one of Cicero's alleged "aspersions" in the *First Catilinarian*: "I will also pass over the financial ruin which you will find hanging over you on the thirteenth of this month" (1.14; monthly interest on debts was payable on that date, the ides). Catiline's statement does, however, flatly contradict what he said in the address he gave at his house shortly before the elections, when he told his supporters (if Cicero has reported his words truthfully) that "those who wished to recoup what they had spent and recover what they had forfeited should look at the size of his debts, the limits of his possessions, and the lengths to which he was prepared to go; and that the man who was to be the leader and standard-bearer of the desperate should be the one who was the least afraid and most desperate himself" (Cic. *Mur.* 50). The affectionate references to Orestilla convey an impression of kindness and decency. The reference to Catulus' children does not make sense to us but presumably made sense to Catulus, and it is an indication that the letter is authentic. Overall, the letter is entirely consistent with the character sketches of Catiline found in Cicero and Sallust and with the impression of his character given by the various reports of his utterances.

On the day that followed Catiline's departure, 8 (or 9) November, Cicero addressed the people from the rostra in the forum, while the senate was being summoned (*Cat.* 2.26). The speech was later published as the *Second Catilinarian*. In it, he informs the people of Catiline's departure, justifies his own handling of the situation, and attempts to dissuade the people from joining the conspiracy

---

[67] The point is made by Ramsey 2007b: 157.
[68] On the reluctance of Romans to refer to personal enemies by name, see Steel 2007.

themselves. In spite of this, some people who had not been members of the conspiracy did leave Rome and set out after Catiline. One of those who did so, a certain Fulvius, was brought back on the orders of his father, a senator, and executed by him (Sal. *Cat.* 39.5).

About ten days later, news reached Rome that Catiline had arrived in Manlius' camp. He was calling himself a consul and dressing as one (Sal. *Cat.* 36.1; Plut. *Cic.* 16.4; App. *B. Civ.* 2.3; Dio 37.33.2). There could now be no further doubt as to his guilt. The senate declared him and Manlius public enemies (*hostes*). This meant that the two men were legally stripped of their Roman citizenship, they forfeited their right to hold political office or a military command, and their property would be confiscated.[69] Antonius was given the command against them, and Cicero was to defend the city. An amnesty was offered to any of Catiline's followers who surrendered before a certain date, but no one took advantage of the offer.

It was at this point, toward the end of November, that Sulpicius' and Cato's prosecution of Murena for electoral malpractice came to trial.[70] To Sulpicius' disappointment and annoyance, Cicero undertook the defense, along with Hortensius and Crassus. Cicero's argument was that whether or not Murena had infringed the *lex Tullia*—and he argued of course that he had not—Murena ought to be acquitted because of the threat posed by Catiline. He and Antonius would cease to hold office at the end of December, and it was essential to the safety of the state that there be another two consuls ready to take over from them. Moreover, Murena was a military man, whereas Sulpicius was a jurist, and in the current emergency it was the soldier who was needed. This argument persuaded the jury, and Murena was unanimously acquitted (Cic. *Flac.* 98).

Shortly after the trial was over, Cicero, by an extraordinary stroke of good fortune, was given the chance to acquire the evidence he needed to prove the guilt of Catiline's leading associates in the city. The Allobroges, a tribe from Narbonese Gaul who were

---

[69] Allély 2012: 119.
[70] See Alexander 1990: 111–12 (no. 224).

overwhelmed with debt and were also suffering from the rapacity of Roman magistrates, had sent two envoys to Rome to ask the senate for help,[71] but the senate had done nothing for them. Shortly afterwards, the envoys were approached in the forum by a certain Publius Umbrenus, a freedman who was acting on the instructions of the most senior of Catiline's followers, the patrician Publius Lentulus—the former consul of 71, who had been expelled from the senate in 70 (together with Antonius and Curius) and was now praetor.[72] Umbrenus told the envoys that if they helped the conspirators, they would get what they wanted. He took them to the nearby house of a female member of the conspiracy, Sempronia, the wife of Decimus Junius Brutus (consul in 77), who was away from Rome.[73] Once there, he introduced them to a conspirator of equestrian rank, Publius Gabinius Capito,[74] and revealed the names of others who were in the plot. The aim of the conspirators was to receive a commitment from the Allobroges to supply cavalry for Catiline's army. After debating with each other what to do, the envoys decided to report what they had learned to their tribe's patron, Quintus Fabius Sanga; he informed Murena, who took them to Cicero.[75] Seeing this as an opportunity to acquire incriminating evidence, and well aware of how it would look if the Catilinarians were caught red-handed conspiring with Rome's traditional enemy, the Gauls, Cicero told the envoys to ask Gabinius for a meeting with the most important conspirators and to request from them written oaths that they could show to their people. The meeting was held, and three of the conspirators provided the documents requested: Lentulus, Cethegus, and Lucius Statilius, an equestrian. A fourth conspirator, Cassius, the man who appears to have advertised his support for Catiline by

---

[71] The number of the envoys is given only by Plutarch (*Cic.* 18.3).

[72] Levick (2015: 71, 75–76) argues that Lentulus saw himself not as a follower of Catiline but as his equal or superior. Lentulus' colleague as consul, Gnaeus Aufidius Orestes, is likely to have been the father of Orestilla; see Evans 1987: 70–71.

[73] On her identity and possible connections, see Cadoux 1980; Syme 2016: 173–81 (cf. 363–66).

[74] Perhaps a cousin of Aulus Gabinius, the consul of 58: see Dyck: 2008: 175.

[75] On this chain of events, see Dyck 2008: 170, 172.

providing free food in inscribed bowls, declared that since he was going to Gaul anyway, he need not put anything in writing—and then promptly left Rome. It was decided that the envoys would leave Rome by the Via Lata and cross the Mulvian Bridge, about two miles north of the city (see Map 1); they would be escorted up the Via Cassia as far as Faesulae by Titus Volturcius, a native of Cortona, a town about fourteen miles south of Arretium (see Map 2);[76] and then, after a meeting with Catiline, they would complete their journey to Gaul on their own. In addition to the statements that the envoys were to take with them, Volturcius would convey a personal letter from Lentulus for delivery to Catiline, informing him that Volturcius could give him an oral report[77] and urging him to enlist slaves. This was something that Catiline had hitherto refused to do, since his rising was one of oppressed citizens, not slaves, and it would be highly damaging to his cause if it were perceived as being a slave revolt or could be represented as being one.

The envoys duly informed Cicero of the plan that had been arranged. He then ordered two of the praetors, Lucius Valerius Flaccus[78] and Gaius Pomptinus, both military men, to place an ambush at the Mulvian Bridge on the appointed night, that of 2 December. Soon afterwards, the envoys and Volturcius walked into the trap. The envoys surrendered immediately. Volturcius made some resistance, and then he too surrendered. The praetors arrested the whole party, confiscated the letters, which were sealed and in a case, and sent messengers to Cicero to inform him of what had happened. At dawn on 3 December, they brought the arrested men and the case of letters to Cicero at his house.

Cicero immediately gave orders that five of the conspirators—Lentulus, Cethegus, and Statilius, who had given letters to the

---

[76] Sallust (*Cat.* 44.3) says that Volturcius came from Croton (a town in Bruttium, in the "toe" of Italy), but see Forsythe 1992.

[77] On the meaning of Lentulus' letter (Cic. *Cat.* 3.12; Sal. *Cat.* 44.5), see Cairns 2012.

[78] Flaccus was the city praetor (Cic. *Flac.* 6, 100; cf. Broughton 1986: 212) and had been resolute in resisting the pleas of debtors (Cic. *Cat.* 1.32; Sal. *Cat.* 33,1, 5). In 59, Cicero successfully defended him on a charge of extortion; the speech was published as *Pro Flacco*.

envoys, together with Gabinius and a further conspirator, Marcus Caeparius of Tarracina—should be brought to him at once. The first four were fetched (they would not have known of the ambush at the Mulvian Bridge). Caeparius, however, had heard of the discovery of the plot and had left for Apulia, where he was intending to stir up a slave revolt among the shepherds. (Evidently Metellus Creticus had been successful in putting down the earlier rising there.) The envoys told Cicero that he would find the conspirators' weapons at Cethegus' house, and Cicero therefore sent another praetor, Gaius Sulpicius, probably also a military man, to recover them. Sulpicius discovered and took away an immense quantity of daggers and swords, all, according to Plutarch (*Cic.* 19.2), newly sharpened. Meanwhile, a large number of leading senators arrived at Cicero's house and urged him to open the letters, just in case they should contain nothing incriminating, but he refused to do so. He did not even take possession of them, but asked Flaccus to keep them and then bring them with him to a meeting of the senate that he had called for later in the morning.

The meeting was held in the Temple of Concord at the western end of the forum. Cicero had had the building surrounded by an armed guard. Out of respect for Lentulus' status as a praetor and fellow magistrate, he led him in by the hand. The other three conspirators, together with Volturcius and the envoys, were taken under guard through the forum to the temple. At the same time, it happened that a new statue of Jupiter was being set up in the forum, on the instructions of the soothsayers two years previously after lightning had destroyed the earlier statue (Cic. *Cat.* 3.20–21; *Cons.* fr. 10.60–65; *Div.* 2.46–47). Volturcius, the envoys, and the individual conspirators were brought into the temple one at a time when it was their turn to be questioned. So until that moment came, they must have been held securely nearby. Inside the temple, the meeting began. Flaccus produced the case of letters. Volturcius was brought in and questioned first. Initially he denied all knowledge of the conspiracy; but when he had been promised immunity from prosecution in return for his evidence, he revealed what he knew and named Gabinius, Caeparius, Autronius, Servius Cornelius Sulla (a senator and distant relation of the dictator Sulla), Vargunteius, and many others. Next, the envoys told their story, which corroborated Volturcius' evidence: they incriminated Lentulus and revealed that the conspirators who had given them letters, together with Cassius, had told them to send cavalry to Italy as soon as possible. After this, the three conspirators whose letters had been intercepted were made to acknowledge their seals, and the letters were opened and read out. The contents were found to be sufficiently incriminating. Cethegus did not deny his guilt, although he initially claimed that the weapons discovered at his house were collectors' items. Statilius and Lentulus admitted their guilt. Gabinius did not deny his guilt either, though he had written no letter. Lentulus was denounced by his brother-in-law, Lucius Julius Caesar (a cousin of the famous Caesar), the consul of 64.

At the end of the meeting, the senate passed a decree (Cic. *Cat.* 3.13–15). Cicero was thanked in the most generous terms for having saved Rome from extreme danger; the two praetors who carried out the ambush were thanked; and Antonius was commended for having distanced himself from the conspirators (this must have been well meant but inevitably sounds damning). Lentulus was to resign his office, and each of the five men summoned by Cicero was to be placed in the custody of a senator: Lentulus was taken by the aedile Publius Cornelius Lentulus Spinther (the future consul of 57), Cethegus by a former praetor Quintus Cornificius, Statilius by Caesar, Gabinius by Crassus, and Caeparius (after he had been captured and brought back to Rome) by Gnaeus Terentius. A further four conspirators—Cassius, Umbrenus, and two others, a Sullan colonist from Faesulae called Publius Furius and a senator, Quintus Annius Chilo—were also to be placed in custody as soon as they were captured. (It is strange that only four people fell into this category and not, for instance, Cicero's two would-be assassins, Cornelius and Vargunteius; the senate must have decided only to proceed against those who were implicated by unimpeachable evidence.)[79] Finally, a thanksgiving (*supplicatio*) was to be offered to the

---

[79] See further March 1988–89.

gods in Cicero's name—the first time such a thing had ever been done in honor of a civilian. In addition (not part of the decree), Catulus hailed Cicero as the "father of his country" (*parens patriae*, Cic. *Pis*. 6; Plin. *Nat*. 7.117; or *pater patriae*, Cic. *Sest*. 121). Lucius Gellius Poplicola (the consul of 72 and censor of 70, whose good judgment in expelling Lentulus from the senate had just been dramatically confirmed) declared that in his view Cicero deserved the civic crown (*corona civica*), a decoration normally awarded only to soldiers who had saved a citizen's life in battle (*Pis*. 6; Gel. 5.6.15). The senate certainly made amends for its earlier failure to heed Cicero's warnings about Catiline.

By the time the meeting ended, it was evening. Cicero walked out of the temple into the forum, ascended the rostra, and from there gave the people a full account of everything that had taken place. The speech he gave was later published as the *Third Catilinarian*. It was followed by a complete reversal of public opinion.[80] Until that point, the entire plebs had apparently supported Catiline (Sal. *Cat*. 37.1, 48.1; cf. Cic. *Cat*. 2.8).[81] Now, as a result of the revelation of Catiline's plans for burning the city (Sal. *Cat*. 48.2; cf. Cic. *Cat*. 3.1, 2, 8, 10, 14, 15, 22, 25), the people cursed Catiline and lauded Cicero to the skies. Sallust says they reacted as if they had been freed from slavery (*Cat*. 48.1).

The next day, 4 December, an informer, Lucius Tarquinius, gave information in the senate incriminating Crassus but was disbelieved and imprisoned. It certainly seems unlikely that a man of Crassus' wealth and an ally of the equestrian financiers would

---

[80] Sallust says that the turnaround happened "upon the revelation of the conspiracy" (*coniuratione patefacta*, *Cat*. 48.1). Scholars (e.g., Ramsey 2007b: 185) take that as being an allusion to the *Third Catilinarian*, but this is unlikely to be what Sallust had in mind, because earlier he used the phrase *coniuratione patefacta* to refer to the arrest of Volturcius and the envoys (*Cat*. 46.2). Nevertheless, the majority of the people could have heard about the exposure of the conspirators' plotting only when Cicero informed them of it, and so, whatever Sallust means, it must have been Cicero's speech that produced the change in public opinion.

[81] Sallust's statement to that effect is accepted by Yavetz 1963 but rejected by I. Harrison 2008. No doubt Sallust is guilty of overgeneralization, but he was in a better position to pronounce on this question than modern scholars are.

have supported a movement for the cancellation of debts and pro-scription of the rich, and in any case he had earlier demonstrated his loyalty by passing to Cicero the letters that had been delivered to his house. Later Crassus accused Cicero of being behind the allegation (Sal. *Cat.* 48.8–9). But this seems unlikely too, since Cicero refused to accept a false allegation made against Caesar by Catulus and Gaius Calpurnius Piso, men who had personal scores to settle with him: Caesar had recently defeated Catulus in the election for pontifex maximus ("chief pontiff") and prosecuted Piso (unsuccessfully) for extortion allegedly committed in Gaul in 66–65.[82] After dealing harshly with Tarquinius, the senate voted rewards for Volturcius and the envoys of the Allobroges. Finally, the nine conspirators whose cases were discussed the day before were declared "to have acted against the state" (*contra rem publicam fecisse*, Sal. *Cat.* 50.3). (This was a formulaic expression of disapproval, but one without generally accepted constitutional significance.) While the senate was meeting, Lentulus' freedmen and some of his clients attempted to recruit a force to set him free, and Cethegus urged his slaves and freedmen to do the same for him. Other conspirators made approaches to leaders of mobs, men who were used to stirring up riots for payment (Sal. *Cat.* 50.2).

On 5 December (the "nones of December") a third meeting of the senate was held, also in the Temple of Concord, to decide what should be done with the five conspirators who were being held in custody (these, by this time, included Caeparius) and the other four, should they be apprehended. Seventeen years later, in 45 BC, Cicero claimed credit "for having come to a judgment myself be-fore consulting the senate" (*ante quam consulerem ipse iudicaverim, Att.* 12.21.1). This presumably means that he made a public statement of his own view on the punishment of the conspirators at some point prior to his asking the senate for its view.[83] His choice of words at *In Catilinam* 4.6 may reflect that: "Nevertheless I have chosen to refer the matter to you, conscript fathers, as if it were still an open

[82] See Alexander 1990: 112 (no. 225).
[83] Lintott 1999a: 77.

question: I want you to give your verdict on what has been done and decree the punishment." The view that he gave is not recorded. As to when he gave it, it has been suggested that he could have done so in the spoken version of the *Third Catilinarian*;[84] alternatively, he could have given it at any time between the meeting of the senate on 3 December and the point at which he asked the senate for its view on the fifth.

The debate in the senate on 5 December was a full and free exchange of views, with many senators changing their minds in reaction to the powerful and persuasive speeches that were made.[85] The speeches that most influenced the course of the debate were those by Caesar and Cato, the former of whom recommended that the conspirators be imprisoned for life in various unspecified Italian towns and their property confiscated, while the latter recommended that they be executed. Both courses of action were unlawful: the conspirators were Roman citizens and therefore entitled to a trial in a court established by the Roman people. Caesar's proposal was utterly impractical, as he must have been aware, but it marked him out as a popular (*popularis*) politician, that is, one who championed the rights of the people against arbitrary action by the senate (cf. Cic. *Cat.* 4.9). Such a reputation would help him when he came to stand for the consulship in 60. Cato's proposal, on the other hand, was eminently practical, but it amounted to murder in cold blood. Versions of Caesar's and Cato's speeches feature in Sallust's account (*Cat.* 51–52). Sometime after Caesar's speech but sometime before Cato's, Cicero intervened in the debate by delivering a short speech, a version of which is embedded within the speech later published as the *Fourth Catilinarian*.[86] It was not one of the important speeches, and it achieved nothing (see pp. 190–191). At the end of the debate, it was Cato's speech that carried the day, and a decree was passed to implement his proposal "that punishment be imposed according to the

---

[84] Shackleton Bailey 1966–70: 5.317.
[85] For an account of the debate, see pp. 165–173.
[86] It will be argued in chapter 2 that §§ 7–11a and 14–18 of the speech derive from the intervention (see pp. 73–79).

custom of our ancestors" (Sal. *Cat.* 52.36). In putting the motion to the senate, Cicero left out the clause about confiscation of property, which was the one part of Caesar's proposal that Cato had accepted.

The senate's decree gave Cicero the moral authority he needed to carry out the executions, but it did not overcome the illegality. The emergency decree may have been thought by some to provide a measure of justification for the executions. However, when Cicero in later years countered the accusation that he had illegally put Roman citizens to death, he did so not by invoking the emergency decree but by parading his obedience to the senate and claiming to have had the approval of "all loyal citizens" (*omnes boni*). Technically, the claim that he was only obeying orders was misleading and invalid: however impressive the senate's decree may have been, it constituted advice only, not an instruction.[87]

When the meeting ended, it was evening. Cicero decided to act on the senate's decree at once. One after another, the five conspirators were fetched from the places in which they were being held and were led through the forum toward the state prison. Again, Cicero personally escorted Lentulus. Leading senators accompanied their consul, forming a great ring round him and acting as his bodyguard, while the people looked on in hushed awe (Plut. *Cic.* 22.1). The conspirators were each taken into the prison and lowered by a rope into a squalid subterranean execution chamber, the Tullianum, where they were strangled.[88] When the last of the five had been executed, Cicero announced to the crowd, "They have lived" (Plut. *Cic.* 22.2; Plutarch explains that he did not say "They are dead," because that would have been taken as a bad omen). As he made his way back through the forum in the direction of his house, the people pressed round him, applauding him and calling him the savior and

---

[87] The emergency decree and the legality of the executions have been endlessly debated: see Drummond 1995: esp. 95–102, 108–13. Drummond makes the important point that Roman discussion of these issues was political rather than legalistic.

[88] The prison was immediately adjacent to the Temple of Concord, which must have concentrated the senators' minds during the debate. The Tullianum still exists and is open to the public. Despite the addition of a staircase, it remains much as Sallust describes it at *Cat.* 55.3–4 and has a chilling atmosphere.

founder of his country. Women holding lamps stood on the rooftops and watched the scene.[89] Cicero had overwhelming public backing for the action that he had taken and had undoubtedly saved the city from a bloody conflict. Among the compliments that he received was one from the consul-elect Murena, who declared that Cicero had saved him not once but twice: first by securing his acquittal on the bribery charge and a second time along with the whole nation (Cic. Dom. 134).

A week or so before these events, at the end of November, the army of Antonius approached Catiline's forces from the south; Catiline abandoned his camp at Faesulae and took to the mountains.[90] The news from Rome was consistently bad. First, Catiline learned that Cicero had secured the acquittal of Murena. This meant that there would be a consul with considerable military experience—and a less friendly opponent than Antonius—ready to attack him in January. Then, in early December, came the news of the discovery of the conspiracy in the city—again achieved by Cicero, with help from Murena—and the execution of the conspirators. This prompted most of Catiline's followers to desert, reducing his force from ten thousand to three thousand men. He persevered in his refusal to enlist slaves, but it is not impossible that in the end some slaves did attach themselves to him.[91]

---

[89] This account of Cicero's warm reception in the forum comes from Plut. Cic. 22.5–7; but, given that Plutarch's main source is likely to have been Cicero's lost account of his consulship in Greek (see pp. 66–67), there may be some exaggeration in Cicero's favor. See Pelling 1985: 312–18.

[90] On Catiline's movements, see Sumner 1963 (a speculative attempt to link the chronology of Catiline's defeat with the chronology of events in Rome). The importance of Antonius in the area at this time is perhaps reflected in the wording of an inscription found at Modena in which his name, contrary to the normal practice of placing first the name of the consul who had been elected first, is put before that of Cicero: C·ANTONI·M·TVLI·COS (CIL I².2.750, = 11.843).

[91] See Sal. Cat. 56.5 (Catiline turned away slaves), 61.5 (no freeborn citizen was taken alive); Suet. Aug. 3.1 (Gaius Octavius, the father of Augustus, destroyed a band of slaves, survivors of the risings of Spartacus and Catiline, near Thurii in 60); Dio 37.33.2 (Catiline ultimately accepted slaves). The evidence is discussed by Yavetz 1963: 493–95 and Bradley 1978.

The suppression of the conspiracy in the city put a march on Rome out of the question. Catiline therefore decided that there was nothing for it but to cross the Apennines into Cisalpine Gaul and then make for Narbonese Gaul, where he would perhaps find the Allobroges sympathetic to his cause. But to the north he found his way blocked by the three legions of Metellus Celer (who was probably at Bononia). Deciding that he would fare better against Antonius, who might perhaps not fight too hard, he turned back to face him at Pistoria (twenty-one miles northwest of Faesulae). He was right in thinking that his friend did not relish the contest: pleading an attack of gout, Antonius handed over the command to his legate Marcus Petreius, a former praetor and a professional soldier of more than thirty years' experience. In the ensuing battle of Pistoria, at the beginning of January 62, Catiline's army fought long and hard but in the end was annihilated. Manlius was one of the first to fall. Sallust relates that Catiline, after seeing that his forces had been routed, "mindful of his family and his ancient rank" (*memor generis atque pristinae suae dignitatis, Cat.* 60.7) threw himself into the thickest of the enemy and was run through. When his body was found, he was still just breathing, and his face retained the fierce look that had characterized it during his life (*Cat.* 61.4). Antonius had the head cut off and sent to Rome as proof that Catiline was no more.

Three series of coins were struck to commemorate the defeat of Catiline. One moneyer, Scribonius Libo, issued denarii with the head of Bonus Eventus ("Happy Outcome") on the obverse and the Puteal Scribonianum, a stone wellhead in the forum connected with his family and at this time the meeting place of the moneylenders, on the reverse (see Fig. 1.5).[92] Different versions of the coin show a hammer, tongs, and an anvil—tools for making coins—placed in front of the Puteal. The message being transmitted seems

---

[92] Crawford 1974: 1.441–42, 2.pl.51.4 (no. 416/1a–1c). Crawford 1.442 makes the connection between the obverse and the defeat of Catiline. Harlan (1995; 11–13) interprets the reverse as representing opposition to Catiline's proposed cancellation of debts.

52 | CICERO'S CATILINARIANS

(a)   (b)

FIGURE 1.5 Silver denarius of Scribonius Libo commemorating the defeat of Catiline, 62 BC. Obverse: head of Bonus Eventus; LIBO / BON · EVENT. Reverse: Puteal Scribonianum decorated with garland and two lyres, with anvil at base; PVTEAL / SCRIBON. Crawford 1974: 1.441–42 (no. 416/1c). ANS 1950.103.47. American Numismatic Society.

to be that, following the happy suppression of the conspiracy, the moneylenders are open for business—and from this it should perhaps be inferred that the lending of money at Rome had come to a halt while the conspiracy was in progress. Another moneyer, Lucius Aemilius Paullus, issued denarii with the veiled head of Concordia ("Harmony") on the obverse and a historical scene, the triumph of Lucius Aemilius Paullus over Perseus of Macedon and his two sons in 168 BC, on the reverse; the legend, TER ("three times"), refers to the supposed three triumphs of the famous Paullus (see Fig. 1.6).[93] To my knowledge, this coin has not previously been associated with the defeat of Catiline but surely should be. Cicero specifically mentions the *concordia* between senators and equestrians following the suppression of the conspiracy in the city at *In Catilinam* 4.15. Moreover, Paullus was the man who had attempted to prosecute both Catiline and Cethegus for violence (see p. 33), and he was in

---

[93] Crawford 1974: 1.441, 2.pl.51.3 (no. 415/1).

(a)   (b)

FIGURE 1.6 Silver denarius of Lucius Aemilius Paullus commemorating the defeat of Catiline, 62 BC. Obverse: veiled head of Concordia; PAVLLVS · LEPIDVS / CONCORDIA. Reverse: trophy with, *left*, three captives (Perseus of Macedon and his sons) and, *right*, figure in toga (Lucius Aemilius Paullus); TER / PAVLLVS. Crawford 1974: 1.441 (no. 415/1). ANS 1896.7.90. American Numismatic Society.

addition a firm supporter of Cicero during his consulship (Cic. *Vat.* 25; *Fam.* 15.13.1–3). Such a man would naturally have shared Cicero's view that the defeat of Catiline represented a restoration of national harmony. Later, under the principate, Concordia was again to feature on the coinage following periods of internal convulsion, on coins of Vitellius, Vespasian, and Nerva. That Paullus and Scribonius took the same view of recent events is indicated by their issue of a series of denarii jointly, showing the veiled Concordia and Paullus' name on the obverse of the coins and the Puteal Scribonianum and Scribonius' name on the reverse.[94] Through their coins, the two men seem to be saying: Catiline is dead (Bonus Eventus), the moneylenders are back in business (Puteal), and Rome is once more united (Concordia).

After defeating Catiline, Antonius went off to the province Cicero had given him, Macedonia, where he remained governor until 60. There he suffered military defeat and oppressed the

---

[94] Crawford 1974: 1.442, 2.pl.51.5 (no. 417/1a–1b).

provincials. On his return to Rome, he was prosecuted in 59, probably for extortion, by the young Marcus Caelius Rufus, Cicero's future client.[95] Cicero believed that if the man nominally responsible for defeating Catiline were to be convicted, it would constitute a public repudiation of the action that had been taken against the conspirators. He therefore defended Antonius with vigor, but lost.

On the day of Antonius' conviction, a group of "violent criminals and internal enemies" (Cic. *Flac.* 95) made their way to Catiline's tomb, decorated it with flowers, performed funeral rites for Catiline, and held a feast—raising their cups, no doubt, to the memory of their fallen comrade.

[95] See Gruen 1973; Alexander 1990: 119–20 (no. 241).

·2·

What Are the *Catilinarians*?

Any discussion of Cicero's *Catilinarians* must first establish what these speeches are—what it is that we, as readers, are dealing with. It is a question that Cicero does not want us to dwell on: the point of *Quo usque tandem . . . ?* ("How far, I ask you . . . ?", *Cat.* 1.1) is, partly, to immerse us immediately into a situation, created by our imaginations, in which Cicero is denouncing Catiline in the Temple of Jupiter Stator in November 63 BC. But since we are at this moment not reading the *Catilinarians* but reading (or, in my case, writing) a book about them, let us pause to consider: What exactly *are* the *Catilinarians*? Before answering that, though, it is necessary to take a step back and ask a further question: What are Cicero's speeches?

The question "What are Cicero's speeches?" is a variant of the question whether Cicero's speeches accurately reflect what he said at the time of their original delivery—that is, whether he revised his speeches when he wrote them up for publication. In recent years this has been the most debated topic in Ciceronian oratory. Currently, most scholars are content to treat the majority of Cicero's speeches as reasonably close approximations of what Cicero actually said.[1] Passages might occasionally have been omitted from the published versions[2] or added to them (cf. Cic. *Att.* 1.13.5, 13.20.2), but the fact that Cicero goes so far as to provide headings indicating

---

[1] See Riggsby 1999: 178–84; Powell and Paterson 2004b: 52–57. However, Lintott (2008: 15–32) has argued, on the basis of court procedure, that *Pro Flacco*, *In Vatinium*, and *Pro Plancio* are conflations or otherwise revised. This throws some doubt on the general picture.

[2] On the evidence for omission of passages in Cicero's published speeches, see Dyck 2010.

Cicero's Catilinarians. D. H. Berry, Oxford University Press (2020). © Oxford University Press.
DOI: 10.1093/oso/9780195326468.001.0001

his omissions at *Pro Fonteio* 20 and *Pro Murena* 57 may suggest that he did not normally make substantial changes, at least to speeches published immediately; and substantial changes would in any case have been noticed by those readers who had been present at the original delivery of a speech. The only surviving speech of Cicero that is known to have been read from a script is *Post reditum in senatu* (Cic. *Planc.* 74). Presumably, therefore, the published speech represents more or less exactly what Cicero said. *Post reditum in senatu* does not appear in any way different in style or manner from Cicero's other published speeches.

A modern reader may wonder precisely *how* Cicero could have written out afterwards what he had said. In the first place, like all successful orators, he must have had a remarkable memory. Pliny at *Epistulae* 2.3 talks about an orator called Isaeus who had trained himself to deliver speeches extempore and then repeat them with 100 percent accuracy. If he could do this, then so could Cicero. Secondly, in the case of speeches that were prepared in advance, Cicero would have been able to draw on the *commentarii* (notebooks) that he had written while preparing them. Quintilian explains that, on the evidence of these *commentarii* (which still existed in his day but do not exist now), Cicero's practice was to write out the most important parts of a speech, including at least the introduction, and prepare the rest of the speech in his head but be ready to improvise (*Inst.* 10.7.30–1; cf. Asc. 87 C; Quint. *Inst.* 4.1.69). In that case, the only challenge afterwards would have been to recall the improvised portions accurately (as Isaeus could). Thirdly, it is possible that Tiro and perhaps other secretaries of Cicero's were present at the delivery of many of his speeches[3] and so would have been able to assist him afterwards in reconstructing his original words.

Of course, not all of Cicero's speeches were actually delivered in the first place. In the case of the second *actio* (hearing) of the *Verrines*,

---

[3] Not being senators, however, they would not have been permitted to attend the senate, although they could possibly have stationed themselves at the main door. On the presence of senators' sons at the main door, see Taylor and Scott 1969: 533, 577.

which is usually thought not to have been delivered,[4] the tendency of scholars has been to treat this speech (it is a single speech in five parts) as a hypothetical speech, that is, a speech composed as a rhetorical exercise, like, for example, Brutus' hypothetical defense of Milo, which he composed after Milo's conviction (Asc. 41 C; Quint. *Inst.* 3.6.93, 10.1.23, 10.5.20). However, Thomas D. Frazel has argued that the fact that it happens not to have been delivered is a point of little significance and that it should not be treated any differently from those of Cicero's speeches that were delivered.[5] The *Second Philippic*, on the other hand, is clearly a hypothetical speech of the same type as Brutus' *Pro Milone*. If Verres had attended the second hearing of his trial, Cicero would presumably have delivered the actual (five-part) speech that survives today, or something very like it. But if Cicero had attended the senate on 19 September 44, it is inconceivable, in view of the danger to himself, that he would have delivered the *Second Philippic* in the presence of Antony's soldiers—a speech that in any case he had not yet started writing.[6]

A further category of speeches is those that were published only after a delay—in my view, *Pro Roscio Amerino*, *In Pisonem*, and *Pro Milone*. If a speech was not published immediately, but only after a delay, then it is much less likely that it will be an accurate reflection of what Cicero actually said, either because of the opportunity for revision and amplification afforded by the delay or because of the difficulty of remembering the original speech at a later point in time. In the case of *Pro Roscio*, I have followed other scholars in arguing that the original trial speech of 80 was published in a revised form when Cicero returned from Greece after Sulla's death, in 77.[7] This would explain the ironic criticisms of Sulla and his regime that

---

[4] The evidence for the non-delivery of the second *actio* is Plin. *Ep.* 1.20.10 and Ps.-Asconius 205 Stangl. However, Powell and Paterson (2004b: 56) have pointed out that it is assumed to have been delivered at Tac. *Dial.* 20.1. The question is therefore open. See further Frazel 2004: 132; Lintott 2008: 16.

[5] Frazel 2004.

[6] Lintott (2008: 8–14) proposes *Post reditum ad Quirites* as a further speech that was never delivered. The safest conclusion is that it is not known whether this speech was delivered or not.

[7] Gruen 1968: 268; Harris 1971: 271–72; Gabba 1976: 138; Berry 2004.

the speech contains: such criticisms would have damaged Cicero's chances of securing an acquittal and so cannot have been included in the original speech. In the case of *In Pisonem*, R. G. M. Nisbet has argued that there was an interval between delivery and publication, and that the published speech is probably very different from the original and may have been "expanded . . . out of all recognition."[8] In the case of *Pro Milone*, finally, there is independent evidence of later revision: Asconius, Quintilian, Cassius Dio, and the late antique scholia (i.e., commentaries) all distinguish between the trial speech and the published speech that survives today (Asc. 42 C; Quint. *Inst.* 4.3.17; Dio 40.54.2; *Scholia Bobiensia* 112.10–13 Stangl).[9]

So what, according to current thinking, are Cicero's speeches? In most cases (including, I would argue, *Pro Archia* and *Pro Sestio*, speeches that have sometimes been thought to have been expanded for publication),[10] they are reasonably close approximations of what Cicero actually said; in the case of the second *actio* of the *Verrines*, this is the speech that Cicero would have delivered if he had had the opportunity; the *Second Philippic* is a purely hypothetical speech; and *Pro Roscio Amerino*, *In Pisonem*, and *Pro Milone* are speeches that were published only after a delay and were in all probability, for different reasons, altered by Cicero in the intervening period.

Let us now turn to the *Catilinarians*. The *Catilinarians* are a set of four speeches, of near-identical length (the longest, the first, exceeds the shortest, the fourth, by only thirty-nine lines). These speeches purport to have been delivered on four separate occasions between 7 (or 8) November and 5 December 63. The first and fourth are addressed to the senate, the second and third to the people. In the *Bellum Catilinae*, Sallust mentions only one speech of Cicero, which he describes as "brilliant, and of service to the state" (*Cat.* 31.6); this was the original of the *First Catilinarian*. Important evidence for the initial circulation of the collection is provided by a letter of Cicero's

---

[8] Nisbet 1961: 199–202 (quotation from 202). Powell (2007: 6), however, questions the likelihood of an extensive revision.

[9] See further Berry 2000: 169–71.

[10] Kaster (2006: 36–37) argues that the political excursus in *Pro Sestio* was part of the delivered speech.

to Atticus, *Ad Atticum* 2.1, written two and a half years after Cicero's suppression of the conspiracy at Rome, on around 3 June 60. At § 3 of this letter he writes (tr. D. R. Shackleton Bailey, with modifications):

> I'll send my little speeches, both those you ask for and some more besides, since these things which I write, prompted by the enthusiasm of my young admirers, do also, I know, give pleasure to you. Remembering what a brilliant show your countryman Demosthenes made in his so-called *Philippics* and how he turned away from this argumentative, forensic type of oratory to appear in the more elevated role of statesman, I thought it would be a good thing for me too to have some speeches to my name which might be called "consular". They are: (1) delivered in the senate on 1 January [*De lege agraria* 1]; (2) to the assembly, on the agrarian law [*De lege agraria* 2]; (3) on Otho; (4) for Rabirius [*Pro Rabirio perduellionis reo*]; (5) on the children of the proscribed; (6) when I resigned my province at a public meeting; (7) the one by which I sent Catiline out of Rome [*In Catilinam* 1]; (8) delivered to the assembly the day following Catiline's flight [*In Catilinam* 2]; (9) at a public meeting the day the Allobroges gave their testimony [*In Catilinam* 3]; (10) in the senate on 5 December [*In Catilinam* 4]. There are two further short pieces, chips, one might say, from the agrarian law [*De lege agraria* 3 and 4]. I shall see that you get the whole corpus, and since you like my writings as well as my doings, the same compositions will show you both what I did and what I said. Otherwise you shouldn't have asked—I was not forcing myself upon you.

This passage shows: (1) that Cicero has written down these various speeches delivered during his consulship; (2) that he has done so because there are young admirers of his oratory who want to read them; and (3) that Atticus also likes to read Cicero's speeches but has not seen these ones before (cf. "the same compositions will show you both what I did and what I said"). Atticus was Cicero's oldest and closest friend, and it is scarcely conceivable that Cicero had in fact written and circulated his consular speeches immediately after their delivery in 63 (the view of William C. McDermott) but was only now sending Atticus a copy.[11] It is quite possible, however, that he had in his possession transcripts of his speeches that had been taken down at the time. Plutarch (*Cat. Min.* 23.3) reports that Cicero arranged for Cato's speech on 5 December 63 to be taken down by some "fast writers," that he had previously trained these writers in the use of shorthand notation, and that this was the first time that shorthand was used at Rome.[12] But Cicero cannot have known in advance that Cato was going to make the decisive speech, and so it is more likely that he had arranged for all the speeches to be taken down, in which case there would also have existed a transcript of his own speech for him to draw upon later. In the case of his speeches to the people, he might easily have arranged for Tiro and other secretaries of his to be present to record what he said; again, this would have provided him with transcripts that he could have filed away for future use. The existence of these transcripts is a matter of conjecture, but if they existed, it would obviously have been much easier for him to recall what he had said, and the transcripts would have formed the basis for the final versions that he wrote up and circulated later.

The letter to Atticus does not specify when Cicero wrote his consular corpus, but the most natural inference is that it was in the recent past. He had been pressed by his young admirers to provide them with copies of his consular speeches.[13] It would not be surprising if the speeches had become famous in the meantime and there was a demand for copies. After all, few people, if any, were

---

[11] See Dyck 2008: 10 ("The whole tenor of the passage is hard to explain unless these speeches are so far unpublished"). For the contrary view, see McDermott 1972, followed most recently by Mouritsen 2013: 66 n. 22.

[12] At *Sul.* 42 Cicero mentions that two days earlier he had appointed four fast writers, whom he names, from among the senators to take down the evidence of the informants in the senate. This shows that 5 December was not in fact the first occasion on which shorthand was used at Rome (although it may have been the second). Presumably, the same four senators were employed on both occasions and used the same system of shorthand each time. (Incidentally, translations of the Plutarch passage mention "clerks" or "scribes," but there is no corresponding word in the Greek, and non-senators were not permitted to attend the senate. The four senators chosen by Cicero were all men of high standing, as Cicero emphasizes at *Sul.* 42.)

[13] I attempt to identify two of these admirers at pp. 101–103.

likely to have heard all the speeches, and non-senators would not have heard those that had been delivered to the senate. Although Cicero's usual practice was to publish only his forensic speeches (*De imperio Cn. Pompei* and *In toga candida* were the only significant exceptions), he nevertheless concluded that the preservation of the political speeches of his consulship would be a worthwhile undertaking (cf. "Remembering . . . how he [Demosthenes] turned away from this argumentative, forensic type of oratory to appear in the more elevated role of statesman, I thought it would be a good thing for me too to have some speeches to my name which might be called 'consular'").[14] And, having written them up, he naturally wanted Atticus to see them.[15] One point worth noticing is that at this date Cicero evidently had a following of young admirers, and one of his motives in publishing his speeches was to provide models for aspiring orators to read, admire, learn, and perform themselves.[16] Later, in 57, he tells Atticus that he does not want to keep "our younger generation" (*iuventuti nostrae*) waiting for his *De domo sua* (*Att.* 4.2.2), and in 54 he tells his brother that "all the schoolboys" (*pueri omnes*) are learning his *In Pisonem* by heart of their own volition (*Q. fr.* 3.1.11). In Seneca the Elder, Cicero's son Marcus, hearing an orator, Hybreas, quoting a lengthy passage written by his own father, asks, "Come on, do you think I haven't memorized my father's 'How far, I ask you, Catiline, do you mean to stretch our patience?' [*Cat.* 1.1]?" (*Suas.* 7.14).

The practice of memorizing Cicero's speeches is also attested in late antiquity. A friend of Augustine called Simplicius had learned all of them by heart (he had also learned the whole of Virgil) and used to recite to Augustine and his friends on request any given speech "backwards" (*sursum versus*)—whatever that may mean—as a sort of party trick (Augustine, *De anima et eius origine* 4.7.9).[17]

---

[14] *Pro Murena* is not mentioned in Cicero's list. As a particularly brilliant forensic speech that had resulted in the defendant's unanimous acquittal, it had presumably already been published.

[15] He does not, incidentally, ask Atticus to publish them: see J. J. Phillips 1985–86: 229. Even so, they appear to have been published, because Pliny the Elder shows a familiarity with the collection at *Nat.* 7.117.

[16] Stroh 1975: 21, 52–54.

[17] Hagendahl 1967: 321, 479.

Evidence for the teaching of specifically the *First Catilinarian* is provided by a bronze statuette found in the late 1960s at a late Roman villa at Fendeille, between Toulouse and Narbonne (see Fig. 2.1).[18] The statuette is of a male figure wearing a *pallium* (woolen cloak) and seated on a simple *sella* (stool); in his left hand he holds an open book (a codex, not a scroll), and with his right he makes a rhetorical gesture. Similar figures elsewhere, particularly on sarcophagi, enable the subject to be identified as either a schoolmaster (*magister*), a grammarian (*grammaticus*), or a rhetorician (*rhetor*).[19] On the base of the statuette is written the inscription VERBA CICERO / NIS QVO VSQ(ue) / TANDEM ABVTE / RE CATELINA PA / TIENTIA NOS / TRA ("The words of Cicero: 'How far, I ask you, Catiline, do you mean to stretch our patience?'"; see Fig. 2.2), and on the book is written QVIS / PRI / MV(s) ("Who first . . . ?"), the opening words of the *Ars grammatica* of the grammarian Dynamius.[20] These quotations suggest that the figure should be identified as a grammarian, perhaps Dynamius himself, who is teaching his pupils Cicero's *First Catilinarian*.[21] One answer to the question "What are the *Catilinarians*?" is, therefore, model political speeches to be used for study and recreation. They served that purpose in Cicero's own time, and for centuries afterwards.

---

[18] *A. Epig.* 1971 (1974): no. 254; Passelac 1972. The statuette, like the Wilczek bronze in the Metropolitan Museum of Art, New York (accession number 47.100.42), is likely to have served as an adornment on a luxury covered wagon (*carruca*): see Brown 1983; Ournac, Passelac, and Rancoule 2009: 289; https://www.metmuseum.org/art/collection/search/468204 (accessed 11 October 2018). Unfortunately, the Fendeille bronze was sold privately by its finder soon after its discovery, and its location is unknown. The archaeological service at Montpellier would appreciate any information as to its whereabouts.

[19] Passelac 1972: 189.

[20] QVIS / PRI / MV(s) has not previously been explained, although Passelac (1972: 188) conjectured that the words might be an incipit. The quotation is identified here by my colleague Justin Stover. This discovery enables the statuette to be dated to the end of the fourth century or the first half of the fifth (Michel Passelac, in correspondence).

[21] The identification of the figure as a grammarian would allow the three similar figures on the Wilczek bronze to be identified as two grammarians and, perhaps, a rhetorician. See Brown 1983, who uses the Fendeille bronze to identify the figures on the Wilczek bronze tentatively as two orators and a grammarian.

FIGURE 2.1 Bronze statuette of a grammarian (Dynamius?) teaching Cicero's *First Catilinarian*, from Fendeille. Fourth to fifth century. Owner unknown.

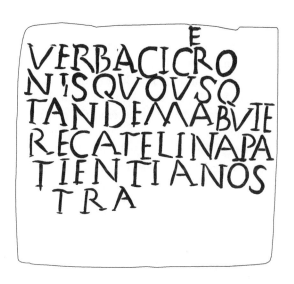

0 1 2 cm

FIGURE 2.2 The inscription on the base of the statuette from Fendeille (Fig. 2.1).

The *Catilinarians*, then, were almost certainly not published until two and a half years after the occasions on which they purport to have been delivered (although some of them, most obviously the fourth, but conceivably also the second and third, may derive from transcripts made at the time). Have they, like *Pro Roscio Amerino, In Pisonem*, and *Pro Milone*, been altered for publication? McDermott believes that the four speeches, being published immediately, were not altered.[22] More recently, Robert W. Cape has accepted that the speeches were published in 60 but denies any revision.[23] He states, however, that the publication in 60 was in fact a republication and that Cicero had previously published the speeches in

[22] McDermott 1972: 283–84.
[23] Cape 2002: 114, 120 ("There is no evidence that Cicero revised the speeches"); 154 ("There is no firm historical or textual evidence for such a revision").

What Are the *Catilinarians*? | 65

63.[24] No evidence is cited in support of this assertion, except that it had been Cicero's practice to publish his speeches. But the letter to Atticus shows that Atticus had not seen the speeches before, and it was in fact far from unusual for Cicero not to publish speeches he had delivered: Jane W. Crawford lists eighteen speeches that he delivered between 80 and 63 but decided for one reason or another not to publish.[25] Since Cape is offering a literary discussion of the *Catilinarians*,[26] he needs to establish at the outset what he is dealing with, and, finding no evidence for revision, he proceeds to offer a discussion predicated on the assumption that the speeches are faithful accounts of what Cicero actually said. However, this raises the question of the burden of proof. If a speech was published some years after delivery (as Cape accepts the *Catilinarians* were), and if there is no evidence of revision, ought it to be assumed that the speech is as Cicero delivered it? One could just as easily argue that the speech is not in its original form unless there is evidence to prove that it is.[27] That being the case, it is methodologically unsound to take non-revision as the default possibility. If there really is no evidence, the correct procedure must surely be to make no assumptions of any kind and admit that one cannot tell what one is dealing with. As it happens, though, the *Catilinarians* do provide a considerable amount of evidence.

In the first place, the fact that the four speeches are of near-identical length and form such a neat group should give rise to suspicion. Cicero gave more than four speeches during the Catilinarian crisis; for example, he gave a speech to the senate the day before the consular elections of 63 were due to take place, calling for their postponement (Cic. *Mur.* 51), he informed the senate about

---

[24] Cape 2002: 114 ("As he had done for nearly twenty years, Cicero published his speeches"). Steel (2005: 52–53) describes this theory of a double publication as possible.

[25] Crawford 1984: 33–91. Crawford argues that of the twenty-two lost or unpublished speeches she lists down to the end of 63, all but four (nos. 7, 10, 18, and 19) were certainly or probably never published.

[26] Cape 2002: 140–53.

[27] The point is made by Batstone 1994: 214: "But, it is equally apt to say of the *First Catilinarian* that we cannot say with certainty that any passage was *not* added later."

the conspiracy on 21 October (*Cat.* 1.7),[28] and he informed the senate about Catiline's attempt to assassinate him shortly before he delivered the *First Catilinarian* (*Cat.* 2.12).[29] The *Catilinarians* that we have, therefore, have been both specially selected and carefully crafted with regard to length. Further suspicion is aroused by the other literary works that Cicero published during 60 (Cic. *Att.* 1.19.10, 1.20.6, 2.1.1–2, 2.3.4; cf. Dio 46.21.3): a prose account of his consulship in Greek (now lost) and a three-book epic poem on his consulship in Latin, *Consulatus suus* (parts of which survive, including seventy-eight lines quoted in his *De divinatione* at 1.17–22).[30] He also contemplated, and may have begun, a further prose account of his consulship, in Latin; as he tells Atticus, with wry humor, he did not want to leave out any form of self-praise (*Att.* 1.19.10). These various works were written as part of what Elizabeth Rawson calls a "propaganda campaign,"[31] intended by Cicero as a counterblast to the attacks on his consulship by Publius Clodius, the man who as tribune in 58 would bring about his exile. To try to determine whether the *Catilinarians* have been altered for publication, one approach would therefore be to look for details or passages in them that would be appropriate to a propaganda campaign in 60 but not to Cicero's campaign against the Catilinarian conspirators in 63.

Between 63 and 60, Cicero came under attack from three people: Quintus Caecilius Metellus Nepos, tribune in 62 and later consul in 57; Lucius Calpurnius Bestia, tribune in 62 and according to Sallust a Catilinarian conspirator (Sal. *Cat.* 17.3, 43.1); and Clodius, who was Nepos' half-brother. On the day of the executions, 5 December, Cicero was the hero of the hour (Plut. *Cic.* 22), and there is no record of any criticism of him from any quarter. But on 29 December 63, the last day of his consulship, the new tribunes Nepos and Bestia used their veto to prevent him from giving the consul's customary retiring speech on the grounds that he had executed Roman citizens without trial. This followed shortly after

---

[28] Crawford 1984: 88–89.
[29] See pp. 35–36.
[30] See Courtney 1993: 156–73.
[31] Rawson 1975: 104.

a public meeting at which Nepos had said that a man who had punished others without allowing them the right to speak in their own defense ought not to be allowed the right to speak himself (Cic. *Fam.* 5.2.8). This is so far as is known the first time that Cicero was criticized for his handling of the conspiracy; and the conclusion that he did not come under attack until shortly before 29 December is supported first by *Ad Familiares* 5.2.6–7 (mid-January 62 BC), in which Cicero dates Nepos' opening of hostilities to 29 December, and by *Pro Sestio* 11 (56 BC), where Cicero specifically dates the two tribunes' attacks to the final days of his consulship.[32] On 3 January 62 Nepos again attacked him in a public meeting; Cicero responded with *Contra contionem Q. Metelli* (the speech was revised and published a year later, in 61; a few meager fragments survive).[33] The senate stepped in to protect Cicero by decreeing that those who had acted against the conspirators should be immune from prosecution and that anyone who prosecuted them would be considered a public enemy (*hostis*). In addition, Cato harangued the people and persuaded them to vote Cicero greater honors than those the senate had voted, including the title "father of his country" (*pater patriae*). Nepos then attempted to have Pompey recalled from Asia to defeat Catiline and restore order, but the senate passed the emergency decree against him and suspended him from office, at which point he fled to Pompey in the east.

Nepos' colleague Bestia remained in Rome, where he kept up the attacks on Cicero. Before long, Cicero was participating in the trials of the conspirators who had survived the conspiracy. Being a tribune and therefore immune from prosecution, Bestia was not brought to trial himself. All the conspirators who were prosecuted

---

[32] At *Mur.* 81 Cicero refers to a public meeting held the previous day at which the "pernicious voice" (*vox perniciosa*) of a tribune designate, namely, Nepos, had been heard. That meeting would have taken place in late November, a couple of weeks before the arrest of the conspirators in the city and their execution. Cicero does not give any indication, however, that the "voice" was directed against him. At Sal. *Cat.* 43.1 the conspirators at Rome agree that when Catiline arrives with his army, Bestia (by then a tribune) will call a public meeting and complain about Cicero's actions; but of course the meeting was only a projected one.

[33] Crawford 1994: 215–26.

were convicted, and in each case Cicero gave evidence against them based on his unique knowledge of the conspiracy. In due course, Publius Sulla (the nephew of the dictator) was prosecuted, and Cicero defended him successfully with the argument that he knew him to be innocent. *Pro Sulla* reveals (§ 31) that at the time Cicero was still being attacked by Bestia, and moreover that public opinion had turned against him: the prosecutor Lucius Manlius Torquatus (the son of the consul of 65), who in 63 had been one of Cicero's supporters, had apparently gone so far as to criticize the executions of 5 December in the course of his speech (§ 30). Cicero was accused of *crudelitas* ("cruelty," §§ 7–8, 20, 43, 93) and *regnum* ("kingship," "tyranny," §§ 21–35, 48); it was claimed that he had acted as a *rex* ("king," "tyrant"), first in his execution of citizens without trial and then in his arbitrary interventions in the Catilinarian trials. His defense of Sulla was undertaken partly to counteract this wounding characterization.

After Sulla's trial, which took place in the summer of 62, there is no record of any more attacks on Cicero until early in 61, when the conservative elements in the senate were pressing for a special court to be set up to try Publius Clodius for sacrilege. In the course of attacking his senatorial opponents, Clodius brought up Cicero's consulship and the executions. When Cicero then gave evidence disproving Clodius' alibi at his trial in May and Clodius was acquitted by bribery, a feud between the two men was begun, which was to flare up seriously in 59 and then culminate in Cicero's exile in 58. In the letter in which Cicero writes to Atticus about his consular corpus, he goes on provide a long list of insulting jokes that he had recently made about Clodius in public (*Att.* 2.1.5). These include the allegation of incest, which he was to bring up regularly against him in the following decade.

So are there any details in the *Catilinarians* that would be appropriate to the situation in 60, but not to that of November and early December 63? In fact, there are. *Pro Sulla*, of 62, contains a strong element of self-justification: Cicero acted correctly in executing the conspirators. His nature is not cruel but gentle; the severity he displayed was a "mask" (*persona*) imposed on him by his public duty as consul (*Sul.* 8). The theme, which may be called the *lenitas* ("lenience") theme, is readily identifiable, and it continues into the 50s as Cicero tries to convince his public that the grounds on which he was exiled were unjustified. In *Pro Sulla*, the key words of this rhetoric are *lenitas* / *lenissimus* ("lenience," "gentleness" / "most lenient," "gentlest," used of Cicero at *Sul.* 1, 8, 18, 47, 87), *misericordia/misercors* ("mercy"/"merciful," 1 twice, 8 twice, 20, 87 twice), *mitis* ("soft," 1, 87), and *mollitia* ("softness," 18). Since all four *Catilinarians* purport to have been delivered before any of the conspirators had been executed and the last of them to have been delivered nearly a month before Cicero began to be criticized, it would be surprising to discover the *lenitas* theme in them. But it is present—as is its counterpart in *Pro Sulla*, the theme of *crudelitas/regnum*. In driving out Catiline, Cicero says that he wants to be *clemens* ("compassionate," *Cat.* 1.4), to act *lenius* ("more leniently," "more gently," 1.12), and to show not hatred but *misericordia* (1.16). On the other hand, if he were to execute him, it would be absurd to imagine that any loyal citizen might consider him to have acted *crudelius* ("too cruelly," 1.5), although doubtless there would be some who would say that he had acted *crudeliter et regie* ("cruelly and tyrannically," 1.30). In reporting to the people in the *Second Catilinarian* on Catiline's flight, he says at the beginning of the speech that he has shown *lenitas*, but that *lenitas* is no longer appropriate (2.6); and at the end he says that his *lenitas* is a deliberate policy, which he is prepared to abandon if necessary (2.27, 28). If he has to abandon it, he says, then he will make sure that the lives of all are saved "by the punishment of a few" (*paucorumque poena*, 2.28)—a curious remark to make almost a month before the conspirators in the city were detected and arrested. As to the possibility that Catiline may go into exile: if he does, then there are some who will consider Cicero a *crudelissimus tyrannus* ("the cruelest of tyrants," 2.14). In the *Third Catilinarian*, when he reveals to the people that a plot against them has been foiled, he says that although the conspiracy is a large one and there are many domestic enemies, the senate has nevertheless shown commendable *lenitas* in decreeing the punishment of only nine traitors (3.14). In fact, the senate had not at this point decreed the punishment of the conspirators, but only that they be held in custody. Finally, in the *Fourth Catilinarian*, there is pleading. If the senate votes for execution, "the Roman people will readily release both you and me from the accusation of cruelty [*crudelitatis vituperatione*], and I shall maintain that this proposal was in fact much the more lenient [*leniorem*] of the two" (4.11). But how can it be *crudelitas* to punish a crime so monstrous (4.11)? He is motivated, he continues, not by vindictiveness—"for who has a milder nature than I?" (*quis enim est me mitior?*)—but by *misericordia* (4.11). Indeed, if a man were to find his wife and children murdered by a slave and he failed to inflict punishment, would he be thought *clemens ac misericors* ("compassionate and merciful") or *inhumanissimus et crudelissimus* ("utterly cruel and inhuman," 4.12)? It is by being *remissiores* ("rather lenient") when our country and its citizens are being destroyed that a reputation for *crudelitas* is incurred (4.12).

Nepos and Bestia are not named in the *Catilinarians*. Nevertheless, there are veiled references to them in the third and fourth speeches. At 3.28 Cicero says, "If the attacks of internal enemies, which you have been saved from, come to be directed exclusively at me, then you will have to consider, citizens, what you want to happen in the future to people who, in order to secure your safety, expose themselves to unpopularity and great danger." Then at 4.9, where Cicero is insincerely praising Caesar for having proposed that the conspirators be spared execution, he says that the proposal "clearly shows what a difference there is between the fickleness of demagogues and the truly popular spirit that has the people's interests at heart." The first of these references, like the references to *lenitas*, seems to show a keen awareness of the position that Cicero would find himself in when he stepped down from his consulship a month later.

In the references to *lenitas* and *crudelitas*, the same rhetoric is found as occurs in *Pro Sulla*, the only difference being that in the *Catilinarians* Cicero is defending himself against the charges of *crudelitas* and *regnum* long before anyone has made them: the conspirators have not even been executed yet. There must therefore be a strong suspicion that at least the *First*, *Second*, and *Fourth Catilinarians* have been revised. It must be admitted, however, that strong suspicion does not amount to proof; it would still be possible to argue that Cicero, by exceptional foresight, anticipated the charges that would later be made against him—and he does actually claim at *Pro Sestio* 47 that when he was suppressing Catiline, death and exile were constantly before his eyes.[34] Nevertheless, this explanation would be difficult to maintain in the light of the reference to the "punishment of a few" at *In Catilinam* 2.28: Cicero could hardly have predicted the lucky chance that allowed him to arrest the conspirators in the city. But let us conclude at this point merely that there are strong reasons for doubting that the *Catilinarians* are faithful accounts of what Cicero actually said.

In trying to determine whether the *Catilinarians* have been altered for publication, another approach would be to look for internal contradictions and repetitions. One example is *In Catilinam* 3.15:

> Although the senate judged, once the evidence had been revealed and his confession made, that Publius Lentulus had forfeited the rights not only of a praetor but of a citizen, he was nevertheless permitted to resign his office. This has the effect of freeing us from any religious scruple in treating him as a private individual when we come to punish him.

Cicero has already reported the senate's decree regarding Lentulus' resignation of his praetorship at 3.14 ("They voted too that Publius Lentulus, after resigning his praetorship, should be placed in custody"); but in this passage, he makes the further claim that the senate had decreed that Lentulus had forfeited his rights as a citizen. This cannot be correct, because, as Jonathan Barlow points out, in the senatorial debate of 5 December the conspirators' status as citizens was still an open question.[35] Moreover, Cicero's claim that Lentulus was no longer a magistrate is contradicted by Cicero's own behavior on the fifth. Sallust relates that Cicero personally escorted Lentulus to his execution (*Cat.* 55.2); this was a clear sign

---

[34] On Cicero's alleged powers of prophecy, see also Nep. *Att.* 16.4.

[35] Barlow 1994: esp. 183.

that he was still a praetor (as Sallust explains at 46.5) and that Cicero considered him to be one. As Barlow argues, what is likely to have happened is that Cicero was afterwards accused of sacrilege for executing a serving magistrate, and so added this passage in retrospective self-justification.[36] If he was accused of sacrilege at the same time as he testified against Clodius at Clodius' trial for the very same offense, then he would have had a powerful motive for his insertion of this passage when he came to publish the *Catilinarians* in 60. And there is one other point of interest: if Cicero personally escorted Lentulus to his execution, then he cannot have foreseen that he would later be criticized for executing a serving magistrate. This destroys the argument against revision that Cicero, even in the first two *Catilinarians*, possessed such exceptional foresight that he anticipated the charges that would later be made against him.

In the *Fourth Catilinarian*, the problem of contradictions and repetitions is more complex. But the more complex the problem becomes, the more clearly it emerges that the speech is a conflation of, on the one hand, passages deriving from different moments in the debate of 5 December and, on the other, passages that were added later in retrospective self-justification. Let us start with the end of the speech. In 1959, Harald Fuchs pointed out that §§ 19 and 24 repeat the content and phraseology of § 18.[37] § 18 begins with a sentence that looks as if it is introducing the *conclusio* ("conclusion"): *Quae cum ita sint, patres conscripti, vobis populi Romani praesidia non desunt: vos ne populo Romano deesse videamini providete* ("Conscript fathers, that is how the matter stands. The support of the Roman people does not fail you: so you make sure that you do not appear to be failing the Roman people"; cf. § 23, which also begins *Quae cum ita sint . . .*). § 18 continues *habetis consulem* ("You have a consul . . . "); § 19 begins *habetis ducem* ("You have a leader . . . "); and the last sentence of § 24 begins *habetis . . . consulem* ("You have a consul . . . "). In the next sentence of § 18 Cicero

[36] Barlow 1994: 182.
[37] Fuchs 1959.

says *omnes ordines . . . consentiunt* ("All the orders . . . are of one mind"); in the next sentence of § 19 he says *habetis omnis ordines, omnis homines, universum populum Romanum . . . unum atque idem sentientem* ("You have a situation in which all the orders, all men, and the entire Roman people . . . are of one and the same mind"). At the end of § 18 he concludes: *praeterea de vestra vita, de coniugum vestrarum atque liberorum anima, de fortunis omnium, de sedibus, de focis vestris hodierno die vobis iudicandum est* ("And it is on your own lives, on those of your wives and children, on your property, on your homes, and on your hearths that you must today reach your decision"); § 19 continues *hodierno die providendum est* ("today you must make sure"); and in the penultimate sentence of § 24 Cicero says *Quapropter de summa salute vestra populique Romani, de vestris coniugibus ac liberis, de aris ac focis, de fanis atque templis, de totius urbis tectis ac sedibus . . . decernite* ("Therefore on the survival of yourselves and the Roman people, on your wives and children, on your altars and hearths, on your shrines and temples, on the houses and homes of all of the city . . . you must now make your decision"). What appears to have happened is that Cicero has taken § 18 and has recast it as §§ 19 and 24, inserting a new passage, §§ 20–23, in between. The new passage begins, "Now before I ask you once again for your views, I should like to say a word about myself" (§ 20), and then there follow nearly two pages in which Cicero enlarges on the magnitude of the service he has done for Rome and the dangers to which he will be exposed as a result. At one point he envisages a future resurgence of Catilinarianism: "But if that gang should ever again be stirred up by the rage and criminality of some individual [*alicuius furore et scelere*], and succeed in overpowering your authority and that of the state, I shall never, conscript fathers, regret the actions and the line I have taken" (§ 20). The "individual" can hardly fail to be Clodius, and the "criminality" (*scelere*) must surely be a reference to his trial for sacrilege.[38] In view of this clear case

---

[38] Not, incidentally, a reference to Clodius' tribunate and Cicero's exile, which occurred two years after the publication of the speeches.

of prophecy *ex eventu*, Fuchs's conclusion should be accepted: that § 18 is the original ending of the speech, that §§ 19–24 are a replacement ending added later by Cicero, and that Cicero or his copyists when adding the new ending failed to suppress the earlier one.[39] The resulting double ending is highly revealing. First, it casts a curious light on Cicero's cut-and-paste method of composition, a method exposed by several remarks in the letters to Atticus.[40] But more importantly, it shows that my earlier supposition[41] that Cicero was working from a transcript of the speech is almost certainly correct. For if he did not possess a transcript of his original speech, the existence of § 18, a part of the text of that speech, is difficult if not impossible to explain.

At this point we should turn back to the *Third Catilinarian*, because the second half of the passage on the magnitude of Cicero's service, 4.22–23, is pretty much identical in content to 3.26–27. In both 3.26 and 4.23 Cicero declares that he does not ask for conventional rewards for his service to the state, but merely that the Roman people do not forget what he has done for them (he makes a similar statement at *Pro Sulla* 26–27). In 3.27 and 4.22, on the other hand, he argues that internal enemies, unlike external ones, can never be completely vanquished, but so long as all loyal citizens give him their backing, he and they will be safe from harm. If the passage from the *Fourth Catilinarian* is a later addition to the speech, as it must be in view of the double ending (and the likely reference to Clodius), then 3.26–27 is likely to be

---

[39] Hence Syme (1964: 106 n. 12) calls the speech a "composite product."

[40] At *Att.* 1.13.5 (61 BC) Cicero says that he has made some additions to a Metellan speech that he has given (i.e., *Contra contionem Q. Metelli*) and also intends to insert a passage of topographical description into a speech. At *Att.* 13.20.2 (45 BC) he tells Atticus that he is not in a position to make additions to *Pro Ligario*, because the speech is already in circulation. At *Att.* 16.6.4 (44 BC) he tells him that he has inadvertently begun his *De gloria* with a preface that he had selected from his file of prefaces without noticing that he had previously used it for Book 3 of his *Academica* (neither work survives); he encloses a replacement and asks Atticus to cut the old preface from his copy and paste on the new one.

[41] See pp. 60–61.

a later addition as well. Moreover, 3.28–29a continue in the same vein, with references to the attacks of "internal enemies" (an allusion to Nepos and Bestia, and perhaps Clodius too) and to the unpopularity (*invidia*) that may attach to Cicero as a consequence of his having saved the state. "My policy," he says, "will be always to keep in mind what I have achieved" (3.29a)—and it is hard for the reader not to complete the thought: "because no one else will." This passage obviously belongs with what has preceded it, and the whole of 3.26–29a, with its fears for the future and allusion to Nepos and Bestia (who had not yet assumed office at the time at which the speech was purportedly delivered), must surely be a later addition. In short, Cicero has added a new *conclusio* to the *Third Catilinarian* as well as the *Fourth*. It has already been noted that the four speeches are of near-identical length. Cicero was presumably motivated to extend the third and fourth speeches partly because he wanted them to match the first two in length. In particular, he must have been concerned that his contribution to the debate of 5 December should serve as the grand finale to his speeches against Catiline rather than as a coda to the first three. Even as it is, the fourth speech is the shortest.

Let us turn now to the beginning of the *Fourth Catilinarian*. Andrew Lintott has recently argued that § 6 of the speech derives from the formal *relatio*, the laying of the issue before the senate.[42] The passage begins: "Nevertheless I have chosen to refer the matter to you [*referre ad vos*], conscript fathers, as if it were still an open question: I want you to give your verdict on what has been done and decree the punishment. I shall state in advance [*praedicam*] the points that it is appropriate for the consul to make." In the rest of the section, Cicero warns the senate that they should not underestimate the seriousness or the extent of the conspiracy and tells them that they must reach a decision by nightfall. However, the reader is in for a surprise, because the very next section begins: "I see that so far we have two proposals, one from Decimus Silanus, who

---

[42] Lintott 2008: 17.

proposes that those who have attempted to destroy Rome should be punished by death, and one from Gaius Caesar, who rules out the death penalty but recommends the strictest penalties otherwise available. Each of them proposes a punishment of the greatest severity" (4.7). This, obviously, is an intervention (*interrogatio*) during the course of the debate, at a point when Silanus and Caesar have spoken but Cato has not. That Cicero made such an intervention is attested by Plutarch (*Cic.* 21.2), but of course Plutarch could have inferred it from the existence of this speech. Lintott states that an intervention by Cicero is "not totally implausible," but he also raises the possibility that the whole of the speech from § 7 onward is an "*ex post facto* invention."[43] In support of this, he cites *Ad Atticum* 12.21, a letter sent by Cicero to Atticus in 45. In the letter, Cicero complains that Brutus, who was writing a book on Cato, has misunderstood Cicero's role in the punishment of the Catilinarian conspirators. What particularly irritates him is that Brutus praised him merely for having referred the matter to the senate (*quod rettulerim*), and not "for having exposed the plot, for having insisted on action, and for having come to a judgment myself before consulting the senate" (*Att.* 12.21.1). If Cicero did deliver a speech during the debate, it is strange that he should not have said so in this letter. However, it is probably more likely that he did make an intervention, because § 18 appears to be its original ending.

For Lintott, then, the only part of the speech that is likely to have been delivered is §§ 1–6; but even that, he feels, is "by normal standards . . . probably somewhat excessive" as a *relatio*.[44] It is an interesting observation, because in fact the opening of the speech has long been under suspicion.[45] The speech begins: "I see, conscript fathers, that the eyes and faces of all of you are turned in my direction: I see that you are concerned not just about the danger to yourselves and the country, but also, if that is averted, about the

---

[43] Lintott 2008: 17–18.

[44] Lintott 2008: 17. The suggestion that §§ 1–6 belong to the *relatio* was previously made by Cadoux 2006: 614. Cadoux suggests that § 10 is also part of the *relatio*.

[45] See, e.g., Winterbottom 1982: 61–62.

danger to me. Your goodwill towards me comforts me in my troubles and relieves my pain" (§ 1). This makes more sense as an intervention than as the beginning of a *relatio* (at § 3 the senators are already in tears), but whether Cicero was putting a matter before the senate or intervening to ask it to decide between two proposals, the note of personal concern at the very opening of the speech and continuing to the end of § 3 is completely out of place. The content of the passage is similar to §§ 20–23, but here the emphasis is on the danger that Cicero will be assassinated: he is ready to die, he says, because unless the senate stands up to Catiline, everybody is going to die in any case (§ 3). In both passages there is a reference to Cicero's infant son: at § 23 Cicero wants the senate to look after his son should he be assassinated, while at § 3 the state is holding his son to its bosom as a hostage for Cicero's consulship. §§ 1–3 therefore derive from the same stage of composition as §§ 19–23, which have been found to be part of an addition made to the speech at the time of publication.

This leaves just §§ 7–18 to be accounted for, of which § 18 has been identified as the end of Cicero's original intervention. §§ 11b (*quamquam, patres conscripti* . . . , "In any case, conscript fathers . . . ") to 13 contain a heavy emphasis on *crudelitas* and *misericordia*, and so are likely to be a later addition; but there seems to be no reason why the rest of this part of the speech, namely, §§ 7–11a and 14–18, should not be a version of Cicero's intervention. In view of the number of speakers in the debate and the necessity of reaching a decision before nightfall, the consul's intervention is likely to have been brief. These sections amount to five pages of Latin text, about 40 percent of the speech.

To recapitulate, this discussion of the *Fourth Catilinarian* has led to the following analysis (the most tentative part of this is §§ 11b–13, because the passage is well integrated with its context):

§§ 1–3 added later (personal concern)
§§ 4–6 Cicero's original *relatio*
§§ 7–11a Cicero's original intervention
§§ 11b–13 added later (*crudelitas, misericordia*, etc.)

§§ 14–18 Cicero's original intervention
§§ 19–24 added later (personal concern)

A further passage worth examining is *In Catilinam* 4.21, from within the new *conclusio* added to the fourth speech. This passage is revealing because it shows that Cicero does not shrink from including a significant anachronism, but merely leaves out the specific details that would make the anachronism obvious:

> Let Scipio have his fame . . . [and the second Africanus, and Paullus, and Marius]; and let Pompeius be rated higher than all of these, since his achievements and merits are bounded by the same borders and limits as the course of the sun. But amid the praise due to these men there will surely be some space left for my own glory—unless perhaps it is a greater achievement to open up provinces for us to go out to than to ensure that those who have gone out to them have a country to which they can return in triumph.

At the end of this passage, in an ironic conditional clause, Cicero compares Pompey's achievement unfavorably with his own, suggesting that Pompey, who in 63 had just added four new provinces to the Roman empire, has merely extended that empire, whereas he has saved Rome itself from annihilation. To argue that this passage is not part of the original speech, one could simply point out that at the time Cicero is supposed to be speaking, Catiline is still in command of a hostile army, and the conspirators at Rome have not yet been executed. But there is a more telling point. Cicero's suggestion that his own achievement surpasses that of Pompey would seem, on the face of it, needlessly and damagingly offensive to Pompey. It is therefore surprising in the extreme to find the remark later being quoted back to Cicero with approval by none other than Pompey himself. At *De officiis* 1.78 Cicero says:

> Gnaeus Pompeius, in many people's hearing, paid me this compliment: he said that he would have brought home his third triumph in vain were it not for the fact that my service

to the state had ensured that there *was* a home to which he could bring it.

It is too much to suppose that Pompey heard that Cicero had compared him unfavorably with himself and then repeated Cicero's words to others with approval. What must be happening at 4.21 is that Cicero is paraphrasing—and reminding his readers of—a gracious compliment that Pompey paid him at some point after his return to Rome at the end of 62. The compliment originated with Pompey, who knew what Cicero wanted to hear; Cicero then gave it the widest possible circulation, writing it into the *Fourth Catilinarian* and, later (in 44), *De officiis*.

A similar compliment paid by Pompey to Cicero is reported at *Ad Atticum* 2.1. In that letter, after giving Atticus a description of his consular corpus, Cicero goes on to say that Pompey has been eulogizing Cicero's achievements in far more glowing terms than his own and that he has declared that whereas he has merely given the state good service, Cicero has saved it (*Att.* 2.1.6, tr. D. R. Shackleton Bailey):

> And in a mild sort of way you take me to task for my friendly relations with Pompey. . . . You may be interested to learn that he eulogizes my achievements, which many persons had prompted him to attack, in far more glowing terms than his own, acknowledging himself as a good servant of the state but me as its savior.

Pompey's remark finds two echoes in the *Catilinarians* (here again it is too much to suppose that the comparison, unfavorable to Pompey, originated with Cicero and was repeated by Pompey to others with approval). First, at 3.15, immediately before the paragraph on Lentulus' resignation of his praetorship, Cicero says:

> And if you compare this thanksgiving with the other ones that have been decreed in the past, you will find that there is this difference, that the others were given for services towards the state, whereas this one alone was given for saving it.

Then, at 4.20 (within the added *conclusio*), he says:

> Others have received your thanks for having served the country well—but I alone for having saved it.

Cicero was clearly flattered by Pompey's compliments (there is yet another reported at *Philippics* 2.12), and it would seem that when he wrote up his speeches he could not resist slipping in allusions to them. He was not able to attribute them to their source, however, because that would have made the anachronism obvious: in December 63, Pompey was still away in Asia. Instead, therefore, he pays the compliments to himself from his own lips.

This discussion has focused on the passages where it can be shown, or at least shown to be overwhelmingly likely, that Cicero altered the *Catilinarians* for publication. But if it is accepted that certain parts of the *Catilinarians* are later additions, it follows that other parts—such as the original ending of the *Fourth Catilinarian* at 4.18—may well represent what Cicero originally said. Those other parts, which on a rough calculation may conceivably amount to as much as 90 percent of the total, may perhaps correspond to Cicero's original speeches to the same degree that the majority of the published forensic speeches correspond to the original trial speeches. If there is much in the *Catilinarians* that reflects the changed political situation of the period following Cicero's consulship, there is even more that reflects the dangerous, uncertain days of November and December 63. There is still a sense in the *Second Catilinarian* that it is not absolutely certain that Catiline has taken himself to Manlius' camp rather than into exile; and even in the *Fourth Catilinarian* there is still a sense that the imprisonment of the arrested conspirators, rather than their execution, is a real possibility.

It is now possible to answer the question posed in the title of this chapter: What are the *Catilinarians*? They are certainly, as Cicero himself says, models of oratory for his young admirers: all Cicero's published speeches fulfilled this function. At the same time, they are also, like the prose account of his consulship in Greek and the epic poem *Consulatus suus*, a major exercise in self-justification, intended to demonstrate, at the very least, that he acted correctly in his handling of the Catilinarian crisis. But then again, the speeches are also, in origin, an attempt to deal with Catiline and his supporters, and to win over public opinion while Catiline was still in the field. They are therefore a complicated and sometimes confusing set of texts originating in different periods and with different purposes, aiming to persuade their audiences, for example, both that the arrested conspirators should be executed in the future and that they were rightly executed in the past. Finally, when Cicero says at 4.21, "Amid the praise due to these men there will surely be some space left for my own glory," he shows that he has yet another audience in mind: posterity.[46] In these speeches, he is speaking directly to us. So let us now turn to the speeches and try to interpret them in a way that acknowledges (rather than ignores or dismisses) the varied nature of their origins and purposes.

---

[46] In 59 BC Cicero wrote to Atticus: "What will history say of me 600 years hence? I am far more worried about that than about the gossip of those who are alive today" (*Att.* 2.5.1). (He need not have worried. Six hundred years later, the *Verrines* were still being copied—in Egypt, which in Cicero's time was not part of the Roman empire (papyrus M-P³ 2919.1 (= PSI I 20), from Oxyrhynchus: see Seider 1979: 133–34; Sánchez-Ostiz 2013: 146–47, 152).)

·3·

Denouncing the Living/Dead Catiline: The *First Catilinarian*

Now that it has been established what the *Catilinarians* are, it is
time to proceed to the second and larger part of this investigation: how they should be understood. But before turning to examine
the *First Catilinarian*, it may be worthwhile to consider, for comparison,
a modern work of literature that has resemblances in the manner of its
composition, although not perhaps in other respects, to the *Catilinarians*.

   In 2005, a former British tabloid newspaper editor, Piers Morgan,
published a book documenting his life from 1994 to 2004, during
which time he had been editor of first the *News of the World* and
then the *Daily Mirror*. The book, which is entitled *The Insider: The
Private Diaries of a Scandalous Decade* and is written in diary form,
details his meetings and conversations with the most prominent
and influential figures of the day, people such as Queen Elizabeth II
and Princess Diana, Prime Minister Tony Blair and his wife Cherie,
Chancellor Gordon Brown, entrepreneur Richard Branson, pop
star Victoria Beckham, and a host of politicians, business leaders,
newspaper executives, showbiz personalities, and celebrities. It was
serialized by the *Daily Mail* under the heading "Piers Morgan knew
everyone. What none of them knew was that he was keeping a dev-
astating secret diary."[1] The book presents Morgan as a top celebrity

---

[1] *Daily Mail*, 28 February 2005.

Cicero's Catilinarians. D. H. Berry, Oxford University Press (2020). © Oxford University Press.
DOI: 10.1093/oso/9780195326468.001.0001

himself, a mover and shaker, operating within the very highest levels of British national life. Through its diary form, it conveys a powerful sense of immediacy, of intimacy, and of authenticity. A large proportion of the entries record private conversations, and if those conversations were written down immediately after they took place, by an experienced journalist, then they are likely to be accurate. On the face of it, the book is a historical record of the highest value—on a par, perhaps, with Cicero's letters.

The "private diaries" are not what they seem, however. Reviewers noticed that they contain astonishing anachronisms.[2] For example, in the entry for 25 January 1996, Harriet Harman is described as the Secretary of State for Social Security; but in January 1996 her party, the Labour Party, was not yet in government, and she was not appointed to her Social Security post until 3 May 1997. On 26 March 1997, the diary claims that Morgan had tea with Tony Blair at 10 Downing Street ("He was yawning a lot and drinking endless cups of tea. I tried to wake him up a bit").[3] But the prime minister at the time was John Major; Tony Blair did not enter No. 10 until 2 May of that year. In the entry for 24 January 1999, Morgan reports that the secretary-general of the United Nations, Kofi Annan, mentioned his name to the US editor of the *Daily Mirror* at a reception in New York; but on that day Mr. Annan was in the middle of a week-long visit to Switzerland. On 3 August 1999, the diary shows Morgan once again taking tea with Mr. Blair, this time at Chequers, the British prime minister's official country residence in Buckinghamshire. After tea, Morgan claims, he and Mr. Blair strolled up to the Cabinet War Rooms, where, Morgan says, Churchill had made his famous wartime speeches; but the Cabinet War Rooms are forty-three miles from Chequers, in London. On

---

[2] The examples that follow are taken from the list at *Private Eye* 1128 (18 March 2005), 5. An analogous and more recent case of a "diary" by a journalist purportedly written "in the heat of the moment" (417) and yet containing patent anachronisms is Tina Brown's *The Vanity Fair Diaries: 1983–1992* (Brown 2017). See *Private Eye* 1459 (15 December 2017), 32–33.

[3] Morgan 2005: 147.

29 November 2001, Morgan is back at 10 Downing Street, at a lunch party with Mr. Blair and members of his inner circle. Finding himself seated between Cherie Blair and Fiona Millar, the partner of Alastair Campbell, the Director of Communications at No. 10, he joked, "Ah . . . the *real* Axis of Evil."[4] But the phrase "axis of evil" had yet to attain political currency, being first used by President George W. Bush in his State of the Union address two months later, on 29 January 2002. Most of these anachronisms, once pointed out, were removed from the book on reprinting.

In fact, Morgan did not keep a diary of his time as a newspaper editor: in his acknowledgements, he thanks his agent for suggesting to him, in 2003, that he write his memoirs "in diary form."[5] The "diaries" are therefore a recollection of events, written some years after they took place (if they did take place), and cast in the literary form of a diary. The anachronisms reveal that the diaries are not entirely accurate and also suggest that they contain a degree of invention. The diaries are obviously designed to show Morgan in as favorable a light as possible, to present him as being supremely well connected and influential, and a tabloid editor of outstanding ability with a buccaneering style and a magic touch. They appear to exaggerate, to some extent at least, his closeness to the prime minister. And they seek to justify decisions that he took, make light of mistakes that he made, and excuse certain actions of his that seriously damaged his reputation (Morgan was dismissed as the editor of the *Daily Mirror* after publishing hoax photographs allegedly showing the abuse of Iraqi prisoners by British soldiers; he was also criticized for buying shares in a company shortly before the shares were tipped in the financial pages of his newspaper).

Reviewers predicted that Morgan's diaries will be of negligible historical importance, because unlike, for example, the memoirs of many former politicians, their factual accuracy cannot be relied upon. It is certainly the case that any given detail in them may or

---

[4] Morgan 2005: 309.
[5] Morgan 2005: v.

may not be true. Nevertheless, taken as a whole, they do provide a revealing picture of the day-to-day life and working methods of a leading tabloid editor, of the relationship between that editor and his proprietor, and of the relationships between politicians and the press at the turn of the twenty-first century. Future historians, if they examine the diaries critically and test their claims, should be able to derive much of value from them (in the same way as much of our knowledge of the ancient world is derived from untrustworthy literary sources). It is simply a matter of arriving at a correct understanding of what the diaries are and making due allowance.

There are clear parallels between Morgan's diaries and Cicero's *Catilinarians*. One important difference is that Cicero did actually deliver speeches against Catiline, whereas Morgan did not keep a diary. But the *Catilinarians*, like the diaries, purport, in their form, to be something they are not: they are not verbatim records of Cicero's original speeches. Like the diaries, they were written up after an interval of some years and contain anachronisms and distortions. But the *Catilinarians* can easily be read as though they are the original speeches, because they have been written as though they are; and as long as readers are aware that they are not, they are unlikely to be led seriously astray. Similarly, the diaries have been written as though they are original compositions set down immediately after the events they describe and can therefore be read, with enjoyment, as authentic diaries. Here too the reader who sees them for what they are is unlikely to be misled. Both works were written in part to promote their authors and to justify controversial aspects of their careers. Moreover, both the *Catilinarians* and Morgan's diaries have value as historical evidence. Cicero does not, so far as it is possible to tell, falsify well-known dates and facts (although he does of course put his own interpretation on events), and in matters of chronology his account of the conspiracy is much more reliable than Sallust's.

Morgan's book, therefore, can help us to think about how we should approach the *Catilinarians*. If the concept of inauthentic speeches with a self-justifying agenda that can be read and enjoyed both as authentic speeches and as the later creations that they are seems difficult to grasp, the reader should reflect on Morgan's book, which can be read both as a genuine diary and as a self-justifying memoir written some years after the events described. Both authors are telling their readers how they handled significant and interesting events in their past lives. Morgan does this by means of an invented diary; Cicero does it by means of speeches that blend public utterances he made at the time with material he composed afterwards. In each case, the result is a complex literary creation that serves the author's purposes well.

How, then, is the reader to interpret the four *Catilinarians*? First of all, it is possible to read them as original speeches delivered in 63 BC. This is not exactly what they are, since they have been revised. Nevertheless, it is legitimate to read them as such, because Cicero has taken care to write them as though they represent what he actually said. If the speeches are read in this way, readers can study, for example, the techniques by which Cicero sets about turning the senate and the people against the conspirators. The exercise is similar to studying how, in Sallust's *Bellum Catilinae* (52.2–36), Cato turns the tide of the debate in the senate on 5 December. The speech that Sallust has put in the mouth of Cato, although based very loosely on fact, is, technically speaking, a fictional one, but it can still be analyzed, and admired, on its own terms. Likewise, the *Catilinarians* are, strictly speaking, fictional (because they are later recreations by Cicero), but they can nevertheless be read and appreciated on their own terms as though they are the original speeches. This first method of reading the *Catilinarians* will be described in this book as Approach A. It is the approach that one would be following if one were to read Morgan's diaries and acquiesce in the fiction that they are real diaries.

Although I have said that this approach consists in reading the speeches on their own terms, it is still necessary to take into account what is known of their original historical context. Suppose that Sallust introduced Cato's speech with the information that Cato had been a member of the conspiracy, and that he had advocated the immediate execution of the conspirators in order to divert suspicion from himself and at the same time remove the witnesses to his own involvement. That would cast the speech in an entirely different light: the reader would need to analyze it as a response to a situation far removed from the situation to which the speech actually responds. Therefore, in analyzing the *Catilinarians*, one must take account of the actual circumstances in which the speeches were delivered (explained in chapter 1)—circumstances that Cicero may not always represent accurately, or with full disclosure.

It is equally possible, however, to read the speeches entirely as productions of 60 BC. This will be described as Approach B. Parts of the speeches are indeed later additions; but even where Cicero has set down exactly what he said at the time, it is still the case that he chose, in 60, to preserve some of his original words and, presumably, to suppress others. His original words of 63 survive, where they do, because he judged them to suit his purposes in 60. It is important to understand that Approach B is valid even if the reader does not accept that any particular passage has been revised by Cicero for publication. All that the reader has to accept is that the speeches that survive were published by Cicero in 60 with the aim of justifying his consulship. Readers who read the speeches as productions of 60 can study, for example, the way in which Cicero seeks to justify the execution of the conspirators in speeches of which the originals were delivered before the conspirators' punishment had been decided.

The whole of the *Catilinarians*, then, can be analyzed using both Approach A and Approach B, and one does not need to hold any particular view on which parts of the speeches are original or revised in order to be able to do this. Even if my own views on this question are entirely mistaken, it is still the case that Cicero intended his four speeches to be read as though they had been delivered, and it is still also possible to read them in the light of the self-justifying agenda that he had at the time when he wrote them up and published them.

Previous studies of the *Catilinarians* have always, to my knowledge, followed Approach A exclusively.[6] This study is different in

---

[6] See, e.g., Cape 2002, who denies that the speeches have been revised. Kennedy (1972: 178), however, seems to hint at the possibility of Approach B when he remarks

that it will make use of both approaches. Thus, a particular passage may be interpreted both as persuading the listening public of 63 that the conspirators should be suppressed and as persuading the reading public of 60 that their suppression was a necessary and indeed praiseworthy act. It would be possible to signal which approach is being adopted at any given moment by referring to the character Cicero who is made to speak in 63 as "Cicero" (in quotation marks) and to the writer Cicero who commits the speeches to paper in 60 as Cicero (without quotation marks). But instead, to avoid confusion, I shall simply write about "Approach A" and "Approach B."

The *First Catilinarian* is the denunciation of Catiline that Cicero delivered before the senate on 7 (or 8) November 63, immediately (or one day) after Catiline's abortive assassination attempt on him at his house. Although in his description of the meeting of the senate at *In Catilinam* 2.12–13, Cicero implies that he merely asked Catiline some questions, his reference to the speech at *Ad Atticum* 2.1.3 as "the one by which I sent Catiline out of Rome" proves that he did deliver a speech on this occasion. Sallust (*Cat.* 31.6) and Diodorus (40.5a) also state that he gave a speech, although arguably they could have been misled by the existence of the *First Catilinarian*. The dramatic circumstances, and the fact that the speech, unlike the other *Catilinarians*, was delivered in Catiline's presence and was addressed to him, makes this an obvious speech for Cicero to have chosen as an introduction to the set. On Approach A, the speech is a denunciation of Catiline in his presence. On Approach B, it is an attack on his memory after his death and a timely reminder of

that the *First Catilinarian* "is also addressed to readers in 60 BC and tries to show them why he was justified in taking as stringent measures as he did." Likewise Batstone (1994: 261 n. 82) writes: "I have on occasion remarked in the notes on the appropriateness of a particular argument to the circumstances of 60 BC." Cf. Gurd (2007: 51), who, discussing the unstable, fluid nature of Cicero's writings and other ancient texts, argues, "We must not only ask, 'How does a given text embody the social or discursive world in which it was produced?' but also, 'How does it, as a variable entity, implicate the *worlds* [his emphasis] in which it was copied, reformed, and subjected to different readings and critiques?'"

Cicero's service to the state, and his personal achievement, in engineering Catiline's suppression.

Like any speech, the *First Catilinarian* should be understood primarily with reference to the goal of its persuasion, that is to say, its purpose. A speech always has a purpose. In the case of forensic oratory (speeches delivered in a court of law), there is invariably a single and obvious purpose: to secure either the conviction or the acquittal of the person who is on trial. In the case of deliberative oratory (speeches to a political assembly) and epideictic oratory (speeches of display, typically of praise or blame), on the other hand, the purpose is often less clear. Deliberative speeches usually involve the recommendation of a particular course of action, in which case the purpose is obvious, but they may involve making a report rather than a recommendation, and in that case the making of the report may involve persuading the audience to take a particular view of what is being reported. The *Second* and *Third Catilinarians* fall into this category, while the *Fourth Catilinarian* is a classic deliberative speech in that it makes recommendations to an assembly, the senate, during a debate that will be followed by a vote. The *First Catilinarian* is also a speech delivered in the senate, but the bulk of it (all except §§ 27b–32) is, crucially, addressed not to the senators but to Catiline, and the speech does not take place in the context of a debate leading to a vote. It is best regarded, therefore, not as deliberative but as epideictic, specifically a speech of blame.[7] The characteristic type of speech of blame is an invective, which is an abusive

---

[7] Batstone (1994: 218–21) argues that the speech is epideictic with forensic elements (220–21: "an *epideixis* which encompasses the forensic in support of deliberative purposes"). Kennedy (1972: 175–76), on the other hand, implies that he considers it to be deliberative: "The rhetorical analysis of the *Catilinarians* is, however, difficult. They do not conform well to the ordinary requirements of deliberative oratory. . . . Only the fourth can be said to deliberate about a course of action." MacKendrick (1995: 58) considers the speech to be deliberative, but with an invective purpose. For Steel (2006a: 66), it is deliberative. Dyck (2008: 61) considers it "basically deliberative," but also "in some ways comparable to a prosecution speech." May (2002: 522) justly remarks that "this speech is notoriously difficult to classify in terms of formal rhetoric and notoriously slippery in terms of defining a rhetorical challenge."

personal attack on an individual. The *First Catilinarian*, however, is a series of specific allegations against Catiline rather than a generalized attack, and is therefore not an invective in the strictest sense but, as already stated, a denunciation.[8] The purpose of a denunciation is to accuse someone of something, and the primary purpose of the *First Catilinarian* may therefore be said to be to expose Catiline as a conspirator (rather than simply to denigrate him, which would be its purpose were it a conventional invective). Accordingly, Cicero asks Catiline in the opening paragraph of the speech, "Do you not realize than your plans have been exposed?" (§ 1).

But to go further than that in defining the purpose or purposes of the speech is not easy. Many readers must have read the speech and been impressed by the force of Cicero's oratory, but nevertheless been unsure precisely what result the speech was intended to produce. George Kennedy says of the *Catilinarians*, "The parts of the speeches do not necessarily perform their usual functions or relate very clearly to each other. Indeed, it is rather difficult to say what is the principal objective of each speech, with the exception perhaps of the fourth. Usually Cicero seems to have several objectives in mind."[9] In order to clarify these objectives, the speech will now be reviewed and its purposes inferred at each point.

In the course of the review, some indication of the structure of the speech will be provided. However, the speech does not have a clear, well-defined structure to the same degree that a forensic speech usually does. To some extent, the structure is fluid, as befits a speech that is intended to be seen as, and in origin almost certainly was (since Catiline joined the meeting of the senate while it was

---

[8] This is the view of Powell 2007: 2. Craig 2007b considers the speech to be an invective and attempts to explain its lack of conventional invective themes; but perhaps the explanation lies in the fact that it is not strictly speaking an invective.

[9] Kennedy 1972: 176. Batstone 1994: 214–15 lists the many different purposes that have been attributed to the *First Catilinarian* by different scholars. None of these scholars consider the purposes of the speech as a written production of 60 BC (Approach B). Batstone himself concludes that the purpose of the speech is to construct and present Cicero's version of his consular ethos (1994: 216).

in progress),[10] a spontaneous outburst. All that can be stated with confidence is that there is an *exordium* (introduction) that takes up some or all of §§ 1–6; there is an argumentative section formally addressed to Catiline (§§ 10b–27a); there is an address to the senate (§§ 27b–32); and there is a brief *conclusio* (peroration) at § 33.[11]

Cicero begins the speech in a burst of anger: "How far, I ask you . . . " (*Quo usque tandem . . .*). The phrase is extremely rare: besides this passage and later quotations of it, it occurs only three times in extant Latin (Sal. *Cat.* 20.9; Liv. 6.18.5; Apul. *Met.* 3.27). At *Bellum Catilinae* 20.9, where Catiline is made to say to his followers, in June 64 BC, "How far, I ask you, shall we put up with this, most valiant men?" (*Quae quo usque tandem patiemini, o fortissumi viri?*), scholars have questioned why Sallust (writing in c. 42) puts into Catiline's mouth the opening words of the speech in which Cicero denounced him and exposed his conspiracy. The correct explanation, in my view, is that of D. A. Malcolm, who suggests that that is how Catiline, demagogue that he was, actually spoke.[12] Cicero would then be mimicking the impatient and reckless conspirator and throwing one of his characteristic expressions back in his face.[13] The reference would have even more point if it had been reported to Cicero that Catiline had used the phrase in the course of the meeting at Laeca's house. At that meeting, Catiline had sought

---

[10] See pp. 35–36.

[11] See the structural analyses proposed, for example, by Kennedy 1972: 178–80; Primmer 1977: 28; Craig 1993: 262–66; Batstone 1994: 226–27, 236; MacKendrick 1995: 58–60; and Dyck 2008: 61–62.

[12] Malcolm 1979, followed by Batstone 1994: 228. The other explanations, that Sallust is parodying Cicero (Syme 1964: 106; Renehan 1976: 99–100; Dyck 2008: 63) or that he is complimenting him (Innes 1977; Oakley 1997: 545–46) seem to me implausible, not least because Catiline's speech is supposed to predate Cicero's historically.

[13] Beard (2013: 85–86) lists some instances of the use of the phrase *quo usque tandem* in modern contexts, and she comments: "The irony in all this is that the political dynamics of the slogan's original context have been consistently subverted. . . . Words which started life as a threat uttered by the spokesman of the established order against the dissident are now almost universally deployed the other way round: as a challenge from the dissident to the established order. Catiline should be smiling in his grave." But if the words were originally Catiline's, there is no irony or subversion.

volunteers to assassinate Cicero (Sal. *Cat.* 27.3–28.1; cf. Appendix 2, no. 5). Perhaps what he had said was something like "How far, I ask you, shall we put up with this upstart consul?" If Catiline had indeed used the phrase *quo usque tandem*, then, on Approach A, the purpose of Cicero's throwing it back at him would have been not just to mock him but to signal to him that Cicero knew precisely what he had said at the meeting. On Approach B, on the other hand, the words provide a memorable opening for a speech that was perhaps already famous. The note of theatricality also helps to establish the dramatic situation for Cicero's readers (see p. 56).

Rudely addressing his would-be assassin as "Catiline" rather than, as senatorial convention and good manners required, "Lucius Catilina" (Cicero nowhere in the speech dignifies him by the use of his *praenomen*),[14] Cicero tells Catiline that his plans have been exposed and that his meeting at Laeca's house is common knowledge (1), and he expresses his outrage that Catiline is still alive and has brazenly entered the senate (2a). The *exordium* may be viewed either as ending at this point or as continuing to the middle or end of § 6. Cicero tells Catiline that he should already have been put to death on the authority of the emergency decree, and he cites historical precedents for the summary execution of traitors by senior magistrates (2b–4). So far his purposes may be assumed, on Approach A, to be to intimidate Catiline with his knowledge and to convince the senate that Catiline is indeed a serious threat and a man against whom he would be justified in taking a firm line (it should not be supposed that he is actually arguing for his execution). He then turns to the senators and tells them that he wants to be compassionate and to take no stricter action than is necessary, but that he finds himself already guilty of failing to act (4). On Approach B, his purpose here is to persuade his readership that he is not a vindictive man and that the actions he took two and a half years previously, in 63, were not excessive. He reminds the senate of

---

[14] Cf. Adams 1978: 146; Shackleton Bailey 1992: 3–4; Berry 1996: 127; Dyck 2008: 63. Cicero allows Catiline his *praenomen* in *Cat.* 2, but not in *Cat.* 3 or 4, after he had taken up arms against his country.

Manlius' army and declares that Catiline is its leader (5); this is an attempt, on Approach A, to convince the senate of Catiline's guilt. Then he ridicules the idea that if he were to order Catiline's immediate execution, he would face criticism; but he will not execute him, he adds, so long as there exist people so criminal as to deny the justice of his doing so (5–6a). The picture that is created is of a Cicero who is fully justified in taking the most extreme action possible against Catiline but who refrains from taking any action that would be controversial. This is plainly an attempt, on Approach B, to justify his actions against Catiline, and more particularly against the conspirators he executed, in 63.

Cicero advises Catiline to call off his plans, because they have been exposed (6b). In what could be viewed as a *narratio* (narration, 7–10a), he lists the plots of Catiline that he has previously exposed and, in some cases, forestalled (7–8a). He mentions the meeting at Laeca's house, states that it was attended by some of those present at this meeting of the senate, and describes what took place: plans were made for raising Italy in revolt, for burning Rome, for Catiline's departure, and for the assassination of Cicero himself, which he also succeeded in forestalling (8b–10a). No names are given, either of the senators who attended the meeting or of the two equestrians who undertook to assassinate Cicero. All this, on Approach A, has two purposes: for Cicero to use his detailed knowledge both to intimidate Catiline and to convince the senate of his guilt—without revealing the identity of his sources, so that he would continue to be supplied with information.

The *argumentatio* (argumentation), which takes up the greater part of the speech (until 27a or, alternatively, 32), begins at 10b. In view of what he has just revealed about Catiline's plans, Cicero urges him to leave Rome and go to Manlius, taking with him as many of his followers as possible. He will not allow Catiline to remain: "I will not tolerate it, I will not endure it, I will not allow it" (10b). This appears, on Approach A, to be an attempt to induce Catiline to leave Rome; but Cicero has just said (9) that Catiline is on the point of leaving Rome anyway. Instead, therefore, the passage must simply be an attempt to persuade the senate that Cicero is in control of events and is taking decisive action.

Cicero thanks Jupiter Stator (in whose temple the meeting is taking place) for enabling him to escape from Catiline, but the survival of Rome should not continue to depend on Cicero alone. Hitherto, he has foiled Catiline's attacks on himself by taking private measures (11); but Catiline is now attacking Rome as a whole, its temples and houses, the citizens, and all Italy. Nevertheless, Cicero will show lenience toward Catiline rather than executing him, because lenience, unlike execution, will result in Catiline's followers being flushed out of the city (12). On Approach A, Cicero is trying to persuade a possibly skeptical senate that Catiline's actions have reached a critical point, but he is also justifying, to any senators who think he ought to punish him, his decision not to do so. On Approach B, on the other hand, he is reminding his readership of his lenient nature, and so defending himself against the accusation of having acted as a tyrant in executing the conspirators on 5 December.

At § 13a Cicero returns to the central question of the speech: what he is going to tell Catiline to do. It is clear by now what action he and the senate are going to take: they are going to take no action. Cicero repeats what he said at § 9, that he knows that Catiline is planning to leave Rome in any case, and then orders him to do this. He represents Catiline as asking whether Cicero is ordering him to go into exile. Catiline does seem to have asked this question at some point;[15] it is an obvious question for him to have asked. Cicero's response is that he is not ordering but is merely advising Catiline to go into exile. Consuls did in fact have the power to send Roman citizens into exile in the public interest (the power was called *relegatio*, "banishment").[16] But if Catiline went into exile on Cicero's order, his guilt would not be proved, and he would appear as an innocent victim of tyrannical power. Cicero's position,

---

[15] Stroh 2000: 73.
[16] Lintott 2008: 144.

then (on Approach A), is that he is ordering Catiline to leave Rome, but is merely advising him to go into exile. It is a fine distinction, made with an eye to Cicero's need to justify himself should Catiline not go on to incriminate himself by joining Manlius.

At § 13b Cicero tells Catiline that there is nothing to detain him in Rome, because everyone there hates and fears him (the argument is circular:[17] Cicero has been trying to persuade the senate that Catiline is to be feared but now tries to persuade Catiline with the argument that everyone fears him).[18] This leads to a passage of invective (13b–14a) in which Cicero denounces Catiline's sexual crimes in vague terms and accuses him of having murdered his former wife and of having committed another, unspecified, crime (explained by Sallust at *Bellum Catilinae* 15.2 as the murder of his son)—all in a series of rhetorical questions. In an instance of *occultatio* ("paralipsis"), a figure by which pretended omission is used as a means of covertly introducing arguments or assertions that will not stand up to more direct scrutiny,[19] Cicero parades a flimsy excuse for not providing further details, before declaring that Catiline faces imminent bankruptcy. This passage serves to denigrate Catiline during his life (Approach A) and after his death (Approach B). It also provides students of rhetoric with a specimen invective (Approach B), illustrating, perhaps, what might be achieved with little or no material.

Cicero moves from Catiline's crimes against individuals to those against the state (14b) and makes a brief reference (15) to his appearance in the forum with a weapon on 29 December 66 and his

---

[17] The point is made by Craig 1993: 258, 260, 263–64.

[18] Tzounakas 2015 detects an allusion, here and at § 17, to the famous lines from Accius' *Atreus*, *oderint, / dum metuant* ("Let them hate, provided they fear!," Acc. *Trag.* 203–4 Ribbeck²), and to Ennius, possibly from the *Thyestes*, *quem metuunt oderunt, quem quisque odit periisse expetit* ("Whom they fear they hate, and whom one hates one desires dead," Enn. *Trag.* 348 Jocelyn). He argues that the allusion to the myth of Atreus serves to mark Catiline as a tyrant who deserves death and, on publication of the speech in 60, to deflect the charge of tyranny from Cicero himself (64–65).

[19] See Usher 1965: esp. 177 (list of instances). There was an example earlier at § 3, "I will pass over precedents that are too old, such as . . . ," and there will be another at *Cat.* 3.18.

alleged plot to assassinate the consuls—presumably the incoming consuls of 65. (One of those consuls, however, was Lucius Manlius Torquatus, who was shortly afterwards to support Catiline at his trial for extortion, and this is perhaps why Cicero does not make much of this allegation: the single reference in the *Catilinarians* to the supposed "first Catilinarian conspiracy" is a mere rhetorical question.) Cicero continues with Catiline's attempts to assassinate him, but no specific assassination attempt is referred to, not even the one that took place outside Cicero's house a matter of hours (or one day) earlier. This lack of specificity gives the passage the air of an invective rather than of an accusation grounded in fact (the oratory has an epideictic rather than a forensic character), and the suspicion of later rewriting is increased by the reference to Cicero's pity (*misericordia*) at the beginning of § 16b. This passage also serves to denigrate Catiline during his life and after his death, and the reference to pity, on Approach B, helps to defend Cicero from the later attacks on his severity toward Catiline and the conspirators.

Next, Cicero describes the scene when Catiline entered the senate (16b). He must have been pleased with the senators' conspicuous shunning of Catiline, and also with his description of it, because he repeats the content of the passage in similar language at *In Catilinam* 2.12. On Approach A, this description at 16b helps to isolate Catiline from the senate; on Approach B, it serves as a contextualization of the speech for its readers, since the first readers did not have the accounts of Sallust and Plutarch to explain to them what it was that they were reading. (The same technique is used at *Pro Roscio Amerino* 59–60, where Cicero describes the nonchalant behavior of the prosecutor before Cicero began his speech and the prosecutor's reaction of panic and alarm once he had begun it. That description too may have been intended as contextualization for the readership of the published speech—although it also makes complete sense as part of the delivered speech, and there is no reason to think that it was not delivered.) Cicero's question to Catiline, "Do you really wait for the insult to be expressed in words?" refers to a point of context made more explicit at § 20, that Catiline has challenged Cicero to put the question of his exile to a vote.

The purpose of § 17 is to serve as a bridge passage, linking Catiline's isolation in the senate with the prosopopoeia that follows. The term prosopopoeia (*fictio personae*, "impersonation") denotes the introduction into a speech of an invented statement by a non-personal entity (Rome, the country) or by a person no longer living (for example, Appius Claudius Caecus at *Pro Caelio* 34). It is also used in a wider sense to refer to any passage where the orator represents another person as speaking (for example, Publius Clodius at *Pro Caelio* 36).[20] Being hated as he is (on the evidence of the fact that no senator greeted him or would sit near him), Catiline ought (if he has any shame) to remove himself from Rome, "which is the common parent of us all."The parent (*parens*), which is the country (*patria*), is then made to allude to Catiline's known crimes, express her fear of him, and demand his departure (18). On Approach A, this passage is a means of isolating Catiline in an extreme way and causing the senate to shun him entirely, when his guilt has not in fact been proved: essentially, Catiline is ordered to leave Rome as a precaution, in case he is a conspirator ("If my fear is justified . . . ; but if it is not . . . ").Many in the senate must have suspected that Catiline was not guilty, and it is easier for Cicero to deal with this uncomfortable possibility when speaking as the *patria* rather than in his own voice.The prosopopoeia also provides a respite from the constant denunciation by Cicero, by causing Catiline to appear to be denounced by a different, and more authoritative, attacker. On Approach B, on the other hand, the passage serves to denounce a Catiline whose guilt has been proved by the subsequent events, while also providing readers of the speech with a piece of theatre, a set-piece prosopopoeia that they could study and admire.[21] The prosopopoeia is something to be performed, by Cicero in the

---

[20] Austin 1960: 90–91.

[21] Nisbet (1964: 62–63) objects to the theatricality of the *Catilinarians*, and especially of the two prosopopoeias in *Cat.* 1, and concludes that this element was written into the speeches in 60: "One does not seem to be listening in on a real debate in one of the most hard-headed assemblies that the world has known."Yet this passage does serve a valuable purpose on Approach A, and the speech was not delivered during a debate (cf. Lintott 2008: 143: "The speech . . . belongs to the period of informal discussion

senate and by his readership in their own homes or in front of their teachers. It is a highlight of both the delivered and the published speech, and was perhaps intended from the outset to acquire classic status.[22]

In § 19 Cicero deals with a point that might be thought to count in Catiline's favor, the fact that he had recently offered to place himself in voluntary custody. This gambit of Catiline's had come to nothing, and Cicero takes the line that no one would accept him. The picture that is created is of Catiline as a pariah, a man whom no one will receive into their house or sit next to in the senate. Cicero's purpose, on Approach A, continues to be to effect Catiline's isolation. This leads naturally to the suggestion (it is not an order) that Catiline go into exile (20a), and then to a second point that might be thought to count in Catiline's favor, his willingness to go into voluntary exile if the senate will decree it (20b). (The words attributed to Catiline, "Put the question to the senate," are not to be supposed to be interjected by Catiline at this point in Cicero's speech, because his offer has already been alluded to at § 16; instead, Cicero is quoting, or paraphrasing, words spoken by Catiline at an earlier point in the meeting.) Cicero peremptorily refuses to put the question of Catiline's exile to a vote: a vote would play into Catiline's hands, either by showing that Cicero did not have the support of the senate, if the senate declined to vote for Catiline's exile, or by casting Catiline in the role of an innocent victim if it did. Instead, therefore, Cicero infers from the senate's silence that they agree with his policy of driving Catiline out of Rome—into exile, if Catiline wishes Cicero to use that word ("Go into exile—if that is the term you are waiting to hear": the condition is significant, and serves to transfer some of the responsibility for the utterance from Cicero to Catiline). The reader should imagine a pause at this point (not indicated in the text), as Cicero suspends his speech

that regularly occurred when information was received or audience granted to foreign representatives").

[22] Tzounakas 2006 provides a valuable study of this prosopopoeia and its pair at §§ 27–29, explaining in particular the inconsistencies between them.

to allow Catiline to hear the senators' silence. All this argument can be understood on Approach A as an attempt to cut Catiline off from the senate's support. On Approach B, it is pure theatre.

To show that the senators' silence really does indicate that they agree that Catiline should be driven out of Rome, Cicero invites Catiline to consider what the senate's reaction would be if he had spoken in this way about two other senators, Publius Sestius and Marcus Claudius Marcellus (respectively, the future tribune of 57, successfully defended in *Pro Sestio*, a quaestor in 63; and the future consul of 51, the subject of *Pro Marcello*, previously a quaestor in 64).[23] Obviously, Cicero says, the rest of the senators would have leapt to their defense. The fact that they have not done this for Catiline demonstrates, Cicero argues, that they approve of the line he is taking; and he adds that he also has the approval of the equestrians and the Roman people (21). On Approach A, the suggestion that the senate would intervene physically to defend two even of its most junior members helps to reinforce Catiline's isolation. But on Approach B, the names of the two senators gain greater significance. Sestius was the quaestor assigned to Cicero's colleague Antonius, and in this role he acted as an agent of Cicero's, ensuring that Antonius remained loyal to the state (Cic. *Sest.* 8). After the meeting of the senate on 7 (or 8) November, he first went to Capua to secure it against the conspirators (*Sest.* 9–11), and then in December he went to Etruria, where he was responsible for persuading a reluctant Antonius to defeat Catiline immediately rather than suspend operations against him for the winter (*Sest.* 12). Marcellus, on the other hand, had on the night of 19 (or 18) October accompanied Crassus

---

[23] Diodorus, in his account of the meeting of the senate on 7 (or 8) November, says that Cicero asked the senators whether he should order Quintus Catulus to go into exile, and the senators all shouted their disapproval (Diod. 40.5a). On the strength of this, some scholars have argued that Cicero originally mentioned Catulus in his speech but when writing it up in 60 substituted the names of Sestius and Marcellus (see Reinach 1904; Ungern-Sternberg 1971; Cadoux 2006: 613 n. 9). This is rightly rejected by Stroh (2000: 76–77) and Dyck (2008: 104). In any case, there can be no doubt about the text here: the rhetorical point that Cicero is making absolutely depends on junior senators, not a senior one, being named.

when he came to Cicero with letters warning of an impending massacre (see pp. 31–32). One of the two men, then, had assisted in providing Cicero with evidence against Catiline, while the other would shortly afterwards contribute to Catiline's defeat. Cicero's mention of them here honors them, memorializes their service, and indirectly records his gratitude.

But there is a further point. Cicero wrote up and published the speeches of his consulship because he had been prompted to do so "by the enthusiasm of my young admirers" (*adulescentulorum studiis*, *Att.* 2.1.3; see p. 60). His reference to "this fine young man here [*huic adulescenti optimo*], Publius Sestius, or to the valiant Marcus Marcellus" is the only place in the *Catilinarians* where a named person is described as "young." Moreover, Sestius and Marcellus were both orators. As tribune in 57, Sestius gave speeches to the people in which he defended the policy of the senate while Cicero was in exile (Cic. *Red. Sen.* 20) and then gave a "frantic" (*furiosissimae*, *Att.* 4.3.4) speech on the subject of the delayed aedilician elections in November. He defended himself when on trial with great relish (Plut. *Cic.* 26.8; it is not certain which trial Plutarch refers to). He also spoke in the senate in support of Cicero and against Antony in April 43 (Cic. *Ad Brut.* 2.5.4). Catullus reveals that his speeches were published: the poet read one of them, an attack on a candidate for office named Antius, because he wanted to be invited to dinner by Sestius, but he found the speech so frigid (i.e., bombastic) that it made him ill with flu (Catul. 44.10–21).[24] Marcellus, on the other hand, is actually described in *Pro Marcello* as "my rival and imitator in my studies and in my work" (*aemulo atque imitatore studiorum ac laborum meorum*, Cic. *Marc.* 2), and in the *Brutus* he is praised as a hardworking student of oratory who lacks none of the oratorical virtues (Cic. *Brut.* 248–50; he is one of only two orators included despite being still alive, the other being Caesar). Dio adds that it was the power of his oratory that won him his consulship for 51 (Dio

---

[24] On the meaning of "frigid," see Fordyce 1961: 197–98. Cicero did not approve of Sestius' style either (*Fam.* 7.32.1; *Att.* 7.17.2). See further Malcovati 1976: 425–26.

40.58.3).[25] I suggest that both Sestius and Marcellus were among the young admirers, or even *were* the young admirers, whose enthusiasm prompted Cicero to publish the political speeches of his consulship.[26] If so, they may have had a personal interest in the publication of these speeches, over and above their desire to possess models of oratory for imitation. If Cicero had actually referred to the two of them, and in complimentary terms, in the speech in which he denounced Catiline before the senate, then they would doubtless have wanted his words about them to be publicized and preserved for posterity. The attractions of being immortalized by Cicero in a literary classic must have been considerable. On Approach B, then, Cicero's reference to the two men at this point in the speech is a friendly nod to two of his supporters who had helped him in 63–62 and who now, perhaps, were his greatest oratorical fans.

The identification of Sestius and Marcellus with the *adulescentuli* ("young men," i.e., young admirers) mentioned at *Ad Atticum* 2.1.3 cannot be proved, but does in my view have a high likelihood of being correct. The sequence of events, I suggest, was as follows. First, Cicero did refer to Sestius and Marcellus in his original speech in the senate. He chose them, rather than any other senators, because they were young, which was necessary for his rhetorical point, and because they were supporters of his: Marcellus had just demonstrated his loyalty to him against Catiline, and Sestius, a serving quaestor, would shortly do so even more strongly. Three years later, the two men urged him to publish his consular speeches partly because they were students of oratory but more particularly because they had been singled out for honorable mention in Cicero's (by then) famous speech against Catiline in his presence, and they wished to see the speech given circulation and permanence. Cicero then published the political speeches of his consulship and retained the reference to his two young friends in the speech that became the *First Catilinarian*, partly because he wished to thank them for

[25] See further Malcovati 1976: 457–58.
[26] Cf. *Sul.* 19–20, where Cicero speaks of his respect for the Marcelli and his strong desire to oblige them.

their support in 63–62, and partly because they deserved the credit for having persuaded him to publish his consular speeches (something that in fact he needed no great persuasion to do, since their publication suited his purposes in 60). *In Catilinam* 1.21 therefore fulfills the function of the acknowledgments of a modern book: "I should like to thank X and Y for suggesting that I write this book." Sestius and Marcellus would understand, be grateful, and continue to support their oratorical idol.

Cicero's words at § 22, "But why am I saying this?," indicate a pause and signal a change of focus, from Catiline to Cicero himself. So let us pause ourselves at this point and recapitulate what Cicero has said so far to Catiline, and what his purposes have been, on Approach A.

First, Cicero has ordered Catiline to leave Rome (§§ 10, 13, 20). But he has not ordered him to join Manlius, because that would be equivalent to ordering him to make war on Rome. He has also been reluctant to order him to go into exile (he did this only at § 20, where he qualified the word "exile" with "if that is the term you are waiting to hear"). Even though it would not be unlawful, ordering Catiline into exile could be considered an abuse of Cicero's authority (since Catiline has not been convicted in a court of law) and might well be viewed as the persecution of an innocent man. Instead, therefore, Cicero has merely advised him to go into exile or suggested that he go into exile (§§ 13, 20). If Catiline went into exile, then, he would be doing so of his own free choice; he could not claim that the consul had forced him. As far as Cicero is concerned, advising Catiline to go into exile rather than make war on Rome is entirely uncontroversial. He is merely advising Catiline to put the state's interests above his own. By a strange coincidence, he would later do the same himself: on his return from exile in 57, he claimed that by yielding to force and withdrawing from Rome, he had put the interests of the state above his own, and so prevented civil violence and bloodshed (Cic. *Red. Sen.* 6, 33–34; *Red. Pop.* 1, 13; *Mil.* 36).

Secondly, Cicero's purposes. Cicero knows, regardless of whatever he says to him, that Catiline intends to leave Rome and join

Manlius (§§ 9, 13, 24, 27, 30), that he is actually on the point of leaving Rome (§ 9), and that he has made arrangements to join Manlius on a particular day (§ 24). This information must be correct: Cicero wants to demonstrate to Catiline that he is aware of his plans ("Do you not realize that your plans have been exposed?" § 1), and this demonstration would fail if the details that he revealed were not true.[27] His strategy is to disclose information that Catiline knows to be true, while implying that he knows much more (the rhetorical technique is called *reticentia*). It is not the case, therefore, that Cicero is aiming to persuade Catiline to leave Rome, or to leave Rome sooner rather than later, or to go into exile. He knows that he is on the point of leaving Rome and joining Manlius, and since this is what he wants him to do—so that Catiline can then be defeated and killed while engaged in open warfare against Rome—it follows that he is not trying to persuade him to *do* anything at all. So what, then, is the goal of Cicero's persuasion? He has, in fact, two goals. In the first place, he is trying to persuade those senators who are not convinced that Catiline is a conspirator that he is one. This will have the effect of isolating and weakening him, and of strengthening Cicero's own position. In the second place, he is trying to persuade all the senators that he, Cicero, is in control of the situation and is behaving as a responsible consul should.

All the persuasion in the speech so far, then, on Approach A, has been persuasion of the senate; but it has been attempted not by direct address to the senate but by direct address to Catiline. This may be described as oblique persuasion. Cicero wishes it to appear that he is working on Catiline, whereas in fact he is working, and working hard, on the senate.[28]

At § 22, then, Cicero introduces a new element into the speech—the consul—and he puts the question: How will his order to Catiline, to leave Rome, and his advice to him, to go into exile,

---

[27] In Sallust's account, Catiline is eager to join Manlius but wants to secure Cicero's assassination first (*Cat.* 27.4).

[28] Cf. Kennedy 1972: 179: "The portrayal of Catiline's character is more of interest to the senate or posterity than to Catiline himself."

affect Cicero himself? If Catiline leaves Rome and goes into exile, it will make Cicero unpopular (because Catiline will be wrongly assumed to be innocent), but Rome will be safe. Cicero selflessly presents this as a desirable outcome—although he also admits that it is an inconceivable one, in view of Catiline's bad character. Nevertheless, he urges Catiline to adopt this course of action, and he repeats that it would make Cicero himself unpopular (23): Catiline would be seen as having gone into exile at the consul's command (although Cicero has been careful to recommend exile rather than order it). If, on the other hand, Catiline leaves Rome and joins Manlius, then, Cicero says, this will strengthen Cicero's own position and enhance his glory. This line of argument is presented as an attempt to induce Catiline to damage Cicero's position, and save Rome, by going into exile. But of course Cicero knows (as he is about to admit) that Catiline has already resolved to join Manlius. The sole purpose of the argument, on Approach A, is simply to present Cicero to the senate as in command of the situation and as acting unselfishly by arguing for a course of action that is in Rome's interests but against his own. On Approach B, he also appears as authoritative and selfless. But Cicero's readers know that Catiline did go to Manlius and are here told firmly that this is something that redounds to Cicero's glory. The passage therefore also serves as retrospective self-justification and self-praise.

At § 24, Cicero asks, "Why should I be urging you . . . ?" when he knows that Catiline has sent an armed force ahead to wait for him at Forum Aurelium and has arranged a rendezvous with Manlius on a particular, unspecified day. A literal answer would be "So that the senate will believe that I am in control." But of course the question is rhetorical. When, at *In Catilinam* 2.13, Cicero reports to the people what he said to Catiline in the senate, he says that he told him that he had information that Catiline had sent ahead "arms, axes, rods of office, trumpets, military standards, and also that silver eagle to which he [Catiline] had even dedicated a shrine at his house." In fact, he mentions here only "that silver eagle to which you have dedicated a shrine at your house." The discrepancy is not significant: the silver eagle, a standard that Sallust says had allegedly been used by Marius in the Cimbric War (*Cat.* 59.3), was incriminating enough. Catiline's aristocratic friends might well have been shocked to learn that he apparently venerated the cause of Marius.[29] Cicero's purpose, on Approach A, is to intimidate Catiline and, more importantly, to impress the senators with the extent and specificity of his information, thereby helping to convince them of Catiline's guilt. But he concedes here what he has not conceded earlier, that it is not within his power to influence Catiline's plans. In the next step in his argument, Catiline's departure is therefore now presented as inevitable: "You will go, at long last [*tandem aliquando*], where your unrestrained, insane ambition has long been driving you" (25).

An outburst of invective follows. It is well placed, being the culmination of the passage of argument that began at 10b, and signals Cicero's exasperation. The word *tandem*, "at last," echoes the opening of the speech; the phrase *tandem aliquando*, "at long last," was used earlier in the final words of the rosopopoeial at § 18 and will recur as the opening words of the *Second Catilinarian*. The invective begins with an attack on Catiline's supporters, who are described for the senators (on Approach A) using political vocabulary: "Drawing on the worst of society [*ex perditis*], you have scraped together a gang of traitors [*improborum manum*], men entirely abandoned not just by fortune, but even by hope" (25). The words are far from imprecise: Cicero means that Catiline's followers consist of disreputable men (including senators) who have run out of money and credit, and who know that they cannot restore themselves to solvency without joining Catiline in overthrowing the state. Such men are by definition bad people (26). All this, obviously, denigrates Catiline and his followers both during the meeting of the senate and two years after his death. This leads on to an extraordinary characterization of Catiline (26):

---

[29] One could speculate how Catiline, originally a prominent supporter of Sulla, came to possess a military standard of Marius. But evidently the standard allowed him, as a one-time Sullan appealing to former Marians as well as former Sullans, to be all things to all men—a characteristic of his highlighted by Cicero at *Cael.* 13–14.

Those physical powers of yours we hear so much about have set you up for a life of this kind: the ability to lie on the bare ground has prepared you not just for launching sexual assaults but for committing crime, the capacity to stay awake not just for cheating husbands in their sleep but for robbing unsuspecting people of their property. Now you have an opportunity to show off your celebrated capacity to endure hunger, cold, and the lack of every amenity—hardships which you will shortly find out have finished you off!

Catiline's powers of endurance were evidently a talking point ("we hear so much about," "your celebrated capacity"): the senators must have known about and been impressed by his ability to sleep on the ground, to stay awake,[30] and to endure hunger, cold, and every kind of hardship, all attributes of a well-trained soldier and a model commander. Cicero does not deny Catiline those powers, but he claims that they have been used not for any honest purpose but to commit crime, particularly sexual crime; he says that Catiline will be able to display them in Manlius' camp; and he adds, with a touch of bravado, that they will not prove sufficient to protect him there (cf. "How will they endure the frost and snow up there in the Apennines? Perhaps they expect to endure the glacial temperatures more easily because they have had plenty of practice dancing naked at dinner parties?," *Cat.* 2.23). The passage is a way of dealing with a characteristic of Catiline's that was admirable and well known, and therefore had to be addressed: Cicero associates it with criminality, and then claims, with slight inconsistency, that it will turn out not to be such a strong characteristic after all. In this way Catiline is presented to his contemporaries and to posterity as a rapist, an adulterer, and a thief on the one hand and an inadequate soldier, doomed to failure, on the other.

---

[30] Cf. Cicero's claim at § 8, "I am much more vigilant in defense of the country than you are for its destruction."

This same characterization makes a reappearance in the *Second Catilinarian*, where Cicero is dealing with the same issue before a different audience (2.9):

> Catiline himself, as a result of his repeated sexual misconduct and criminal activities, had acquired the ability to endure cold, hunger, thirst, and lack of sleep, and was therefore hailed as a hero by people of this sort. However, his sexual excess and criminal behavior actually tended to dissipate his physical energy and mental power.

So before the people, too, Cicero needed to counteract a favorable impression that Catiline had made, and he does so in much the same way, but this time with a stronger element of inconsistency: Catiline's sexual and criminal exploits both gave rise to and undermined his physical powers. The self-contradiction allows Cicero to talk up Catiline's criminality while talking down his chances of success. At the same time, a suggestion that Catiline's unusual physical powers are something monstrous and even bestial does not lie far beneath the surface—hence the references to repeated sexual crimes. The audience had been prepared for this by the description of Catiline as "that monster and portent" at the beginning of the speech (*a monstro illo atque prodigio*, 2.1; cf. 2.2).[31] The characterization recurs yet again in the "obituary" of Catiline at *In Catilinam* 3.16–17 ("He could endure cold, thirst, hunger. He was so keen, so bold, so well prepared, so clever, so vigilant in committing crime, and so thorough in depravity"), and it has an afterlife in Sallust at *Bellum Catilinae* 5.1–5 (esp. 3). The similarity of wording in all these passages is striking. But that is how the ancient orator, relying on his rhetorical training and his memory, operated. Cicero knew what he wanted to say about Catiline, and he said it whenever the occasion demanded or allowed.

---

[31] Corbeill 2008 argues that in Ciceronian invective a *prodigium* represents something that must be extirpated in order to secure the survival of the state.

At § 27b, the *argumentatio* completed, Cicero turns to address the senators: "Now, conscript fathers . . . " This section of the speech, to § 32, may conveniently be labelled a *digressio*. (This does not mean that Cicero is straying from the point; *digressio* is the term traditionally used by scholars to denote any section of a speech that cannot be classed as one of the standard parts prescribed by ancient rhetoricians.) Cicero's address to Catiline was also, of course, intended for the senators; but §§ 27b–32 are differentiated from what comes before by the fact that nothing that Cicero says is intended for Catiline. He has dealt with him and now ignores him.

In this section, Cicero, having done his best to convince the senators of Catiline's guilt, justifies his decision to take no action against him and so allow him to go to Manlius (as he knows he will) and make war on Rome. The alternative course of action, summary execution of Catiline, is carefully presented as a suggestion not of Cicero himself but of the *patria*, in a second prosopopoeia. Her first speech was addressed to Catiline, urging him to leave Rome (§ 18); this one is addressed to Cicero, urging him to prevent Catiline from leaving. The first one puts into words the attitude of those senators who are afraid of Catiline but not fully convinced of his guilt; this one puts into words the attitude of those who are convinced of it and want Cicero to take a hard line.[32] The *patria* calls on the consul by name and asks him what he is doing letting loose rather than punishing a man whom he has discovered to be a public enemy (27b; however, Catiline had not yet been declared a *hostis* by the senate). She raises three possible objections to execution— inadequate precedent, illegality, and the potential adverse judgment of posterity on Cicero—and dismisses each of them in turn (28). Precedents exist, she says (although she does not cite any), and rebels always forfeit their civil rights (although this was not actually the case in law). The greatest attention is given to the third objection, the judgment of posterity. Cicero has a duty to place the safety of his fellow citizens above his own reputation and safety, she argues,

---

[32] Dyck 2008: 19–20, 113.

and in any case the alternative course, letting Catiline go, would also be injurious to Cicero's reputation, particularly when Catiline is ravaging Italy and burning her cities (29a). The value of the prosopopoeia to Cicero is that it allows him to avoid, to some extent, the outrage that might be caused if he gave arguments for the execution of Catiline in his own voice. As it is, the execution of Catiline is a hypothetical proposal, put forward not by himself but by an entity that is beyond criticism, the *patria*. The effect of producing those arguments, on Approach A, is to make Cicero's expulsion of Catiline (if that is how the senators choose to interpret Catiline's departure) seem a moderate and reasonable response to the crisis. It underlines his lenience in letting Catiline go, and so protects him from the charge of autocratic behavior. At the same time, it provides him with a justification for taking firmer action, should he need to. From the perspective of Approach B, on the other hand, the passage reads differently. Catiline's supporters, although not Catiline himself, had been summarily executed by Cicero on 5 December, and Cicero had faced severe criticism for that action. The prosopopoeia provides an emotionally powerful justification for the executions as being in the public interest, made all the more effective by being put into the mouth of the *patria* herself.

Cicero addresses his answer to the *patria* to the senators (29b–30). He would certainly have executed "that gladiator" without hesitation if he had judged that that was the right thing to do. Precedents suggest that such a course of action would have done his reputation no harm, but if it had done him harm, then the unpopularity would only have brought him glory (29b). But executing Catiline would have been the wrong thing to do. In the first place, there are some senators who fail to see the danger, or refuse to see it. If Cicero had executed Catiline, people would have believed that he had executed an innocent man and so had acted cruelly and tyrannically. But if he allows him to leave Rome and go to Manlius' camp, as he knows he intends to, then no one will be able to deny that the conspiracy exists (30a). The argument is weak because it takes no account of the statement Cicero has just made, that damage to his reputation was not a factor in his decision because "unpopularity earned by doing what is right is not unpopularity at all, but glory" (29b). But on Approach A, the passage gives a practical reason why Cicero cannot execute Catiline: there are important members of the senate (he is perhaps thinking primarily of Caesar) who would not support him. On Approach B, it provides a reminder that in spite of the executions that he did carry out, those of 5 December, Cicero is nevertheless a consul who did not act "in a cruel and tyrannical manner" (30a).

The second reason why executing Catiline would have been the wrong thing to do is given at 30b. If Catiline is allowed to leave Rome and takes his followers with him, then they can all be wiped out together, and Rome will be safe from future ills. The point has already been made to Catiline himself at § 12: "If I order your execution, all the other members of the conspiracy will remain within the state; but if you leave Rome, as I have long been urging you to do, the voluminous, pernicious dregs of society— your companions—will be flushed out of the city." On Approach A, this is a compelling reason for letting Catiline go. On Approach B, however, it serves no purpose, since Catiline did not take his followers with him when he left Rome.[33]

The end of the *digressio* (31–32) provides a rhetorical amplification of and conclusion to the argument just advanced (the address to the "conscript fathers" in both sections shows that this part of the speech belongs to the *digressio*, not the *conclusio*). In a lengthy simile, the removal of Catiline from Rome, without the removal of his followers, is compared to a drink of cold water given to a patient who is suffering from fever: the drink causes the fever to abate temporarily but then to break out again more violently (31). The comparison is not an exact one, but in an age when most illnesses were more dangerous than they are today, and therefore more to be feared, the graphic description of a fever is an effective way of frightening an audience. Ironically, Catiline would have agreed that the state was diseased, but he would not have accepted Cicero's

---

[33] Cf. Stroh 2000: 77.

diagnosis of the cause. On Approach A, the passage serves to make the senators alive to the danger of removing Catiline while leaving his followers in place. On Approach B it is less effective, again because Catiline did in fact leave his followers behind when he left Rome. The conclusion to the *digressio* invites all the traitors, not just Catiline, to leave Rome (32). Once again, this is only effective on Approach A. But it does contain the best (although not the most famous) sentence of the speech: "Finally, let it be inscribed on the forehead of every citizen what he thinks about his country" (*sit denique inscriptum in fronte unius cuiusque quid de re publica sentiat*)— an expression of the deep patriotism that was always the guiding principle of Cicero's life. A consul who uttered those words in the senate would be listened to carefully. On Approach B, they add to the grandeur of the speech (before the clausula, i.e., the standard rhythmical ending [*publica sentiat*], the sentence consists almost entirely of long syllables) and help to raise it to classic status.

There follows a short *conclusio*, signaled by the change of addressee from the senators back to Catiline (33). But after a mere sentence Cicero turns from Catiline to Jupiter, that is, to the statue of Jupiter Stator that stood in the temple, and makes a double prophecy: you, Jupiter, will drive Catiline and his associates from Rome, and you, Jupiter, will inflict on these criminals everlasting punishment.[34] It is a majestic and apt end to the speech, which, on both approaches, removes responsibility from Cicero while at the same time investing his cause with the highest possible authority. On Approach B, the reference to the imminent divine punishment of criminals serves to place Cicero's execution of the arrested conspirators beyond question.[35]

---

[34] On Cicero's references to Jupiter Stator in the speech, see Vasaly 1993: 49–59; Gildenhard 2011: 273–78 (276: "The audience is to believe that the god's crushing of the enemies of Rome is . . . a predetermined fact, which Cicero has the power to divine. . . . In claiming to know what Jupiter will do, Cicero reinforces the impression that he and the gods . . . have been and will be closely collaborating in the protection of the Roman state").

[35] The point is made by Usher 2008: 52–53.

On a casual reading, the purposes of the *First Catilinarian* are far from clear. The speech is not a forensic speech, and it has no *partitio* (partition, division) stating what the orator intends to prove and how he will organize his argument. It is difficult to follow, and difficult to hold in the mind all at once (it is easier to remember only its highlights). It appears to be an address to Catiline (except at §§ 27b–32), and this gives it an extraordinarily dramatic air, but (on Approach A) it is in fact the senators, not Catiline, whom Cicero is seeking to influence throughout. The speech is full of instructions, exhortations, and unsolicited advice for Catiline: to leave Rome, to go into exile, and even, in the *conclusio*, to initiate civil war. Moreover, in the *Second* and *Third Catilinarians*, Cicero claims to have brought about Catiline's departure from Rome: "When he was driven from the city . . . ," 2.1; "For at the time when I expelled Catiline from the city," 3.3; "When I was driving him out of the city . . . ," 3.16. Writing to Atticus in 60 BC, Cicero describes this speech as "the one by which I sent Catiline out of Rome" (*Att.* 2.1.3). Yet it is clear from the speech that Cicero knew that Catiline was on the point of leaving Rome anyway (§§ 9, 13, 24, 27, 30). At *In Catilinam* 2.1, he gives three possible explanations of his role in Catiline's departure: "This criminal we have expelled from Rome; or released; or followed with our farewells as he was leaving of his own accord." The last of these explanations is the one that comes closest to the truth. Catiline was leaving by his own choice, for Manlius, not exile. Cicero knew it and was happy to see him go. Cicero must have also known that Catiline was not going to take all of his followers with him: even if his spies had not informed him of this, it was obvious that Catiline would need a fifth column within the city. Cicero claims that the reason he has not executed Catiline but is letting him go is because Catiline will take his followers with him and they can all then be destroyed together (§§ 12, 29–32)—but he has to say that, because he cannot admit that he, the consul, is powerless to stop Catiline from going to Manlius and leaving his followers behind. At *In Catilinam* 3.3, he says: "For at the time when I expelled Catiline from the city . . . at that time, when I wanted to get him out of Rome, I imagined that either the rest of the conspirators would leave with him or else those who remained behind would be weak and powerless without him." But of course he imagined no such thing. He knew more or less exactly what Catiline would do, and how little he could do in response.

As far as Catiline is concerned, then, Cicero aims, on Approach A, merely to intimidate and demoralize his opponent. He does not aim to persuade him of anything, or to do anything. For the purpose of persuasion, therefore, on Approach A, the speech is aimed exclusively at the senators—as one would expect a speech delivered in the senate to be. On this approach, Cicero has three aims. First, he aims to destroy Catiline's character in the eyes of the senators, to present him as an object of fear,[36] and to isolate him from the senators, so that they will have no sympathy for him or his objectives and will treat him as a pariah. Secondly, he aims to persuade those senators inclined to give Catiline the benefit of the doubt that his actions have reached a critical point, that he is indeed guilty of plotting to overthrow the government, massacre his opponents, and set fire to Rome, and that consequently Cicero would be justified in taking the strongest possible action against him. Thirdly, he aims to persuade all the senators, including those strongly hostile to Catiline, that he has the situation in hand, and that the course of action he is following (namely, letting Catiline go rather than summarily executing him) is the one that will best protect Rome. Although his position is weak, in that he cannot prevent Catiline from proceeding with his attempted coup, he aims to present himself to his peers as a consul who is authoritative, decisive, and effective.

On Approach B, on the other hand, Cicero's purposes are different. He aims, first, to destroy the dead Catiline's reputation and damn him for all time. Secondly, he aims to persuade his contemporaries, and posterity, not only that he acted correctly when he allowed Catiline to leave Rome, and later when he executed the arrested conspirators, but that his suppression of the conspiracy was a glorious achievement for which he deserves the highest possible

---

[36] On this aspect, see Batstone 1994: 262–63.

praise. More specifically, he aims to persuade his contemporaries, and posterity, that he is not the cruel and vindictive man that his enemies have portrayed him as and that his actions in 63 were unselfish, were not excessive or autocratic, and did not constitute an abuse of power. To these may be added a further aim, one not based on persuasion: he wished to produce a model of oratory for his young admirers to imitate (even though they would be unlikely to be denouncing conspirators themselves) and a literary classic that would confer on him, permanently, the status of Rome's leading political orator and statesman.

It remains to consider the degree to which the *First Catilinarian* was successful.[37] The success of a forensic speech is easy to judge: the client was either acquitted or convicted. Likewise, if a deliberative speech involved the recommendation of a particular course of action, the course of action was either adopted or not adopted. For an epideictic speech, it is less easy to say what result constitutes success, but, generally speaking, a speech is a success if its author's aims are achieved. Sallust makes a favorable judgment about the *First Catilinarian*: the speech was "brilliant, and of service to the state" (*Cat.* 31.6). That may or may not have been the general view at the time when he was writing. If we consider Cicero's aims in the speech, it is of course unknown to what extent, if any, Catiline felt intimidated or demoralized by Cicero's treatment of him. But he was not a man who was easily intimidated. Cicero aimed to change the senators' view of Catiline and of himself, and here too Sallust provides relevant information: he claims that "everyone" (*omnes*) interrupted Catiline's insulting reply to Cicero by calling him "public enemy" and "parricide" (*Cat.* 31.8). This suggests that Cicero's speech had met with general approval but does not quite prove that the skeptics had been won over. As for Cicero's readers in

---

[37] Price 1998 argues that the speech was a failure, because of Cicero's inability to take decisive action (109: "In his speech, the *First Catilinarian*, he urged no particular policy, argued for or against no proposal, proposed no measures and requested no specific action"). But the success of the speech should be judged not against Cicero's position, which was indeed weak, but against its aims.

60 BC, it is unknown whether they revised their view of him, concluding that he should not be blamed for his actions three years earlier or that he should be given greater credit for them. Nevertheless, in the longer term, the speech was entirely successful in destroying Catiline's reputation. Catiline was silenced, for all time, by the force of Cicero's oratory: the speech gives Cicero the last word. In addition, in writing the *First Catilinarian*, Cicero succeeded in creating both a model of oratory and a literary classic.[38] But the speech has come to be more than that. The most famous speech in Latin literature, it is a monument in prose that defines not just Cicero's consulship but his place in history. At the same time, it is a striking symbol of the dysfunctional political culture of the late republic, an epoch when politicians competed first with words and then, all too often, with swords.

---

[38] Sallust's reference to the speech (*Cat.* 31.6) may suggest that it had already acquired classic status by the time he was writing. Quintilian refers to the speech twenty times (for comparison, he refers to the *Second Catilinarian* twice, to the *Third* once, and to the *Fourth* once).

·4·

Persuading the People:
The *Second* and *Third Catilinarians*

Of the ten speeches that Cicero lists in 60 BC as comprising the
bulk of his consular corpus, including the four *Catilinarians*,
six are speeches he made to the people. Besides the *Second* and
Third Catilinarians, there were: "(2) to the assembly, on the agrarian
law [*De lege agraria 2*]; (3) on Otho . . . ; (5) on the children of the
proscribed; (6) when I resigned my province at a public meeting"
(*Att.* 2.1.3; see p. 60). Of the "two further short pieces," *De lege
agraria* 3 and 4, the first was also a speech to the people (it is extant),
while nothing is known about the second. Clearly, then, the collection primarily showcased Cicero's skill in addressing the people—
the Roman citizens who the previous year had raised him, rather
than Catiline, to the consulship. Cicero had given his first speech to
the people only in 66 (Cic. *Man.* 1), yet he had been delivering forensic speeches regularly in the forum since 81, and to the ordinary
people of Rome he must have been one of the most recognizable
and best known senators. In all his surviving speeches to the people,
he addresses them with an easy familiarity, for example, when he
shows knowledge of plebeians who were of no political or social
distinction but were evidently well known to his audience: "I find
that he [Catiline] took with him Tongilius, a man he had first had
sexual relations with when Tongilius was a boy, and also Publicius
and Minucius, men whose unpaid restaurant bills were hardly likely
to destabilize the state" (*Cat.* 2.4). These notorious characters are

Cicero's Catilinarians. D. H. Berry, Oxford University Press (2020). © Oxford University Press.
DOI: 10.1093/oso/9780195326468.001.0001

not mentioned elsewhere in Latin literature. It would be surprising if many other senators had heard of them.

De lege agraria 2 (delivered in January 63 BC) is a speech that perfectly illustrates Cicero's ability to win over the people.[1] In it, he uses his oratorical powers to persuade the people to reject a bill that, at least at first sight, appears to have been strongly in their interest (or, at any rate, in the interest of many of them).[2] The *lex agraria* of Publius Servilius Rullus, a tribune of 63, was a Gracchan-style agrarian bill for the purchase of agricultural land in Italy and for its distribution, together with the fertile public land in Campania, among poor Roman citizens. Cicero argued that the scheme was a con, that it was in reality designed to give unlimited wealth and power to the ten officials (including Rullus) who would administer it ("kings," he calls them) and to their shadowy backers, that it would lead to large-scale corruption, that it would benefit those who had profited from the Sullan proscriptions,[3] that it was an attack on Pompey, that it would bankrupt the treasury, and that the land assigned, being uncultivable and unhealthy, would not be worth having anyway. At the outset, Cicero argues vigorously that he is a *popularis* (popular) consul and that neither the bill nor its proposers are popular (6, 7, 9, 10, 15, 27); he criticizes those who claim to be popular but are not (7); and he reminds his audience that, unlike recent consuls, he is a "new man," without the advantages enjoyed by the nobility—although in this context his newness

---

[1] See Lintott 2008: 137–42 (142: "Pliny [*Nat.* 7.117] is right to see the second and third speeches [*De lege agraria*] . . . as testimony to Cicero's remarkable control over the people in *contiones*").

[2] Yavetz (1963: 490) makes the point that not all of the urban plebs wanted to leave Rome and become farmers.

[3] Cicero argues that the bill would provide a means for the purchasers of the estates of those proscribed by Sulla (Rullus' father-in-law was one such purchaser, Catiline another) to escape from their unpopularity by selling their property to the state (68–70, 98; cf. 1.14–15); and in *Agr.* 3 he tells the people that the bill would bestow on Sullan occupiers the best legal title to their land (3.3, 7–14). In the *Second Catilinarian*, similarly, he capitalizes on the resentment felt against those who have acquired property under Sulla by claiming that Sullan colonists form a significant part of Catiline's support (*Cat.* 2.20).

becomes an advantage (1, 3–4). Praising the Gracchi,[4] he maintains that he is not opposed to land bills in principle (10; cf. 31), but only to this one. Interestingly, he claims that some of his predecessors avoided appearing before the people and addressing them, while others did so reluctantly (6). This was no doubt true. The speech achieved its aim, and the people voted down the bill ("Upon your speaking to them, the tribes rejected the agrarian law, that is, their own sustenance," Plin. *Nat.* 7.117, apostrophizing the long-dead Cicero; cf. Plut. *Cic.* 12.5).[5]

The speech "on Otho" (*De Othone*), of which only a single fragment survives, must have been an even more striking example of Cicero's control over the people.[6] It was delivered on the first day of the Ludi Apollinares, on 9 July.[7] Plutarch describes what happened (*Cic.* 13.2–4, tr. Andrew Lintott, with modifications):

> Formerly the equestrians were mixed with the masses in the theatres and watched with the common people in whichever seats they happened to find. Marcus Otho in his praetorship was the first to separate the equestrians from the rest of the citizens as a mark of honor and to assign them special seats. . . . [8] The common people took this as a humiliation and, when Otho made an appearance in the theatre, they hissed at him insultingly, while the equestrians received him with enthusiastic applause: the people in turn

---

[4] By contrast, Cicero takes a negative (but not entirely hostile) view of the Gracchi when addressing the senate: see *Cat.* 1.30, 4.13. See further Murray 1966 (296: "He [Cicero] is generally quite pleased with the actions of those who opposed them"); Blom 2010: 103–7.

[5] Stockton (1971: 88) describes the speeches *De lege agraria* as "masterpieces of misrepresentation," although he also points out that "it would be rash to assume that the authors of the bill were selfless, disinterested men with no object but to increase the happiness and well-being of the deserving poor." Many of Cicero's criticisms of the bill must have been valid, even if they were overstated.

[6] Crawford 1994: 209–14.

[7] I accept the arguments of Ryan 2006: 99–100.

[8] Lucius (not Marcus) Roscius Otho was (presumably) urban praetor in 63 and president of the Apollinares (Ryan 1997) and had carried his law reserving the first fourteen rows in the theatre for the equestrians when he was tribune in 67.

intensified their hissing, and the equestrians their applause. After that they turned to abusing each other, and the theatre descended into chaos. But Cicero, hearing of this, arrived on the scene and called the people out to the Temple of Bellona, where he rebuked them and gave them his advice. They then went back to the theatre and greeted Otho with enthusiastic applause, competing with the equestrians in showing him honor and glory.

Cicero's influence must have extraordinary for him to be able to achieve such a complete change of mind and behavior in so many people; had he failed, his authority would have been dealt a serious and very public blow. It is not known what he said: the surviving fragment, "The festivals of Ceres and Flora, and the games of Apollo, belong to the immortal gods, not to us" (*Cerealia, Floralia ludosque Apollinares deorum immortalium esse, non nostros*), reveals little.[9] But Cicero was always a supporter of the equestrians, having originated from that section of society himself, and it is possible that he took the opportunity to remind the people that such prosperity as they enjoyed was ultimately dependent on the provincial taxes that the equestrians collected.[10] His triumph in the matter of seating would be echoed four months later when he denounced Catiline in the senate, causing the leading senators to move away from the benches where Catiline was sitting (*Cat.* 1.16, 2.12).

The *Second* and *Third Catilinarians*—two speeches to the people, originally delivered nearly a month apart—are a pair, and so will be discussed in a single chapter.[11] Their original audiences must have consisted of much the same people as had listened to *De lege agraria*

---

9 Crawford 1994: 213–14 suggests that Cicero may have been criticizing the people for politicizing a religious event.

10 See Berry 2003: 225–26 ("It is obvious that he must have lectured the people on the dignity of the equestrian order," at 226); cf. Wiseman 1994: 352 ("Cicero . . . preached the harmony of good citizens").

11 The first and second speeches may also be viewed as a pair but are less closely linked than the second and third. The fourth speech does not form a pair with any of the other speeches.

2 and 3 and *De Othone*. So the experience of being persuaded by what Cicero had to say would not have been new to them. Both speeches are primarily speeches in which news is reported to the people; they are therefore deliberative (see pp. 90–91). In the *Second Catilinarian*, originally delivered the day after Cicero's denunciation of Catiline in the senate, that is, on 8 (or 9) November, Cicero informs the people that Catiline has left Rome during the night. In the *Third*, originally delivered on 3 December, he tells them that four of the leading conspirators have been arrested, interrogated in the senate, and been proved guilty, and that another five have also been found to be involved in the conspiracy. The two speeches were presumably included among the *Catilinarians* because they show Cicero as consul interacting with the people in a complex and impressive way and showing strong leadership at pivotal moments in the crisis. In their focus on mass persuasion they relate well to the other speeches to the people in the larger corpus, and they also serve the self-justifying agenda of the *Catilinarians* and the corpus as a whole.

The *Second* and *Third Catilinarians* both have a much more strongly demarcated structure than the *First*.[12] As is common in Cicero's speeches to the people, the unfolding of the narration and argument takes a linear course, and hence is easy to follow.[13] The *Second Catilinarian* begins with an *exordium* (introduction) in which Cicero announces Catiline's departure and presents him as a bestial creature and as a carrier of disease (§§ 1–2).[14] With the exception of a short stretch of narration at §§ 12–13, all of §§ 3–27 consists of *argumentatio* (argumentation), divided into four blocks. First there is a block (called *praemunitio*, "advance argument," by Andrew R. Dyck)

---

[12] For structural analyses of *Cat.* 2, see MacKendrick 1995: 60–62; Dyck 2008: 125; and of *Cat.* 3, MacKendrick 1995: 92–93; Dyck 2008: 165–66.

[13] Grillo 2015: 20.

[14] On Catiline and disease, see Liong 2016. Liong cites evidence that the months of September, October, and November were a time of sickness and greatly increased mortality at Rome (Murena was ill at his trial in November 63: Cic. *Mur.* 86) and argues that Cicero employs a "rhetoric of season" here to portray Catiline as a danger to the health of the republic and its citizens.

in which Cicero justifies his having allowed Catiline to escape, expresses contempt both for Catiline's supporters in the field and for those he has left behind in Rome, delivers a passage of invective against Catiline and his followers, and proclaims himself the leader of the internal war (*domesticum bellum*) against them (§§ 3–11). Then there is a block (called *narratio*, "narration," + *refutatio*, "refutation," by Dyck) in which he justifies himself against a different kind of critic: those who accuse him of having driven an innocent man into exile. He narrates what happened on the previous day, when Catiline appeared in the senate and Cicero confronted him with his knowledge of his plotting (the encounter is represented as involving an interrogation of Catiline rather than the delivery of a continuous speech, the *First Catilinarian*, against him). He then rejects the view that Catiline has gone into exile rather than to Manlius, and he denies that Catiline was driven out of Rome (§§ 12–16). The third block is the famous categorization of Catiline's supporters into six types (§§ 17–24a). In the fourth block, Cicero compares the government forces with those of Catiline, explains the defensive measures he is taking, and gives a warning to Catiline's supporters in the city (§§ 24b–27). Finally, there is a *conclusio* (peroration) in which Cicero says that he will put down the conspiracy with the minimum of force and with the help of the gods (§§ 28–29).

The *Third Catilinarian* also opens with an *exordium* containing a dramatic announcement: Cicero declares that Rome has been saved, by the gods and by himself, from fire and the sword, and he says he will now give an account of how this has come about (§§ 1–3a; 3a may be regarded either as the close of the *exordium* or as a separate *partitio* [partition, division]). A lengthy *narratio* follows (§§ 3b–15): Cicero describes the sequence of events in Rome from Catiline's departure down to the present moment (the evening of 3 December). For the later readers of the speeches, who may not know the historical context, this helpfully explains what has taken place since the delivery of the *Second Catilinarian*. Cicero narrates Catiline's departure without his followers; Lentulus' approach to the envoys of the Allobroges; the ambush on the Mulvian Bridge and the capture of the incriminating letters; the arrest of the envoys and Volturcius; the summoning of Gabinius, Statilius, Cethegus, and Lentulus; the convening of the senate; the confiscation of the conspirators' arsenal; the taking of evidence from Volturcius and the envoys; the interrogation of Cethegus, Statilius, Lentulus, and Gabinius; and the ensuing senatorial decree—the votes of thanks given to Cicero, Flaccus, Pomptinus, and the consul Antonius; the order for the confinement of the four conspirators just interrogated and for the arrest of a further five; and finally the decree of a thanksgiving (*supplicatio*) to the gods in Cicero's name. All these events are narrated in chronological order, except that Lentulus' resignation of his praetorship, which is noted in its correct place at § 14, is narrated a second time at § 15 (with the further claim that he had also forfeited his rights as a citizen) in a coda to the main account.

A section of *argumentatio* follows, in which Cicero provides his commentary on the events he has just narrated (§§ 16–22). There are two blocks. In the first, he draws a distinction between Catiline, who was a capable and energetic leader and organizer (he speaks of him in the past tense, as though he were no longer alive), and his fellow conspirators in the city, who were hapless bunglers. Their signal incompetence proves that he was right to expel Catiline from Rome (he no longer claims that he merely allowed him to leave): had he not driven him out, the conspirators would have had an effective leader, and it would have been much more difficult to put down the conspiracy in the city (§§ 16–17). In the second block, he argues that various recent natural phenomena and the timely erection of a new statue of Jupiter on the Capitol show that his suppression of the conspiracy is the result of divine providence (§§ 18–22). The *conclusio* (§§ 23–29) also falls into two blocks, with a final coda. In the first block, Cicero tells the people to celebrate the thanksgiving and their deliverance from death, and he contrasts his (so far) bloodless victory with the civil wars of the 80s and 70s (§§ 23–25). In the second, he turns the spotlight on himself: comparing himself with Pompey, he asks the people never to forget his achievement; he appeals for their future protection against traitors and internal enemies; and he pledges to speak out in defense of his consulship (§§ 26–29a). The final coda consists of two sentences: the people are told to worship Jupiter and defend their homes (§ 29b).

The *Second Catilinarian* appears to be the least altered of the four speeches. This gives it greater authenticity and immediacy than the other *Catilinarians* have. Even so, the *lenitas* ("lenience") theme makes several appearances (§§ 6, 27, 28; see pp. 69–71). Cicero is worried about being thought of as "the cruelest of tyrants" (14); he says he will try to ensure "that not a single traitor inside the city shall pay the penalty for his crimes" (28); and yet he also makes a reference to the state prison (27), the place where the conspirators were later to be executed, and he promises to ensure "that all your lives are saved by the punishment of only a few individuals" (28). When the speech was originally delivered, he did not know that he was going to detect and execute some of the conspirators in the city, and so it is difficult not to conclude that at least some of these remarks were added to the speech on publication in 60.

In the *Third Catilinarian*, however, the signs of later revision are much more glaring. The *lenitas* theme appears just once (§ 14): Cicero praises the "lenience" of the senate in decreeing the punishment of only nine conspirators—even though the senate had not yet decreed any punishment, but merely that the men be held in custody. There is an echo of a gracious compliment that Pompey did not pay him until 60, as shown by *Ad Atticum* 2.1.6 (15; see pp. 80–81). There is the second, expanded account of Lentulus' resignation of his praetorship, placed out of order and presumably added at a later date in order to counter accusations that Cicero had committed sacrilege by executing a serving magistrate (15; see pp. 72–73). There is the "obituary" of Catiline, inexplicably written in the past (imperfect) tense at a time when, according to the dramatic date of the speech, Catiline was in Etruria preparing to march on Rome (16–17; see p. 5). Then there is the second "block" of the *conclusio* (26–29a), in which Cicero begs the people to remember what he has done for them and to protect him from his enemies. Since the content of 26–27 is virtually identical to that of *In Catilinam* 4.22–23, which has been found to be a later addition to that speech, it is likely that the whole of 26–29a is also a later addition and that the original *conclusio* of the speech consisted only of the first "block" (23–25) and the coda (29b; see pp. 75–76). The subtraction of 26–29a would reduce the *conclusio* to a length less out of line with the extremely brief *conclusiones* of the *First* and *Second Catilinarians*; as it stands, the *conclusio* of the speech accounts for 22 percent of its length. If 26–29a is indeed a later addition, the reference to "internal enemies" at 28 would be an allusion to the tribunes of 62, Nepos and Bestia, who had not yet taken office at the time of the original delivery of the speech and did not begin their attacks on Cicero until 29 December 63 (Cic. *Fam.* 5.2.6–7; *Sest.* 11); it would perhaps even allude to Clodius as well. Finally, if 26–29a is a later addition, then the *exordium* of the speech (1–2) is likely to be one as well, because of its similar content: in that passage, Cicero asks to be honored for saving the city (his fear is that he will not be). In the interpretation of all these passages in the *Second* and *Third Catilinarians*, Approach B will be the more productive.[15]

This brings us to the purposes of the two speeches, on Approaches A and B. Happily, their purposes are much easier to discern than those of the *First Catilinarian*, and it will not be necessary to analyze either of the speeches paragraph by paragraph in order to do this. In the case of the *Second Catilinarian*, Cicero actually states what his purpose is: "I have now achieved my objective, to make all of you see that a conspiracy has been openly formed against the state" (6). If that were his only objective, and he really had achieved it, he would have no need to say anything more. But of course he has other objectives (listed here not in order of importance but roughly in the order in which they become dominant in the speech). In the first place, he wants to inform the people that Catiline has left Rome: "He has gone, departed, cleared off, escaped" (*abiit, excessit, evasit, erupit*, 1). Secondly, he wants to represent Catiline's departure as a victory, to take credit for it, and to avoid blame for it (1). More specifically, he wants to defend himself against accusations, from different sets of critics, of having let Catiline go (3–4) and

---

[15] Approaches A and B are articulated at pp. 87–89.

of having forced him into exile (12–16). Thirdly, he aims to influence the view that the people take of Catiline and his followers, in order to dissuade them from joining the conspiracy themselves. He does this, for example, by characterizing the conspirators as alien and immoral (5, 7–10, 17–24), casually mentioning their plans for arson (1, 10, 19), arguing that they have no chance of success (5, 17–25), and claiming that the gods are on his side (19, 25, 29). He also aims to deter Catiline's associates in the city from continuing with their schemes (27). Fourthly, he aims to defend his own character (14), convince the people that he is managing the crisis correctly (6, 26), and present himself as an important military leader (11). On Approach B, on the other hand, he is addressing not the Roman people in the forum but an educated literary readership. Nevertheless, some of his original purposes still apply: he still wants to denigrate Catiline and his followers, even after their deaths; he still wants to defend his own character and his management of the crisis; and he still wants to present himself as an important, and by this time successful, military leader. In particular, he is anxious to represent his character as lenient and moderate (6, 14, 27–28) and to justify the executions of 5 December (27–28). Finally, he wants to advertise and illustrate, as in *De lege agraria* 2 and *De Othone*, and to posterity as well as to his readership in 60, his skill in using oratory to persuade the people.

In the *Third Catilinarian*, Cicero's primary purpose is to inform the people of his actions since Catiline's departure and of the meeting of the senate that has just concluded, and to present his own interpretation of them (1–15). In the second place, he wants to proclaim that Rome has been saved by himself and the gods and to ensure that he is given the credit for this (1–15). Thirdly, he aims to demonstrate that he has acted correctly throughout and that criticism of his actions is unwarranted (4–15). Fourthly, he wants to put forward his own view of Catiline and his fellow conspirators in the city, in order to justify his expulsion of Catiline from Rome (16–17). Fifthly, he wants to emphasize the Catilinarians' plans for arson (1, 2, 8, 10, 14, 15, 22, 25). The burning of Rome features much more prominently in the *Third* and *Fourth Catilinarians* than in the *First* and *Second*, because firm evidence for it only became public when Volturcius and the envoys of the Allobroges gave their testimony (*Cat.* 3.8, 10); Cassius had requested that the task of supervising the arson be assigned to him (*Cat.* 3.14, 4.13; Cic. *Sul.* 53). Sixthly, Cicero wants to claim divine support for his actions (4, 15, 18–23, 29); and, finally (seventhly), he wants to make an equally grand claim, that the war against Catiline is "the single greatest and most brutal war in history" (25). In this way he aims to maximize the glory of his achievement and make his position less open to challenge in the future (24–25).

On Approach B, some of these purposes remain (most obviously, the second, third, and seventh). But there are additional purposes—more than for the *Second Catilinarian*, because the speech has been more altered. For his readership in 60, Cicero aims to justify the executions of 5 December and attribute responsibility for them to the senate (14); to justify his execution of a serving magistrate (15); to set down a particular view of Catiline for posterity in an "obituary" (16–17); and to persuade the people to stand by him and protect him against Clodius' attacks on his consulship (26–29). Also, of course, he wishes once more to advertise his skill and his achievement as a deliberative orator.

In the rest of this chapter, I will examine three aspects of that skill: Cicero's dissuasion of his audience from joining the conspiracy, his use of narration, and his exploitation of religion. The method of interpretation will be Approach A throughout (the revised parts of the speeches do not overlap with the passages in which these topics feature, except at *In Catilinam* 3.14–15, where the narration has been revised, and perhaps also at 3.1–2).

One of Cicero's chief aims in the *Second Catilinarian* is to dissuade his audience from throwing in their lot with Catiline. Like Rullus, who offered the Roman people plots of land, Catiline was offering something that many of them would find attractive: "new accounts" (*tabulae novae*), that is, cancellation of debts (see pp. 29–30). At the end of his life, Cicero was to comment on the threat, and his success in overcoming it (*Off.* 2.84):

Never was the pressure for debts not to be repaid stronger than when I was consul. Arms and military camps were the means of attempting this, by men of every class and type. But I opposed them so forcefully that the evil was totally eradicated from the state.

When Cicero addressed his audience, there was a real danger that some of them would follow Catiline to Etruria, give their support to the conspirators in the city, or (most dangerous of all) welcome Catiline into the city when he appeared at the gates with his army. Of course, Catiline's plans did not only include debt relief but also an illegal seizure of power through civil war, a massacre, and the burning of parts of Rome. For Cicero, one means of turning the people against him was to point this out, and he does, repeatedly. Another was to insist that Catiline was doomed to fail, and he does this also. But he needed to turn the people against debt relief itself. In the case of Rullus' *lex agraria*, his strategy was to present himself as a *popularis* and expatiate at length on all the negative aspects of the proposal. But it is curious that Cicero nowhere in the *Catilinarians* describes himself as a *popularis*. Presumably the reason is that he could no longer convincingly claim to be one. Perhaps his authorship of a new bribery law, the *lex Tullia*, in the summer had made it obvious to the people that he was not a consul who would put their interests above those of the senate. But there is also an uncomfortable suggestion at *In Catilinam* 4.10 that Lentulus was considered a *popularis*, because of his lavish expenditure of money on the people.[16] This must have made it harder for Cicero to pose as one himself.

---

[16] His oratory was slow and dignified (Cic. *Brut.* 235), which suggests that he was not a demagogue (it was possible to be a *popularis* and not a demagogue: see Cic. *Cat.* 4.9). There are no reasons, incidentally, for thinking that Catiline was considered a *popularis*, and in his early years he was a conspicuous and brutal supporter of Sulla (Asc. 84 C). Cicero accuses him of having scant regard for the people in *Tog. Cand.* ap. Asc. 87 C ("He showed what regard he had for the people when, in full view of the people, he beheaded an extremely popular man [*hominis maxime popularis*]").

The method Cicero uses to turn the people against debt re-lief (and, more generally, the conspiracy itself) is to define the sup-porters of Catiline who are eager for it, and to do so in such a way that his audience will not identify with them, will have no sympathy for them, and will disapprove of them. His audience is plebeian, and poor; he therefore draws attention to the fact that Catiline's leading supporters are men of high birth, and in some cases patrician.[17] At § 4, he comments on the men Catiline has left behind in Rome: "What debts they have, what power, what noble birth!" At the end of the speech he mentions the gladiators at Rome, who, though slaves, "are more loyal to the country than some of our patricians are" (26). Patricians are mentioned again in the *Third Catilinarian*: Cicero attributes to the gods the stroke of good fortune by which the Gauls chose "to forgo the prospect of immense power and wealth offered to them by patricians without their asking" (3.22). The message is clear: Catiline's supporters are not friends of the people, nor do they resemble the people in any way. They are bankrupt aristocrats who have taken up arms against their country for their own personal gain.

The core of the *Second Catilinarian* is what Dyck calls the "soci-ological dissection of the conspiracy" into six types of conspirator at §§ 17–24.[18] Scientific though this categorization may appear, it is far from objective, and Cicero leaves out one significant element of Catiline's following.[19] According to Sallust, the plebs were all sup-portive of Catiline's plans and eager for revolution (Sal. *Cat.* 37.1, 48.1). Indeed, earlier in the speech Cicero confirms that Catiline had substantial urban support when he exclaims, "O happy country, if it gets rid of this urban trash!" (7), and, shortly afterwards, "How

---

[17] Five patricians are known to have been involved in the conspiracy: Catiline himself, Lentulus, Cethegus, Publius Cornelius Sulla (not the man defended by Cicero in 62), and Servius Cornelius Sulla.

[18] Dyck 2008: 124. With this passage, cf. *Red. Pop.* 21, where Cicero, again addressing the people, divides his enemies into four types; as here, he mentions no names (Lintott 2008: 13). On Livy's allusion to this passage in his account of the Bacchanalian con-spiracy of 186 BC (Liv. 39.8–19, at 39.15.9), see Nousek 2010: 163–64.

[19] Yavetz 1963: 488.

quickly he [Catiline] succeeded in assembling a vast crowd of the worst of society—not only from the city, but from the countryside as well!" (8). In his list of conspirators, Cicero says nothing about the urban plebs, because they are his audience, and he wants them to believe that the conspirators are an entirely different group of people from themselves—different in wealth, class, and morality— and that the conspirators' interests do not coincide with theirs. In particular, he wants to stir up resentment of the lifestyles of the rich, so that his audience will feel hostile toward the conspirators and be disinclined to support them. At times, he addresses the six types of conspirators directly (cf. "I will then give each group, if I can, the medicine of my advice and persuasion," 17), but, unlike the urban plebs, it is not to be supposed that many of them were actually present among his audience.[20]

First come the indebted, greedy owners of country estates: "people who have large debts and more than enough property to pay them off, but who are so attached to that property that nothing can set them free" (18). Catiline may have fallen into this category himself: in his letter to Catulus he admitted that he had debts, but he claimed that he was capable of paying them off from out of his own property and that of his wife and daughter (Sal. *Cat.* 35.3; see pp. 38–41). On the other hand, in his address to his supporters shortly before the consular elections in 63, as reported by Cicero (not necessarily truthfully) at *Pro Murena* 50, he implied that his debts greatly exceeded the value of his assets. Antonius, a friend of Catiline but not of course a conspirator, had previously taken a different and more honorable course: he had incurred large debts in the 70s but had turned over his estates to his creditors and was consequently expelled from the senate in 70 for failing to meet the property qualification (Asc. 84 C).[21] Catiline aside, no names

---

[20] In the poetic version of the *Second Catilinarian* in *Consulatus suus* (two fragments survive), Cicero also appears to have addressed the conspirators in their absence: see Courtney 1993: 159.

[21] Cicero claims in *Tog. Cand.* (ap. Asc. 87 C) that Antonius had turned over his livestock and grazing to his creditors but had retained his shepherds (commonly seen as men of violence, because they carried weapons to protect their flocks). His financial

of any conspirators belonging to this first type are known, and it is likely that Cicero is for the most part describing people who were on the fence rather than people who had actually committed themselves to Catiline's cause.[22] They would then be in the same position as Cicero's audience themselves: sympathetic to Catiline, but without having taken any definite action. Cicero, however, prefers to highlight their difference from his audience. Addressing an imaginary member of this group (with an insistent *tu*, "you," spoken five times), he asks him about his "land, buildings, silver, slaves, and everything else" and questions whether, amid the devastation of war, he really imagines that his property will remain intact and that Catiline will implement a cancellation of debts: "New accounts? Those who expect that from Catiline are mistaken" (he does not explain why). But his questions are intended not so much for Italy's indebted landowners as for the plebeians standing in front of him. Do *they* think that their property will be safe if Catiline takes Rome by force? Do they believe he will help *them* financially?

The second type also consists of people who are in debt and greedy—but they are greedy not for country estates but for political office (19). They are "overwhelmed with debt" but nevertheless "look forward to ruling [*dominationem tamen exspectant*], are hungry for power, and think that with the country in turmoil they will be able to obtain offices they have no hope of obtaining when the country is at peace." Cicero names no names, but a number of Catiline's known supporters appear to fit the description. Cassius had, like Catiline, stood unsuccessfully for the consulship in 64;[23] Asconius says that "at that time he seemed more stupid than bad" (82 C). At *In Catilinam* 3.16, Cicero calls him "obese"—not a description that would endear him to a starving populace. Lentulus and Curius had been expelled from the senate in 70; Lentulus had secured readmission by being elected praetor in 64 but apparently

---

embarrassment explains his governorship of Macedonia (62–60 BC) and his subsequent conviction, probably for extortion (59 BC).

[22] Hardy 1924: 53–54.
[23] Broughton 1991: 10 (Cassius); 16–17, 29–30 (Catiline).

suffered from the delusion that "he was the third Cornelius who was destined to attain kingship and dominion over this city, the first two being Cinna and Sulla" (*Cat.* 3.9; cf. *Cat.* 4.12; Sal. *Cat.* 47.2). In the *Third Catilinarian*, Cicero twice refers to his laziness (3.6, 16). In the first of these places, he plays on the literal meaning of the word *lentulus* ("somewhat slow," "tardy"): "Lentulus was very slow [*tardissime*] in coming—I imagine because, unusually for him, he had stayed up late into the night writing letters."[24] Autronius had been elected to the consulship in 66, but had then been convicted of bribery, deprived of his consulship, expelled from the senate, and permanently debarred from public office (see p. 15). Presumably he still wanted to be consul, because in December 64 he used violence in an attempt to force through a bill that would have allowed his immediate return to the senate; the bill was withdrawn in the face of senatorial opposition (Cic. *Sul.* 62–66).[25] Vargunteius had also been put on trial for electoral bribery; since Cicero refers to him as an equestrian at *In Catilinam* 1.9, he had probably been expelled from the senate too.[26] There may have been other conspirators who felt that their birth had not been given its just reward. Cicero declares that the conspirators of this type intend to burn the city and massacre the citizens in order to make themselves "consuls, dictators, even kings." His audience can have felt no sympathy for them—and if senators were electorally unsuccessful, the reason must often have been that the people did not think them deserving of office. The reference to dictators suggests a return to the time of Sulla, with its massacres, confiscations, and proscriptions; and Cicero had previously defeated Rullus' bill with the accusation that he and his fellow land commissioners wanted to be kings.

The terrifying threat of a revival of a Sullan dictatorship under Catiline is made more explicit in the third type (20). These are certain of the Sullan colonists (Cicero does not damn the whole

---

[24] Corbeill 1996: 95 n. 108.
[25] See Berry 1996: 8–9, 257–64.
[26] Berry 1996: 141.

class)[27] who have thrown away the wealth that Sulla suddenly and unexpectedly gave them: "Building as if they were aristocrats, delighting in coaches, litters, armies of servants, and sumptuous banquets, they have fallen so deeply into debt that, if they are ever to become solvent again, they would have to call up Sulla from the underworld!" Manlius, Cicero says, is one of their number: he was a former centurion of Sulla's. Dio adds that he was a spendthrift who had squandered a large fortune that he had obtained under Sulla (37.30.5). Another of them is named at *In Catilinam* 3.14: Publius Furius (he is not otherwise known). The colonists, Cicero continues, "have also driven quite a few poor and needy farmers into hoping, as they do, that the plundering of former times [i.e., of the Sullan period] is going to be repeated." These poor and needy farmers would have included, but not been limited to, those whom Sulla had dispossessed (the dispossessed are not mentioned specifically because Cicero's audience may have had some sympathy with them, and indeed there may have been some of them present). Cicero brands both the colonists and the other farmers as "plunderers and thieves" and advises them to give up "their insane thoughts of proscriptions and dictatorships" before concluding, with a rhetorical flourish much more typical of his earliest speeches (such as *Pro Roscio Amerino*, delivered under Sulla): "The horror of that time is branded so deeply on our national psyche that today not only men but even, I think, animals would refuse to countenance its return."[28] Speaking before an audience that had hated Sulla (among other things, Sulla had stripped the tribunate of its powers and abolished the corn dole),[29] Cicero paints a picture of men who gained wealth under him that they did not deserve, squandered it on luxuries and in living above their station, fell into debt, and are now seeking a new dictatorship so that

---

[27] Harris (1971: 291) infers that there were Sullan colonists in the audience.

[28] Cf., e.g., the references to wild animals at *S. Rosc.* 63, 71, 150.

[29] On the people's hatred of Sulla, see, for example, Morstein-Marx 2004: 56–57, 111–13, who discusses, inter alia, the gilded equestrian statue of Sulla set up on the rostra in 81 and torn down after Pharsalus in 48.

they can do the same all over again. He recalls Sulla's victory later at *In Catilinam* 3.24: "I do not need to remind you how many citizens lost their lives and what a catastrophe it was for Rome."[30] Naturally, the *First* and *Fourth Catilinarians* contain no references to the Sullan period; Sulla had added three hundred equestrians to the senate, and many of these new senators would have been in Cicero's audience when he delivered the originals of those speeches. But in the *Second Catilinarian*, reminders of the Sullan period and of those who had benefited from it were a highly effective means of turning the people away from Catiline, Manlius, and their rural followers. As far as the people were concerned, such men—or, rather, men presented in the way that Cicero presents them—deserved their fate.

The remaining three types of conspirator are less sociologically distinct. The fourth one consists of feckless characters who have fallen into debt or are bankrupt because they are idle and incapable of managing their own affairs (21). They have already left the city (before Catiline, presumably) and the country districts and have joined Manlius. Cicero expresses complete contempt for them (they are "lazy backsliders") and declares that it would be better for all concerned if they died as soon as possible (i.e., by their own hand), rather than dying fighting against their country. The fifth type are murderers and criminals who will never abandon Catiline and who need to be killed en masse (22). The analysis gives way to invective completely in the final type, who are "Catiline's very own, his elect, his darling bosom pals" (22). These wastrels have already been described in a passage of invective at § 10:

> They think of nothing except murder, except arson, except pillage. They have squandered their inheritances, mortgaged their properties. Their money ran out long ago, and now their credit has begun to run out as well; but those tastes they had in their days of plenty remain the same. If, in all their drinking and gambling, they were concerned only with revelling and prostitutes, they would indeed be beyond

---

[30] For a study of Cicero's expressed views on Sulla, see Diehl 1988.

hope. . . . Reclining at their banquets, embracing their whores, heavy with wine, stuffed with food, wreathed with flowers, drenched with perfume, and worn out by promiscuous sex, they belch out their plans for the massacre of decent citizens and the burning of Rome.[31]

Here at §§ 23–24 they reappear as the sixth type of conspirator and are described again in similar terms but at greater length. They are young men who fuss over their grooming and appearance, dress in feminine clothing, sleep all day and party till dawn, sing, dance naked, gamble, commit adultery, take the passive role as well as the active sexually—and commit murders, by dagger and poison. So they are not only immoral but criminal. The unfortunate Fulvius, later executed by his father, may have been one of them (see pp. 41–42). Cicero does not say so here, but he spelled out at § 10 that they are deeply in debt. As with the fourth and fifth types, he wants all of them dead: "Unless they leave Rome, unless they die . . . I tell you that they will be a nursery of future Catilines in our country" (23). They are seducers, not soldiers. Their soft, unmilitary natures are mocked in a series of rhetorical questions, before Cicero concludes, "What a truly terrifying war this is going to be, with Catiline in command of this praetorian cohort of bumboys!" (24).

This talk of categories of people who should die or be killed serves a very direct purpose: Cicero is threatening his audience. It is a veiled threat, because it is ostensibly made only against the last three types of conspirator. But it is the people, not the conspirators, that he is addressing and seeking to persuade. Effectively

---

[31] Invective of this kind is alive and well today in the popular press. An editorial in the *Mail on Sunday* lambastes the behavior of Britain's deputy prime minister, John Prescott (30 April 2006): "Here are the tawdry details of the Deputy Prime Minister's office romance, and what a miserable business it is. . . . A powerful Government department and its staff on a seemingly endless round of parties and dinners, their heads ringing with hangovers as they superintend plans to concrete over the country, destroy local democracy and slice England into alien Euro-regions" (continues at length in the same vein). The editor of the *Mail on Sunday* at that time, Peter Wright, has kindly informed me that the colleague of his who wrote the editorial had not read the Cicero passage.

he is saying: "If any of you join Catiline, then the forces of the state, which are under my control, will kill you." This is an entirely different kind of persuasion from the persuasion normally encountered in Cicero's speeches. We are a long way here from the *lenitas* theme so characteristic of the revision of 60 BC, and a long way from the Cicero who is anxious to justify the executions of the arrested conspirators. His uncompromising attitude gives the speech the authenticity and immediacy already noted. Here, there is no sense at all that controversial executions have taken place and that the consul has blood on his hands. Cicero, unusually, appears ignorant of the future.

One of Cicero's main tasks in the *Second Catilinarian*, then, is to dissuade the people from joining the conspiracy, and, as part of that, to reduce the attractiveness of debt relief. He does this not by posing as a *popularis* but instead by defining Catiline's followers very precisely as men who are utterly unlike the people themselves. They are nobles, patricians, landowners, senators, Sullan colonists with aristocratic pretensions, and fashionable but disreputable men about town. All these people live lives of luxury, and all have fallen hopelessly into debt through their own fault (the only conspirators not described as being in debt are the murderers and criminals, to whom Cicero devotes just a few words). Why should impoverished plebeians risk their lives in order to help such people escape the consequences of their own actions? But if they do go over to them, Cicero suggests that the consequence will be a renewal of the Sullan dictatorship, in which case the outcome might be not a general cancellation of debts benefiting all classes of society (Sulla had not canceled debts) but instead a fresh proscription and confiscation benefiting only the privileged people that he has described. His persuasion through characterization is extremely skillful. Any plebeian member of his audience who considered carefully what he said about the types of men who supported Catiline would probably conclude that the risks of joining the conspiracy would be so high and the likelihood of benefit so low that the best course of action would be to follow the consul's instructions: to guard his home, pray to the gods, and leave everything else to Cicero (26, 29).

Let us now turn to examine a different topic, Cicero's use of narration. Narrations were most often useful in forensic oratory, and narrations in any kind of speech could have served as models for aspiring forensic orators.[32] They were probably more useful in prosecutions than in defenses: a narration could easily be used to represent someone as having committed a crime but was less suitable for representing a person as not having committed one. Much of *In Verrem*, a prosecution, consists of narrations of crimes allegedly committed by the defendant. Where narrations occur in defenses, they are sometimes used, as if in a prosecution, to suggest that the prosecutors themselves are in some way implicated in the crime of which the defendant is accused (*Pro Roscio Amerino*, *Pro Milone*). The narrations in the *Second* (§§ 12–13) and the *Third Catilinarian* (§§ 3–15) both have the character of a prosecution: in each instance, Cicero does not merely recount a sequence of events but sets out a forensic case for, respectively, Catiline's guilt and that of his followers in the city.

In the narration at *In Catilinam* 2.12–13, Cicero ridicules the idea that he has forced an innocent man into exile. He gives an account of his confrontation with Catiline in the senate the previous day, highlighting Catiline's guilt, lack of a defense, and fixed intention to go to war. But he does not say that he gave a speech against him. Instead, he says that he asked him a series of questions, to which Catiline gave no reply (*Cat.* 2.13):

> Then I, the stern consul who forces citizens into exile with a mere word, asked Catiline whether or not he had spent the night in a meeting at the house of Marcus Laeca. To begin with, the criminal, aware of his guilt, declined to answer: so I revealed further details. I explained what he had done during the night, where he had been, what he had planned for the following night, and how he had drawn up his strategy for the entire war. He hesitated: he was trapped.

---

[32] Winterbottom 1982 gives examples of passages in Cicero's speeches that evidently served a pedagogical function.

I therefore went on to ask him what was keeping him from setting out on the journey for which he had long prepared.

While formally a narration within a deliberative speech, this account of an interrogation has an argumentative and forensic character: Cicero delivers accusations, against which Catiline offers no defense. The people are thereby encouraged to conclude that Catiline's guilt was demonstrated by Cicero's argument, just as it had been by the other senators' refusal to sit near him, which Cicero also describes in his narration. It is certain that Cicero did actually give a speech: at *Ad Atticum* 2.1.3 he tells Atticus of the speech "by which I sent Catiline out of Rome." Moreover, in this passage, the points that he says he put to Catiline do occur in the *First Catilinarian*, at §§ 8–10: "I declare that yesterday evening you went to the scythe-makers' quarter—I will be absolutely precise—to the house of Marcus Laeca. . . . Do you dare to deny it? Why do you say nothing?" and so on (1.8). But it was not in his interest to tell the people that his interrogation of Catiline had been only a small part of a lengthy denunciation. He wanted to show, and in as graphic a way as possible, that Catiline was unable to reply to his allegations. He was able to achieve that much more effectively by an account of an interrogation, with Catiline being given ample opportunity to reply to each point but failing to do so, than by a report of a continuous speech during which Catiline was effectively silenced.

The *narratio* of *Pro Milone*, in which Cicero describes the death of Clodius, is famously misleading: he represents Clodius as having been killed without Milo's knowledge in an ambush of Clodius' own devising (*Mil.* 24–31). The extent of his misrepresentation is known only from what we should like to have for all of Cicero's forensic speeches, an independent account of the facts, in this instance the one written by Asconius in the mid-first century AD. However, in the case of the narration at *In Catilinam* 3.3–15 of the events in Rome since Catiline's departure, we are similarly fortunate in having an independent account to set against that of Cicero: the narrative of Sallust at *Bellum Catilinae* 32–47 (which also covers events outside Rome). Sallust's account reveals that Cicero tells his audience only half of the story. The crucial point that Cicero omits, and never mentions in any of his works, is that he tricked the conspirators into incriminating themselves.

Cicero begins his account with Catiline's flight from Rome and with the conspirators who have been left behind; they are described as "fearsome leaders" (3) and as "set on fire with the greatest possible rage and criminality" (4). Of course, at the time that Cicero is speaking, some of these men are in custody, but he still wishes to represent them as dangerous criminals. He tells the people, but only in the most general terms, of the action that he took to protect the city from them (3–4):

> I have been constantly on the alert, citizens, and have been looking to see how, amid such widespread and well-concealed plotting, our safety might best be ensured. . . . I spent all my time, night and day, trying to find out and see what it was they were doing and what it was they were planning. . . . I therefore found out as much as I could.

Then he says that he discovered (*comperi*) that Lentulus had interfered with the envoys of the Allobroges with a view to stirring up a revolt in Gaul, that the envoys had been sent back to Gaul "with letters and instructions" (*cum litteris mandatisque*), that they were to visit Catiline on the way, that they were to be escorted by Volturcius, and that Volturcius had been given a letter for Catiline. He says nothing about how he had achieved this outstanding feat of detection, except that it had been very difficult, and he adds that it had always been his hope that the immortal gods would send him such an opportunity (4).

Sallust goes into more detail. After several pages describing the various actions taken by Catiline on and after his departure from Rome (which is not Cicero's subject), he turns at § 39.6 to events in the city. He describes how Lentulus instructed Umbrenus to seek out the envoys of the Allobroges, and how Umbrenus then met them, took them to the house of Decimus Junius Brutus (the husband of Sempronia; he was away from Rome), introduced them to Gabinius, revealed the conspiracy to them, and secured from them a promise of help (40.1–6). Cicero, by contrast, tells the people simply that Lentulus interfered with the envoys. The interference is attributed to Lentulus, not Umbrenus; Lentulus, being the most important of Catiline's followers, an ex-consul and a praetor, currently being held in custody, was the conspirator whose guilt Cicero most needed to demonstrate. Umbrenus is mentioned only once in the *Catilinarians*, at § 14, where Cicero is reporting the terms of the senate's decree; the man is described merely as "a freedman who was shown to have introduced the Gauls to Gabinius." Sallust next relates how the envoys decided to reveal what had occurred to their patron, Sanga (41.1–4). Then (41.5):

> Cicero, on being informed of the plan through Sanga, instructed the envoys to make an earnest pretense of enthusiasm for the conspiracy, to approach the other members of it, to give them nice promises, and to do their best to render them as red-handed as possible.

Cicero omits all mention of this.[33] It was in fact the heaven-sent opportunity for which he had been hoping, and it proved to be no less than the means by which it became possible for him to put down the conspiracy.

After this, Sallust outlines the preparations of the conspirators within the city and then describes the envoys doing exactly as Cicero had told them (44.1):

> As for the Allobroges, in accordance with Cicero's instruction they had a meeting with the others, brought about by Gabinius. From Lentulus, Cethegus, Statilius, and likewise Cassius they demanded an oath which, once sealed, they could take to their fellow citizens; otherwise, they said, it would not be easy to induce them into so great an enterprise.

---

[33] At *Dom.* 134 (57 BC) he lets slip that the envoys had come to him with proof of the conspiracy, but he does not admit that he directed their subsequent actions. Some modern scholars, perhaps misled by Cicero's silence, appear not to have noticed that Cicero did not merely intercept the letters that the envoys were carrying but had caused them to be written (Wiseman 1994: 356; Manuwald 2015: 40).

Before this, the only conspirators whom the envoys had met were Umbrenus, Gabinius, and presumably Sempronia—a freedman, an equestrian, and a woman of bad character and reputation.[34] But now, "in accordance with Cicero's instruction," they met a patrician ex-consul and serving praetor, another patrician, an ex-praetor, and another equestrian. Cicero of course says nothing about this meeting, which he had set up.[35] Sallust says that Lentulus, Cethegus, and Statilius provided sealed documents as asked, but that Cassius did not. He then goes on to quote the further letter that Lentulus wrote to Catiline urging him to enlist slaves (44.4–5). This letter is quoted later by Cicero in his narration, at § 12, at the point when it was read out in the senate.

At § 5 Cicero describes how, having "discovered" that Lentulus had interfered with the envoys, he sent for the praetors Flaccus and Pomptinus and "showed them what I wanted done" (Sallust says that he "commanded" them): they were to take a force and set an ambush at the Mulvian Bridge. Sallust provides the same information, but adds that Cicero knew when and where to place the ambush because he had been "briefed in detail about everything" (*cuncta edoctus*) by the envoys (45.1–2). Sallust then describes the ambush itself. In his account, the envoys did not know about the ambush in advance, but they were on Cicero's side, and when they realized what was happening, they offered no resistance and surrendered to the praetors; Volturcius, on the other hand, defended himself with a sword and then, when he saw that the envoys had abandoned him, surrendered (45.3–4). In Cicero's account, also, no one other than the praetors knew what was happening, but there is

---

[34] Sallust gives a character sketch of Sempronia at *Cat.* 25 ("To her, everything was always dearer than reputation and chastity; whether she was less sparing of her money or her reputation, you could not easily have told," 25.3). Her son (or possibly stepson), Decimus Junius Brutus Albinus, was a conspirator too, being one of the assassins of Caesar in 44. This may help to explain Sallust's interest in her, something that has puzzled scholars (see Syme 1964: 134; but Sallust need not have been hostile to Decimus to be interested in him).

[35] At *Sul.* 36–39 (62 BC), however, he describes at length a meeting between the envoys and Cassius. That is likely to have been the same meeting as this one.

no mention of any information having passed between the envoys and Cicero. "Swords were drawn on both sides," Cicero says, and "a fight broke out," but the praetors intervened and stopped it; it is implied that the envoys resisted the praetors with violence (6). Of course, if Cicero was going to conceal that he had set up the conspirators, he also had to represent the envoys as guilty. His account continues: the letters were all handed over to the praetors, their seals unbroken, and Volturcius and the envoys were arrested and brought to him at dawn. He then sent for Gabinius, "the villain who had coordinated this criminal plan," and the three conspirators who had written the letters (6). Sallust leaves out the handing over of the letters and the bringing of Volturcius and the envoys to Cicero but reports the summoning of the four conspirators (46.3). He adds that a fifth conspirator, Caeparius, was also summoned but was tipped off by someone and fled the city, intending to start a slave revolt in Apulia (46.3–4). Later he mentions that Caeparius was afterwards captured and brought back to Rome (47.4); this must have been between the delivery of the *Third Catilinarian* (Caeparius is still at large at 3.14) and 5 December, when he was executed. The reason why Cicero omits Caeparius is probably because Caeparius had nothing to do with the envoys and the letters and played no part in the events that Cicero has been relating. He does appear later, though, when Cicero lists the conspirators named in the senate's decree (14).

Cicero next reports that many leading senators came to call on him and urged him to open the letters before putting them before the senate, in case they contained nothing incriminating. He makes a virtue of his refusal to do so—but of course he already knew what they contained (7). While the senate was being summoned, he says, "I did as the Allobroges advised me" and sent the praetor Sulpicius to confiscate the weapons that were stored at Cethegus' house (8). This is his first indication that the envoys were cooperating with him. Sallust does not mention these events.

Cicero and Sallust both describe the meeting of the senate of 3 December. Cicero's account is long (8–15), Sallust's short (46.5–47.4): Sallust does not want either the meeting of 3 December or the one of 4 December to detract from what he regards as the pivotal meeting, the one on 5 December at which the debate on the punishment of the conspirators took place. Sallust's account does not contradict Cicero's on any points of importance, and it differs from it mainly in that the reading of the letters and the decree of the senate, which in Cicero take up §§ 10–15, are covered in only two sentences (47.3–4). For Sallust, the guilt of the conspirators is sufficiently demonstrated by the evidence of Volturcius and the envoys: the letters addressed to the Allobroges contained (so far as is known) nothing but oaths and promises that unspecified verbal undertakings would be honored, while the one from Lentulus to Catiline has already been quoted in full at 44.5. For Cicero, on the other hand, the letters are crucial because they are documentary evidence written in the conspirators' own hands and sealed with their personal seals; as such, they are the only evidence that the conspirators cannot easily deny. As regards the decree of the senate, all Sallust is interested in are the arrangements for keeping the conspirators in custody. Cicero, by contrast, wishes to highlight the senate's declaration that the conspirators are guilty and the exceptional honors it has paid to him; together, these serve as the most impressive vindication possible of the policy that he has followed with regard to Catiline ever since his delivery of *In toga candida* in the senate in the summer of 64.

Cicero begins his account of the meeting of the senate by saying that he brought in Volturcius without the Gauls (8). This is directly contradicted by Sallust, who says that he brought Volturcius into the senate with the envoys (46.6). It was in Cicero's interest that the envoys should not hear the evidence of Volturcius (evidence given independently would make his case stronger), and his account should therefore be preferred. Sallust tells his readers that Cicero led Lentulus into the senate by the hand, because he was a praetor (46.5), but Cicero had no reason to include such a detail; he refers to Lentulus' praetorship only in the context of Lentulus having resigned it (14–15). He reports that he gave Volturcius immunity from prosecution "on the order of the senate"; as with the statement that he brought him in without the Gauls, he is concerned to show that the procedure he followed cannot be faulted and that he has acted correctly throughout. In his account, the evidence given by Volturcius appears nothing less than spectacular. Volturcius gave a verbal summary of the "letter and instructions" (*mandata et litteras*) from Lentulus to Catiline—that Catiline should enlist slaves and march on Rome as soon as possible, the plan being that once the conspirators in Rome had set fire to every part of the city and had massacred an unlimited number of citizens, Catiline would be on hand to mop up any who had escaped, and would then join forces with the leaders in the city (8).[36] According to Sallust, Volturcius said that he had been recruited by Gabinius and Caeparius only a few days before, and that he had heard from Gabinius that Autronius, Servius Sulla, Vargunteius, and many others were in the conspiracy (47.1). Cicero omits these details. It was not in his interest to inform the people that Volturcius' knowledge of the conspiracy was recent and limited. The reason he leaves out the names of all the conspirators except Lentulus is probably because he knew that Volturcius was not a strong witness and because the senate had not regarded the guilt of Autronius, Servius Sulla, and Vargunteius as sufficiently proven for their names to be included in the text of its decree.

Next Cicero says that the Gauls were brought in, and he reports their evidence, which was just as sensational as that of Volturcius (9). They said that Lentulus, Cethegus, and Statilius had given them "an oath and letters" (*ius iurandum et litteras*) to take back to their people, and that those three conspirators and Cassius had told them to send cavalry to Italy as soon as possible, there being no shortage of infantry. They reported that Lentulus had told them that according to the Sibylline prophecies and the responses of the soothsayers, he was destined to follow in the footsteps of Cinna and Sulla and be the third Cornelius to attain "kingship and dominion over this city"

---

[36] Butler (2002: 95) regards the substance from "the plan being that . . . " (in my paraphrase) as an inference by Cicero rather than a statement by Volturcius. But it seems unlikely that Cicero would not have succeeded in eliciting this "plan" from the terrified Volturcius, especially if he had primed him beforehand (as he did the envoys: see two paragraphs below).

(*regnum huius urbis atque imperium*). He had also said that this year, being the tenth since the acquittal of the Vestal virgins (Fabia and another Vestal, Licinia, in 73)[37] and the twentieth since the burning of the Capitol (an accidental fire in 83 in which the Sibylline books were burnt), was destined to be the one in which the city and the empire would be destroyed (9). They added that Cethegus had disagreed with Lentulus and the other conspirators over the timing of the massacre and the burning of the city: this was to have happened on the Saturnalia (17 December), but Cethegus had wanted the date brought forward (10). Sallust provides the same information as Cicero about Lentulus' predictions, although the prophecy that Lentulus would be the third Cornelius to rule Rome he attributes to the Sibylline books alone. In addition, whereas Cicero reports that Lentulus had said that the city and the empire would be destroyed, Sallust says merely that he had told the envoys that according to repeated responses of the soothsayers, there would be a bloody civil war (47.2). The other details given by Cicero do not appear in Sallust's account.

As narrated by Cicero, the evidence of the envoys is surprising, because it is self-incriminating: they were told of a plot against the state but did not report it and did what the plotters asked them to. It would have been more natural for them to tell the truth and testify that they had been told of a plot, had reported it to their patron, and had then done as they were instructed by the consul. The fact that they did not say this demonstrates beyond a doubt that they had been primed by Cicero at their meeting with him before the meeting of the senate: he would have told them to say nothing about their cooperation with him and would have promised them that in return they would be well rewarded. At the meeting of the senate the following day, Volturcius and the envoys were indeed voted generous rewards; as Cicero tells the senate on 5 December, "Yesterday you granted the most handsome rewards [*praemia . . . amplissima*] to the envoys of the Allobroges and to Titus Volturcius" (*Cat.* 4.5; cf.

---

[37] See Alexander 1990: 83–84 (nos. 167–68).

4.10). It would be interesting to know how Cicero persuaded the senate to grant the envoys these rewards, since on his account they did not report the conspiracy to the authorities and did everything that the conspirators asked of them. In their favor, all that he would have been able to say was that they did not resist arrest and then testified willingly.

The rest of Cicero's narration (10–15) is the part that Sallust covers in only two sentences. In §§ 10–12, he describes how Cethegus, Statilius, and Lentulus reacted when confronted with their seals and letters, and then he reports the interrogation of Gabinius, who had written no letter but had been the envoys' main contact, and did not deny their allegations. He mentions that Statilius and Gabinius were each "brought in,"[38] which helps to confirm that he would have brought in Volturcius and the envoys separately too. In the case of Cethegus, Statilius, and Lentulus, he describes first the conspirators' acknowledgment of their seal, then the reading out of the letter, then the contents of the letter, and finally the conspirators' admission of their guilt. He reports how he gave Lentulus a brief lecture on the patriotism of his grandfather, whose head was depicted on his seal (the elder Lentulus, consul in 162, had helped to suppress Gaius Gracchus, although Cicero does not tell the people this: see *Cat.* 4.13). Each letter was read out aloud to the senate; in the case of the first letter, Cicero says that it was he who read it out, and so it was presumably he who read out the other ones as well. The contents of the letters were less impressive than Cicero's theatrical presentation of them—before the senate and in his narration—would suggest, and this must be why he does not quote them: the conspirators undertook to do what they had promised to the envoys, and they requested "the senate and people of the Allobroges" to do in return what the envoys had promised to them. The most damaging point in each case, therefore, was not the letter to the Allobroges but the admission of guilt,

---

[38] The word Cicero uses, *introductus*, is a term regularly used to describe the bringing of a non-member before the senate. Statilius and Gabinius were not members of the senate, but Cethegus and Lentulus were members. See Dyck 2008: 177.

or at least the failure to deny the allegations, which the reading out of each letter prompted. Cethegus had attempted to explain away the swords and daggers found at his house (he claimed that they were collectors' items), but when his letter was read out, "he suddenly seemed weakened and crushed by his sense of guilt, and fell silent" (10). Statilius "confessed," although Cicero does not say to what.[39] Lentulus put up more of a fight. When his letter to the Allobroges was read out, he initially declined to comment. Then he cross-examined the envoys and Volturcius. But when they asked him in return "whether he had not said anything to them on the subject of the Sibylline prophecies," he gave up: "Suddenly driven mad by his crime, he showed what a guilty conscience can do. Although he could have denied what they had said, all of a sudden to everyone's surprise he confessed that it was true" (11). This is Cicero the lawyer speaking: he was well aware that if Lentulus had denied everything and insisted on his right to a public trial once his term in office was over, he could have saved himself. But Cicero then delivered—in the senate and in his narration—the coup de grâce: Lentulus' second letter, the one to Catiline, was produced, Lentulus again acknowledged his seal, and the letter, which called on Catiline to enlist slaves, was read out. Cicero quotes it verbatim, here at the point of maximum impact (12). Although it was cautiously phrased, its meaning was transparent. Cicero does not need to provide any explanation or commentary: it was utterly damning. It must have made as big an impression on the people as it had made on the senate: whether rich or poor, no Roman citizen wanted a slave revolt.

The account of the interrogation is concluded with a graphic description of the four men's demeanor (13). It is a fine example of how narration can be used to persuade, and it helps the people (and us, Cicero's readers) to imagine that they (and we) too had been

---

[39] Butler (2002: 94) points out that if the conspirators had confessed in any detail, Cicero would have quoted their words. He justly observes that "Cicero misleads only by suggestion; here and generally, he takes almost maniacal legalistic care to avoid expressing a literal untruth."

present in the senate and able to see the conspirators' guilt written in their faces:

> Let me add, citizens, that although I thought the letters, seals, handwriting, and finally the confession of each person were totally convincing evidence and proof of their guilt, still more convincing was their pallor, the looks in their eyes, the expressions on their faces, and their silence. So stunned were they, so intently did they stare at the ground, and so furtively did they steal occasional glances at each other that they looked not as if they had been incriminated by others, but as if they had incriminated themselves.

The irony is that they had in fact incriminated themselves, having been tricked by Cicero and his agents, the envoys of the Allobroges, into doing so.

In the last part of the narration, Cicero sets out the terms of the senate's decree and adds his own commentary (14–15). He reports the thanks paid to himself ("Thanks to my courage, wisdom, and foresight the country has been saved from the most extreme danger"), the praise given to Flaccus and Pomptinus (he says that it was given "justly and deservedly"), the praise given to his colleague Antonius (he reports it without endorsing it), the resignation of Lentulus from his praetorship, the placing in custody of the four conspirators who were present at the meeting and of a further five who were not, and finally the thanksgiving decreed to the gods in his name—the first time, he says, that this honor has been granted to a civilian. He quotes the decree from memory (13), but it can be assumed that he quotes it accurately, because in 60 BC he would have been able to check the written text. Most of the commentary that he includes appears to have been added in 60. There is a sentence on the lenience of the senate in punishing only nine conspirators (14: the senate had not yet punished anyone), a sentence that echoes a compliment that Pompey paid to him at least a year later (15), and a sentence in which Lentulus' resignation is discussed, in a rather heavy-handed way, a second time, together with his future punishment (15). Without the added material, the narration would end more impressively, not on a note of apology but with a direct quotation from the decree: "because I had saved the city from burning, the citizens from massacre, and Italy from war."

The narrations in the *Second* and *Third Catilinarians* differ from the narrations in Cicero's forensic speeches in that they are both narrations of events in which he himself featured, and which he controlled—in each case, a meeting of the senate, which is recounted before the people. Each of these narrations is designed to argue guilt: Catiline's guilt in the *Second Catilinarian*, his followers' in the *Third*. They do this well, because not only are the narrations designed by Cicero to incriminate, but so were the events themselves (Cicero's denunciation of Catiline and the interrogation of the conspirators). The interrogation of the conspirators was expertly stage-managed, and that helps the conspirators' guilt to come across in the narration, just as it helped it come across in the meeting. But in each narration, Cicero makes his case appear stronger by remaining silent about a significant detail. In the *Second Catilinarian*, he says that he got the better of Catiline in an interrogation; he says nothing about his delivery of a continuous speech. If he had told the people about the speech now known as the *First Catilinarian*, some of them might have viewed Catiline (as some of the senators may have done) as an innocent and helpless victim of his oratory. In the *Third Catilinarian*, Cicero omits (as Sallust shows) an even more important detail: that he did not merely discover the evidence of the conspirators' guilt but had actually tricked them into creating that evidence. The men he tricked into incriminating themselves were already guilty—but if he had told the people what he had done, they might not have believed them guilty. Both narrations, then, by providing a modified account of recent events, play an important part in winning over the people to Cicero's view of the conspiracy.

The final topic I will examine in this chapter is Cicero's exploitation of religion. This mainly occurs in the *Third Catilinarian*, because in that speech he is reporting a thanksgiving to the gods decreed in his own name. In granting that thanksgiving, the senate handed him a great opportunity to make use of religious arguments in his addresses to the people.

Before the senate itself, however, Cicero makes comparatively few references to religion. In the *First Catilinarian*, he makes rhetorical use of the fact that the meeting is being held in the Temple of Jupiter Stator. There is a sentence at § 11 in which he attributes to the gods and to Jupiter Stator his escape from Catiline's attempts to assassinate him, but he does not dwell on the point. He returns to Jupiter Stator in the last sentence of the speech: "You, Jupiter, who were established by the same auspices as those by which Romulus founded this city," will drive Catiline and his associates from this and the other temples of Rome and will punish them for their crimes (33). In these references, Jupiter is closely associated with the city, its foundation, and its preservation, and these ideas are firmly linked to Cicero's cause, especially by means of the god's protection of Cicero himself. But apart from incidental remarks about Catiline as a would-be destroyer of temples (12) and the gods unfortunately not prompting Catiline to go into exile (22), that is as far as Cicero chooses to go in exploiting religion in the speech.

In the *Fourth Catilinarian*, religion is again a convenient way of ending a speech. At § 18, which is the original ending of Cicero's intervention, the *patria* beseeches the senators to protect her, the citizens, the citadel and the Capitol, the altars of the household gods, the eternal fire of Vesta, the temples and shrines of all the gods, and the walls and houses of the city. Then at § 24, where the content of § 18 is reworked into the ending of the published speech, the senators are asked, not by the *patria* this time but by Cicero, to come to a decision about themselves and the Roman people, their wives and children, their altars and hearths, their shrines and temples, and the houses and homes of the city.[40] More incidentally, Cicero claims at § 7 (from the original intervention) that Caesar does not think that death has been ordained by the gods as a punishment. All the other

---

[40] In this paragraph, later additions to the *Fourth Catilinarian* are read using Approach A, that is, by acquiescing in the fiction that they were spoken by Cicero in the senate.

religious references occur within the added parts of the speech. At § 2, Cicero says that if the immortal gods intend him to save the Roman people from massacre, the senators' wives and children and the Vestal virgins from rape, and the temples and shrines and the fairest *patria* from fire, then he will submit to whatever fortune has in store for him. This is followed up by a hope that "all the gods who protect this city" will reward him as he deserves (3). There is a reference at § 12 to his shuddering at the thought of Vestal virgins being raped by Catiline's supporters. Finally, there are two references to Lentulus' having been persuaded by seers (*inductus a vatibus*, 2) to believe in royal power for himself and destruction for Rome (2, 12; Cicero does not in this speech mention either the Sibylline prophecies or the responses of the soothsayers). Cicero's choice of the word *inductus* suggests that Lentulus had been taken in, and in fact Plutarch claims that Lentulus was corrupted by "fake prophets and charlatans" who invented oracles and passed them off as prophecies from the Sibylline books (*Cic.* 17.4).[41] The conclusion to be drawn from all these passages in both speeches is that religion could be used to sharpen the oratory and heighten the drama of Cicero's words, but it was not an important factor, and probably not a factor at all, in changing the senators' minds. The senators were more likely to be influenced by talk of the *patria* than by talk of the gods.[42]

It would be natural to expect religion to play a much larger part in the speeches to the people. In the *Second Catilinarian*, however, there are not many religious references, and those that there are occur, once again, mainly in the *conclusio*. Nevertheless, two significant ideas appear in the speech. The first is that the gods are involved in the fate of Rome and are on the side of the government

---

[41] See further Gildenhard 2011: 284–85; Santangelo 2013: 144–45.

[42] In *Cat.* 1 Cicero mentions the *patria* six times and puts two speeches into her mouth; in *Cat.* 4 he mentions her eleven times (five times in the original parts of the speech and six times in the added parts). By contrast, he mentions her only four times in *Cat.* 2, and in *Cat.* 3 the only time he mentions her is when he is quoting words that he spoke in the senate (3.10).

and against Catiline.[43] At § 19, where he is discussing the second type of conspirator (unsuccessful politicians who are in debt), Cicero states that "the immortal gods will bring help in person to this unconquered people, this glorious empire, and this fairest of cities against the terrible criminal violence that we face." The moral contrast suggested there is brought out more strongly at § 25, where Cicero declares that the imminent war with Catiline will be a struggle of all the virtues against all the vices, and he suggests that the gods themselves will intervene to ensure that virtue triumphs over vice. Then in the *conclusio* he says that the gods are present among his audience and are protecting the temples and the houses of the city (29). The other idea, put forward in the preceding sentence, is that his promise that the conspiracy will be put down with the minimum possible force derives not from his own foresight (*mea prudentia*) but from "many unambiguous signs from the immortal gods, under whose guidance I have arrived at these hopes and this policy" (29).[44] But he does not elaborate or reveal what those signs are. Before the senate he does not claim to be guided by the gods or to have been sent signs by them. The only other religious references in the *Second Catilinarian* are a declaration that he will never pray to the gods to hear, in order to be proved right about Catiline's intentions, that Catiline is leading an enemy army (15), and, in the last sentence of the speech, an exhortation to the people to pray to the gods to defend the city from citizen traitors (29).

The *First*, *Second*, and *Fourth Catilinarians*, then, are sparing in their use of religious argument. Cicero is a little more venturesome when addressing the people in the second speech than when addressing the senate, but even so, it is the smallness of the part that religion plays in these speeches that is most striking. Religion is used mainly as a way of elevating and universalizing the subject matter at the end of the speeches.

---

[43] Dyck 2008: 148.
[44] On the meaning of *prudentia* in this passage, see Santangelo 2013: 59–60.

In the *Third Catilinarian*, however, the picture is different.[45] Here, the second and larger part of the *argumentatio* is entirely concerned with religion (18–22), and there are further religious moments at the beginning and end of the speech (only the part of the *conclusio* that appears to have been added, 26–29a, is entirely devoid of religious references). The speech opens with a solemn declaration that Cicero's audience and their families, together with Rome itself, have been saved "as a result of the great love that the immortal gods feel for you, and also as a result of my own physical toil, mental effort (*consiliis . . . meis*), and readiness to accept personal risk" (1).[46] Now that the conspiracy in the city has been suppressed, Cicero is not inclined to claim that his own abilities did not play a part. In fact, he goes further (2):

> Surely then, since we have elevated the founder of this city to the immortal gods by our gratitude and praise, you and your descendants ought also to honor the man who saved this same city once it had already been founded and grown to greatness. For what I have done is to extinguish the fires that were being set to the whole of the city, the temples, the shrines, the houses, and the walls, and were about to engulf them; and I have beaten back the swords that had been drawn against the state, pushing away their tips as they were held to your throats.

The sequence of thought is: (1) Romulus founded the city; (2) Romulus has therefore been elevated to the gods; (3) I saved the same city from destruction; (4) I should therefore be honored. Cicero does not actually claim to be a re-founder of Rome, but he does imply that his achievement is comparable to that of Romulus. Nor does he claim himself that he should be honored as a god, but

---

[45] For a recent analysis, see Gildenhard 2011: 278–92.

[46] Cole (2013: 55) detects "a decided tilt toward the latter" (i.e., toward Cicero, as opposed to the gods), but it seems to me that the parallelism of the clauses gives the gods' love and Cicero's actions equal weight. Cole 2013: 53–60 provides a valuable discussion of divinity in the *Catilinarians*.

he invites his audience to make that inference. In this way he uses a kind of syllogistic logic to compel his audience (or readership, on Approach B) to arrive by themselves at the most favorable judgment possible about his actions.[47] The reference to Romulus also serves to link the beginning of this speech to the end of the *First Catilinarian* (1.33).[48]

In the *narratio* (3b–15) Cicero is not much concerned with religion, although at § 4 he describes the conspirators' provision of letters to the Allobroges as an opportunity sent to him by the gods. At § 9 he relates how the Allobroges had reported Lentulus' remarks about the Sibylline prophecies and the responses of the soothsayers. Before the senate, Cicero implies that Lentulus had been taken in by seers (4.2), but here there is of course no suggestion that religious claims should invite skepticism. He presents Lentulus to the senate as gullible, but to the people as merely wicked. At § 15, he comments on the thanksgiving that the senate has decreed to the gods in his name.

The deployment of religion in full force begins at § 18:

> And yet, citizens, the way I have managed everything would seem to suggest that the action that has been taken and the foresight that has been shown derive from the will and wisdom of the immortal gods.

In other words, Cicero's thoughts (i.e., his *prudentia*) and his actions are the result of divine intervention in Rome's favor (this is a similar idea to that put forward at 2.29: it is signs from the gods that enable Cicero to predict the future). Various portents are cited in support of this, but there is nothing specific, and *occultatio* ("paralipsis")[49] is used to make the list sound less flimsy than it is: "To say nothing of the burning torches[50] that have appeared at night in the western

---

[47] Classen (1998: 39–41) argues that the reference to Romulus suits the context of 60 BC better than that of 63. At pp. 124–125 I suggested that §§ 1–2 is an addition of 60, because of its similarity to §§ 26–29a.

[48] On Cicero's use of Romulus in the speech, see further Vasaly 1993: 74, 79–80.

[49] On *occultatio*, see p. 96.

[50] That is, meteors (Dyck 2008: 193).

sky, to pass over the bolts of lightning and the earthquakes, to say nothing of the other phenomena . . . " Cicero hurries past these weak points in order to arrive at the one piece of evidence that he calculates will have a strong effect on his audience.

During the consulship of Cotta and Torquatus (65 BC), Cicero tells the people, various statues of gods and men on the Capitol, including one of the infant Romulus being suckled by a wolf, were struck by lightning and overturned, and the bronze tablets of the laws were melted. Etruscan soothsayers predicted murder, arson, civil war, and the fall of Rome unless the gods were appeased (19). On the soothsayers' instructions, a new, larger statue of Jupiter was commissioned, to face not west, like the previous statue, but east toward the forum and senate-house, in the hope that plots formed against Rome would thereby be made visible to the senate and people.[51] The new statue, however, was not set up until this very day (20)! Cicero infers from this that the gods are controlling the destiny of Rome, that the soothsayers' warnings of plots were well founded, and that Jupiter himself is responsible for the coincidence by which the statue was set in place just as the conspirators, together with Volturcius and the envoys, were being led through the forum to the Temple of Concord. Once the statue was in position, facing the people and senate, the senate and the people saw the plots against them revealed and laid bare (21).

In § 22, Cicero expands on the implications of this intervention from Jupiter. He declares both that it was Jupiter who prevented the conspirators from setting fire to the houses of the people and the temples of the gods ("But if I were to claim that it is I who have stopped them, I would be being intolerably presumptuous: it is Jupiter, Jupiter who has stopped them")[52] and that he stopped

---

[51] The statue surmounted a column in an elevated position: see *Cons.* fr. 10.55, 63 Courtney (cf. Courtney 1993: 169); Quint. *Inst.* 5.11.42; Dio 37.9.1–2; Arnobius 7.40; Obsequens 61 (the last three authors state explicitly, which Cicero does not, that the earlier statue was toppled by a bolt of lightning).

[52] As Taylor (1949: 87) notes, Cicero should be imagined as gesticulating toward the new statue.

them himself under guidance from the gods ("It is under the guidance of the immortal gods that I have shown the determination and purpose necessary to come upon these conclusive proofs of guilt"). There is an element here of having his cake and eating it—a rhetorical technique not mentioned in the handbooks[53] but common enough in Cicero's speeches (as, for example, at 2.1 and elsewhere when he claims both that he drove Catiline from Rome and that he let him leave of his own accord). As at 2.29 and 3.18, where there are references both to his foresight and to the intervention of the gods, he wants to be given personal credit for the detection and suppression of the conspiracy and to claim divine endorsement for his actions, while at the same time transferring responsibility from himself to the gods. If anyone wishes either to defend the conspirators or to criticize him, they will, he implies, be opposing Jupiter. The passage ends with the idea that the gods drove Lentulus and the other conspirators mad in order to destroy them. This parallels Cicero's description of Lentulus' behavior under questioning in the senate: "Suddenly driven mad by his crime, he showed what a guilty conscience can do" (11).

The part of the *conclusio* that appears to be original contains brief references to religion. In § 23, Cicero draws out the implications of a thanksgiving decreed in his own name. The people should thank the gods for rescuing them, but at the same time, "Without an army, without fighting, and as civilians, and with me alone, a civilian, as your leader and commander, you have been victorious." He is also concerned here, as he is throughout, to make it clear that only one of the consuls deserves credit for what has happened. The speech ends with an injunction, as Cicero gestures upward toward the statue: "Worship Jupiter above, the guardian of this city and of yourselves" (29; cf. 1.33).

Cicero's exploitation of religion to enhance his own status (even hinting that he should be viewed as another Romulus) and to put

---

[53] Quintilian is making a different point when he says that Cicero variously attributes the suppression of the conspiracy to the courage of the senate and the providence of the gods (*Inst.* 11.1.23).

himself beyond criticism is a major element of the *Third Catilinarian*. To our eyes, he appears as a sophisticated politician cynically taking advantage of the ignorance of a superstitious and credulous audience. It has even been suggested that he made arrangements with the contractors that the statue of Jupiter should be erected just as he was about to make his speech.[54] I have argued elsewhere that this is unlikely,[55] but it is not impossible. In Book 2 of *De divinatione*, written in 44 BC, Cicero represents himself as putting the case against divination to his brother, Quintus. In a discussion of thunder and lightning, Quintus mentions that Cicero, in his actions (the speech he made on 3 December 63) and in his writings (the published *Third Catilinarian* and the poem on his consulship), has made much of the remarkable coincidence by which the statue of Jupiter was put into position just as the evidence of the conspiracy was being presented to the senate and asks him how, in view of that, he can argue against divination (*Div.* 2.46). But Cicero brushes the point aside, as though Quintus were being naive.[56] The implication is that the concurrence of the two events is best explained by simple coincidence, and nothing further should be read into it. Shortly afterwards, at 2.47, he says explicitly that Quintus attributes the timing of the erection of the statue not to chance (*casu*) but to divine power. But if, on the other hand, he had made private arrangements with the contractors at some point, we should not expect him to say so—just as he does not anywhere reveal his secret dealings with the envoys of the Allobroges. In any case, Dio, in a rare

---

[54] Heibges 1969: 844 ("One wonders about this 'accidental coincidence'"); Goar 1972: 43 ("One cannot help suspecting that the orator may have perpetrated a pious fraud here"); Vasaly 1993: 81 (stated as a fact); Fantham 1997: 114 (stated as a fact); Butler 2002: 97 ("Most now regard the statue as a prop in an elaborate stunt orchestrated by the consul and his friends").

[55] Berry 2006: 312 ("But at the height of the conspiracy, was Cicero really sending messages to the workmen to ask them to speed up or delay their work so that its completion would coincide with his discovery of incriminating evidence, should he happen to discover any—merely in order that he could make a point in a speech which he might or might not then happen to give?").

[56] Santangelo 2013: 26.

comment on the effectiveness of a point made in one of Cicero's speeches, reports that the argument from the statue of Jupiter was highly successful: the people made much of the evidence of divine intervention and became more angry at the conspirators (37.34.4).

It is tempting to assume that Cicero's statements that he was guided by divine providence (*Cat.* 2.29; 3.4, 18, 22) are as cynical as his claim that Jupiter exposed the conspiracy as a result of the erection of the statue. But perhaps in some sense he did believe it. His declaration at *Pro Murena* 82 that he has been saved from assassination "not just by my own personal precautions, but far more by those of the gods" can be discounted as being, like the statements in the *Catilinarians*, an argument designed to win over the credulous. But a private letter to Atticus is another matter. Writing to him in July 61, Cicero laments how Clodius' recent acquittal on a charge of sacrilege has upset the political harmony established by the authority of his consulship "which you [Atticus] attribute to my policy and I to divine providence" (*quem tu meo consilio, ego divino confirmatum putabam, Att.* 1.16.6).[57] It seems quite possible, therefore, that he really did view the Allobroges and their procurement of written evidence from the conspirators as aid sent to him by the gods for the purpose of saving Rome (*Cat.* 3.4). *De divinatione* ends with the conclusion that superstition should be cast aside but traditional religious observance should not be; and he adds, "The celestial order and beauty of the universe compels me to admit that there is some excellent and eternal natural force [*praestantem aliquam aeternamque naturam*] which deserves the respect and veneration of the human race" (*Div.* 2.148). But, whatever Cicero's personal beliefs may have been, religious arguments are used in the *Third Catilinarian* in an entirely self-interested way, and he makes full use of the readiness of the people to be persuaded by them.

The religious element is even more prevalent in the surviving fragments of Cicero's three-book epic poem on his consulship, *Consulatus suus*. He had written up the *Catilinarians* and the rest of

---

[57] Cole 2013: 53 n. 84.

his consular corpus by around 3 June 60 BC (*Att.* 2.1.3). *Consulatus suus* was planned by 15 March 60 (*Att.* 1.19.10), and was complete at some point before the end of December of that year (*Att.* 2.3.4).[58] It therefore looks as if either the speeches and the poem were written concurrently or the poem was completed soon after the completion of the speeches. In either event, Cicero must have been thinking about each when he wrote the other, and so it is no surprise to find strong connections between the two.

In Book 1 of the poem, an omen of Cicero's forthcoming consulship was described (fr. 5).[59] There was a council of the gods, to which Cicero was summoned by Jupiter and from which he was sent to guard Rome and its citizens (fr. 5a). At some point he was also taught the arts by Minerva (fr. 5a). There was a version of the *Second Catilinarian* in which he attacked the conspirators for their luxury and degeneracy (frr. 6–7). The next fragment in Edward Courtney's edition is the famous verse *o fortunatam natam me consule Romam* ("O happy Rome, while I am consul, born!," fr. 8).[60] Because of the first-person reference, the fragment must come from a speech by Cicero within the poem.[61] Since *In Catilinam* 2.7 contains the words *o fortunatam rem publicam, si quidem hanc sentinam urbis eiecerit!* ("O happy country, if it gets rid of this urban trash!"), Courtney attributes this fragment also to the poem's version of the *Second Catilinarian*. But at the time of the *Second Catilinarian* Catiline was setting out for his army and Cicero was trying to prevent the people from joining him. The consul could not possibly

---

[58] Courtney 1993: 173.

[59] All references to *Cons.* are to Courtney's edition (1993: 156–73). Knox 2011 provides a most attractive assessment of Cicero's poetry, and of *Cons.* (200–202), in its original historical context (Cicero is seen as a Hellenistic but not a Callimachean poet, and as unsympathetic to the poetry of the neoterics). He makes the equally attractive suggestion that Catullus 49 is a (double-edged) poem of thanks to Cicero for the gift of a copy of *Cons.* (202).

[60] An alternative translation, preserving the homoeoteleuton and assonance, would be: "How fortunate the Roman state, born in my consulate!" Such jingles were a feature of early Roman poetry. For a full discussion of the verse, see Allen 1956.

[61] Allen 1956: 144–45.

have claimed at that point that Rome had been reborn. The fragment therefore probably belongs instead to a version of the *Third Catilinarian* within the poem. It is in fact a poetic distillation of *In Catilinam* 3.2. In that passage, Cicero claims that the day on which we are saved is at least equivalent to the day on which we are born, before going on to suggest that his saving of Rome places him on a level with Romulus:

> We consider the day on which we are saved to be at least as jubilant and joyful as the day on which we are born: when we are saved, our happiness is assured, whereas when we are born, we cannot take anything for granted; and also, of course, we are born with no feelings, but feel pleasure when we are saved. Surely then, since we have elevated the founder of this city to the immortal gods by our gratitude and praise, you and your descendants ought also to honor the man who saved this same city once it had already been founded and grown to greatness.

This passage provides an exact context for the fragment: on 3 December, with the arrest of the conspirators and the discovery of written evidence against them, Rome was saved, and therefore born again, in the year of Cicero's consulship.[62]

In Book 2, perhaps in order to reassure Cicero after the executions of the conspirators (fr. 9), the Muse of astronomy, Urania, delivered a long speech, of which seventy-eight lines survive, preserved in *De divinatione* 1.17–22 (fr. 10). Burning with celestial fire, Jupiter (conceived not as the god of the *Third Catilinarian* but in Stoic terms) illuminates the world and penetrates the thoughts and lives of men. When you became consul (*te consule*, 11), the Muse

---

[62] At *Flac.* 102 Cicero describes the fifth of December of his consulship "the birthday of this city, or at least the day of its salvation." This continues the rhetorical theme. But since he did not make a speech after the executions (Plut. *Cic.* 22.2), 5 December cannot provide a context for the fragment. (There are no references in the *Fourth Catilinarian* to Rome being born or founded.) Allen (1956: 140 n. 46) believes that the verse alludes to 5 December, but his view requires the text to be changed from *me consule* to *te consule* ("while you are consul").

tells Cicero, you performed the prescribed ceremonies on the Mons Albanus and observed fiery comets that presaged nocturnal slaughter. There then followed an eclipse of the moon, the death of a Roman citizen struck by lightning, an earthquake, and frightening apparitions at night—all signs from Jupiter that portended war. At this point, the prophecies made in 65 were on the point of being fulfilled. Jupiter had sent lightning that destroyed the statues on the Capitol, including the one of Romulus and the wolf, and melted the tablets of the laws; this had given rise to predictions of a great massacre to be perpetrated by citizens of noble stock, together with the burning of the city and its temples. This disaster could have been averted only by the erection of a new statue of Jupiter facing toward the east. This statue was at last set up in your consulship (*consule te*, 61), Cicero—and, in the very same hour, the Allobroges revealed to the senate and people the torches and swords that had been prepared against the *patria*. Rightly, therefore, did your ancestors venerate the gods. The *patria* called you, Cicero, from your youthful philosophical studies to public service; and now you seek release from your anxieties by devoting such time as the *patria* allows to philosophy and to us, the Muses.[63]

At the end of Book 3, Calliope, the Muse of epic poetry, ordered Cicero to continue to win fame and the praise of patriots (*famam laudesque bonorum*) by continuing on the same political path that he had followed when he was consul (fr. 11). Such praise (*laus*), won by a civilian, exceeds that owed to successful generals: *cedant arma togae, concedat laurea laudi* ("Let arms to the toga yield, the laurel to praise give way," fr. 12)—in other words, "Let military triumphs take second place to civilian glory."[64] The line neatly encapsulates the view of his achievement that Cicero wanted to promote in both *Consulatus suus* and the *Catilinarians*. Without an army, he had saved

---

[63] For another summary of this exceptionally difficult passage, see Gildenhard 2011: 294–96 (*Cons.* is discussed at 292–98).

[64] See Allen 1956: 133–34. I am not persuaded by the ingenious argument of Volk and Zetzel 2015 that the line occurred twice in the poem, once in this form and once with the final word as *linguae* ("tongue") rather than *laudi*.

Rome, and had thereby performed a greater service to his coun-trymen than successful generals, such as Pompey, who had merely extended the empire (see *Cat.* 2.28, 3.15, 3.26, 4.20, 4.21; cf. Cic. *Sul.* 33). In both the poem and the *Third Catilinarian*, religion plays a central role in elevating the status of Cicero and his consulship, and in seeking to put his political actions beyond question.

So how successful were the two *Catilinarians* addressed to the people? Did these speeches have the same magical effect as *De Othone*? Unlike *De Othone*, the *Second* and *Third Catilinarians* had a great many purposes (see pp. 125–127), and in many of those pur-poses Cicero's success is unknowable. After the delivery of the *Second Catilinarian*, several people (*complures*) who were not members of the conspiracy did leave Rome to join Catiline (Sal. *Cat.* 39.5), but there was not a general exodus. Sallust says that the entire plebs supported Catiline's schemes (*Cat.* 37.1; cf. Cic. *Cat.* 2.8), but "upon the revelation of the conspiracy" they changed their minds, cursed Catiline, and praised Cicero to the skies (*Cat.* 48.1). Two conclu-sions can be drawn from these passages. The first is that the *Second Catilinarian* may have prevented a general exodus, but it did not in fact induce the people to switch their allegiance from Catiline to Cicero. Secondly, it was, strictly speaking, the revelation of the con-spiracy that brought about the transfer of the people's allegiance: if Cicero had not given the *Third Catilinarian*, but the people had learned of the arrest of the conspirators, the evidence against them, and their confessions by some other means, they would still have abandoned Catiline and supported the consul. And yet Dio, not a historian favorable to Cicero, explicitly states that Cicero's argu-ment from the statue of Jupiter was effective in making the people angry at the conspirators (37.34.4). Overall, the picture that emerges from these sources is one in which the *Second Catilinarian* had only limited success, doing nothing to improve the situation but stop-ping it worsening, while in the *Third Catilinarian* Cicero success-fully capitalized on a victory that he had achieved by action, not words. These speeches, then, should not be classed with *De lege agraria* 2 and *De Othone* as supreme examples of Cicero's influence over the people.

If, on the other hand, we consider the *Second* and *Third Catilinarians* as written productions of 60 BC, what judgment should we come to about their success? Even though Cicero was exiled two years later for executing the arrested conspirators without trial, it is quite possible that the speeches convinced many of their readers that he was a consul who had exercised his authority correctly, had handled the people with consummate skill, and deserved the highest praise for his achievements. We do not know. But one conclusion we can state with confidence is that the speeches have been successful in their influence on posterity. Over two millennia, they have persuaded most of their readers that Catiline and his followers were bad men whom Cicero was right to oppose, and that his handling of the people showed everything, and more, that could have been expected of a man whom Sallust calls "the best of consuls" (*optumo consuli, Cat.* 43.1). Furthermore, readers of these speeches have always been swept along, as many of his original listeners must have been, by Cicero's energy and emotional intensity, the brilliance of his language, the forthrightness of his expression, his skill in characterization, the excitement of his narration, his appeals to patriotism and to the gods, and the deadly power of his denunciations.

But what of the *Fourth Catilinarian*? That speech shows Cicero back before the senate again, but this time taking the role of a moderator in a debate in which the critical contributions were made by others. Moreover, the speech as published is patently an artificial conflation of passages spoken and written at different times. What are we to make of it? Should it be judged a success? These are the questions that will be addressed in the next chapter.

·5·

Pro Cicerone:
The *Fourth Catilinarian*

The *Fourth Catilinarian* purports to be a speech given to the senate on 5 December (the "nones of December") 63 BC during the debate on what should be done with the four men who had admitted their guilt on 3 December—Lentulus, Cethegus, Statilius, and Gabinius—and a fifth man arrested later, Caeparius. We found in chapter 2, however, that it is, in the words of Ronald Syme, a "composite product":[1] §§ 4–6 are likely to be the original *relatio* (the laying of the issue before the senate), §§ 7–11a (to *leniorem fuisse*, "the more lenient of the two") and 14–18 Cicero's original intervention (*interrogatio*) in the debate, and the rest of the speech later additions written in 60 BC.[2] § 18 is the original ending of the speech which Cicero later recast as §§ 19 and 24 and which he or his copyists failed to suppress.[3] The speech as it survives takes roughly 35 minutes to read out aloud and is therefore probably too long to be an intervention in a debate that Cicero was anxious should be concluded quickly ("You must make up your minds before nightfall," 6; "You must reach your decision today," 18).[4] Before turning to analyze the speech, I will first

---

[1] Syme 1964: 106 n. 12.
[2] See pp. 73–79.
[3] Fuchs 1959.
[4] Nisbet 1964: 63 criticizes the "artificiality" of the speech: "A decision had to be reached by nightfall, but Cicero finds time for eloquent digressions and unseasonable *exempla*."

Cicero's Catilinarians. D. H. Berry, Oxford University Press (2020). © Oxford University Press.
DOI: 10.1093/oso/9780195326468.001.0001

reconstruct the course of the debate, noting Cicero's contributions as they arise.[5]

The opening words were spoken by Cicero (Sal. *Cat.* 50.3; Plut. *Caes.* 7.4), and a version of them survives as §§ 4–6 of the *Fourth Catilinarian*. Cicero tells the senate that the crisis they are facing is more serious than those precipitated by Tiberius Gracchus, Gaius Gracchus, and Lucius Saturninus; the conspirators being held under arrest plotted to burn Rome, massacre the senators, admit Catiline into the city, call in the Allobroges, and rouse the slaves to revolt. Their guilt has been proved by letters, seals, and handwriting, and each of them has confessed. "And a plot has been formed to ensure that, following a universal massacre, there should not be a single person left even to mourn the name of the Roman people or to lament the destruction of so great an empire" (4). The senate has heard the evidence and the men's confessions and has taken all the appropriate action, including requiring Lentulus to resign his praetorship and placing him and the others in custody. "All these actions go to show that the named men who have been placed in custody have been visibly and indisputably condemned by you" (5). Nevertheless, Cicero is referring the matter to the senate, "as if it were still an open question: I want you to give your verdict on what has been done and decree the punishment" (6). The senators must do this by nightfall. Many people are implicated in the conspiracy: the evil has crept[6] across the Alps and has taken hold of many of the provinces. The senate must therefore act immediately to impose punishment (6). In 45 BC, Cicero claimed in a letter to Atticus that he deserved credit for having come to a judgment himself before he consulted the senate (*Att.* 12.21.1). This presumably means that he made a public statement of his own view on the punishment of the conspirators in advance of the debate of 5 December.[7] That statement has not found its way into the *Fourth*

---

[5] This reconstruction supersedes Berry 2006: 147–49. The speakers' proposals are generally clear enough, but the order of speakers is not absolutely certain.

[6] Like a snake: Nousek 2010: 165 n. 27.

[7] Lintott 1999a: 77.

Catilinarian, although Cicero may allude to it with his words "as if it were still an open question."

Cicero first called on Decimus Junius Silanus, the consul-elect, for his opinion.[8] Silanus recommended that *supplicium* (punishment) be exacted from the arrested men, and from Cassius, Furius, Umbrenus, and Annius if they should be captured (Sal. *Cat.* 50.4). This was assumed to mean the ultimate punishment, that is, execution in the state prison (assumed by Caesar, Sal. *Cat.* 51.16–24; assumed by Cicero, Cic. *Cat.* 4.7; cf. Plut. *Cic.* 20.3, 21.3; *Cat. Min.* 22.3, 5; App. *B. Civ.* 2.5). Execution would certainly have had a deterrent effect on Catiline's supporters, but it would not have been legal, since citizens could not be put to death without trial, and the senate was not at this date a criminal court (the senate's various decrees, including the emergency decree, could not alter the fact that the conspirators were citizens and were entitled to citizens' legal rights).

Next Cicero called the other consul-elect, Lucius Licinius Murena. Murena expressed the same opinion as Silanus, and so did fourteen former consuls (Cic. *Att.* 12.21.1; Plut. *Cic.* 20.3; *Caes.* 7.5; Dio 37.36.1). After that it was the turn of the praetors-elect to give their opinion. Caesar was called (Sal. *Cat.* 50.5; Plut. *Cic.* 20.3), and he proposed a different punishment: confiscation of property and life imprisonment. Each of the arrested men should be held under guard in a different Italian town, and no one should ever be allowed to raise the question of their release; moreover, the towns should be severely punished should any of the men escape (Cic. *Cat.* 4.7–8, 10;

---

[8] The most complete ancient account of the debate is Plut. *Cic.* 20.3–21.4. Plutarch makes one serious mistake: he says that Caesar's proposal was to imprison the men in Italian towns only temporarily, until Catiline had been defeated (21.1, disproved by Cic. *Cat.* 4.7–8, 10). The other major account is Sal. *Cat.* 50.3–53.1 (gives versions of the speeches of Caesar and Cato, but omits the minor interventions, including Cicero's). Further details are supplied by Cic. *Att.* 12.21.1 (lists the consulars who spoke); Vell. 2.35.1–4; Plut. *Caes.* 7.4–8.2; *Cat. Min.* 22.3–23.3; Suet. *Jul.* 14; App. *B. Civ.* 2.5–6; Dio 37.35.4–36.2; Ampelius 31. The fullest modern account is Drummond 1995. On the order of speaking in the senate (apparently, for each magistracy in order of seniority, magistrates and magistrates-elect before ex-magistrates), see Ryan 1998: 247–59.

Sal. *Cat.* 51.43, 52.13–14; Suet. *Jul.* 14.1; Dio 37.36.1–2; contrast Plut. *Caes.* 7.5, *Cic.* 21.1, and App. *B. Civ.* 2.6: Caesar proposed temporary imprisonment; Plut. *Cat. Min.* 22.4: Caesar demanded that the men be given a trial).[9] A version of the speech is given by Sallust at *Bellum Catilinae* 51: Sallust has Caesar point to the dangerous precedent that execution would set and hint at the legal difficulties.[10] Caesar's proposal was impractical, as Cicero would shortly point out, and was in fact no more lawful than execution was. But it cleverly allowed him to pose before the senate as an implacable enemy of the conspirators while also making it possible for him to present himself before the people afterwards as the man who had attempted to save their lives.

After Caesar had finished, other senators, without making speeches, indicated their agreement either with Silanus or with Caesar (Sal. *Cat.* 52.1; App. *B. Civ.* 2.6; cf. Cic. *Att.* 12.21.1: all the speeches apart from Caesar's were for execution; and contrast Plut. *Caes.* 8.1 and Dio 37.36.2: all those after Caesar agreed with him, until Catulus and Cato). At this point Cicero, presumably worried that Caesar might carry the day,[11] intervened (Plut. *Cic.* 21.2); §§ 7–11a and 14–18 of the *Fourth Catilinarian* are likely to be his intervention. He begins: "I see that so far we have two proposals, one from Decimus Silanus, who proposes that those who have attempted to destroy Rome should be punished by death, and one from Gaius Caesar, who rules out the death penalty but recommends the strictest penalties otherwise available" (7). Both proposals are severe, he argues, but Caesar's, on which he focuses, is considered by its author to be the more severe, since he considers death to be not a punishment but "a release from pain or misfortune." The proposal is unjust to the Italian towns, Cicero adds, and impractical (7); but

---

[9] Pelling argues that Plutarch's account in the *Caesar* "deserves no credence" and that Appian's account is probably dependent on Plutarch's (2011: 164–66, at 165).

[10] Brock (1995: 212–13) argues that Sallust's versions of the speeches of Caesar and Cato are unlikely to be based on accurate accounts of what was said. Tannenbaum (2005), on the other hand, suggests that Caesar published his speech and that Sallust's version is an adaptation of it.

[11] Cadoux 2006: 613.

he will adopt it if the senate decrees it, and will do his best to implement it.[12] Further details of the proposal are spelled out: guards should be appointed; the towns should be punished if any of the men escape; no one should be permitted to reduce the penalties imposed on the men, whether by decree of the senate or by vote of the people; and the men's property should be confiscated (8). Caesar, Cicero points out, is a *popularis* (popular) politician. If the senate adopts his proposal, Cicero may therefore find himself less vulnerable to attacks from popular politicians (presumably he means Nepos and Bestia, tribunes of 62) than he will be if they adopt the proposal of Silanus. But the senate should not be concerned about that: "The national interest ought to prevail over considerations of my own safety." He then distinguishes between Caesar, a true *popularis*, and various unnamed demagogues (9), and he draws attention to one would-be *popularis*, who has supported Cicero and the senate so far but, in order to avoid expressing his opinion, has failed to turn up to the debate.[13] Returning to Caesar's proposal, he declares that Caesar recognizes that the arrested men cannot any longer be considered as Roman citizens, and that the Sempronian law (*lex Sempronia*, 123 or 122 BC, which prohibited the execution of citizens except after trial before the people or in a court sanctioned by the people) therefore does not apply to them. Nor does Caesar think that Lentulus, despite his lavish use of bribery, can any longer be called a *popularis*. Cicero does not claim that Caesar actually made these points in his speech, but only that he "recognizes" (*intellegit*) and "thinks" (*putat*) them; he would therefore seem, outrageously, to be putting words into Caesar's mouth.[14] He then recapitulates Caesar's proposal in language that makes it

---

[12] Before the Social War, Italian towns were not obliged to accept Roman prisoners unless such an obligation was specified in a treaty (Roselaar 2012). It would appear from Cicero's words that this was still the case.

[13] Cicero has usually been taken to be alluding to Crassus. That identification was challenged by Drummond (1995: 14–15), who argued for Nepos or Bestia, but the case for Crassus has been strongly restated by Cadoux 2006.

[14] Lintott 1999b: 170. Dyck (2008: 224), however, thinks it not impossible that Cicero is reporting Caesar's words.

appear horribly severe ("He does not hesitate to consign Publius Lentulus to eternal darkness and chains"), while at the same time describing Caesar as "the mildest and gentlest of men" (10). Finally, he concludes this part of his speech (linking back to the beginning of § 7) by presenting the senate with two choices: either they adopt Caesar's proposal, which will enable Cicero to appear before the people with Caesar at his side in support, or they adopt Silanus', in which case Cicero will defuse any popular unrest by arguing, as Caesar himself has done, that execution is a less severe punishment than life imprisonment (11a).

The general message that he wants his hearers to take from this passage is that the more severe of the two proposals, whichever it is judged to be, is the more suitable, and will be more truly in the people's interests. However, the sophistical, paradoxical nature of the argument he attributes to Caesar at § 7, that death is a release and not a punishment, suggests that he wants the senators to conclude that it is in fact Silanus' proposal, not Caesar's, that is the more severe, and therefore the one to be preferred. Moreover, his lack of enthusiasm for Caesar's proposal is obvious when he talks about its unfairness to the Italian towns (Cicero was always a supporter of the Italians) and the difficulty of implementing it (7–8).

The second part of Cicero's intervention (14–18) picks up where the first part ended. At § 11a he assured the senate that, if they adopted Silanus' proposal and voted to execute the arrested men, he would be able to manage the people. Now he provides further reassurance: he has everything under control. The Romans of every order, class, and age are united. "This is the only issue since the foundation of our city on which everyone holds exactly the same opinion"—a surprising claim in a speech that reviews two opinions, but Cicero is thinking only of the crowds in the forum (14). The sole exceptions, he says, are the conspirators themselves; but, he declares, the men should be considered not as citizens but as enemies (*hostes*, 15). With this remark he encourages the senate to ignore the fact that, as citizens, the conspirators are entitled to the protection of the *lex Sempronia*. Next, he enlarges eloquently on the unanimity and patriotism of the people thronging the forum—the equestrians, the treasury tribunes, the scribes, the freeborn citizens (even the poorest), the freedmen, and the slaves (15–16). The loyalty of the shopkeepers is demonstrated by the fact that a pimp of Lentulus has failed in his attempt to bribe them with money. Shopkeepers rely on peaceful conditions: "If their profits fall when their shops are closed, what will be the effect on those profits, do you think, when their shops have been set on fire?" (17). Cicero concludes his intervention at § 18. It is very obviously the end of a speech. The Roman people are united, and the senate has a duty not to fail them. The *patria*, who addressed both Catiline and Cicero himself in the *First Catilinarian*, stretches out her suppliant hands to the senators and begs them to save the city. The senate must reach their decision today.

Rhetorically, Cicero's intervention is a most unusual piece of persuasion. Normally, an orator will state what he advocates and then provide arguments for it and refute arguments against it. But here Cicero must appear to be impartial. So he reviews the two proposals with apparent neutrality, but makes a series of observations about one of them that he hopes will incline his audience toward the other. However, he did not succeed in inducing the senate to reject Caesar's proposal and rally round that of Silanus. On the contrary, his friends became worried that he would find himself in danger if he executed the arrested men, and so they backed Caesar's proposal (Plut. *Cic.* 21.2). These included Cicero's brother Quintus, who, like Caesar, was a praetor-elect: he changed his mind and went over to Caesar's side (Suet. *Jul.* 14.2).[15] When, after the praetors-elect, the former praetors were called, Tiberius Claudius Nero (probably the grandfather of the future emperor Tiberius) proposed that the guards who were holding the men be increased and that the matter be considered again in the future (Sal. *Cat.* 50.4; App. *B. Civ.* 2.5 says that the proposal was to keep the men in custody until Catiline had been defeated). Perhaps he was concerned by what Cicero had just said about Lentulus' attempt

---

[15] Taylor and Scott (1969: 555 n. 58) suggest that he had already spoken before Caesar.

to bribe the shopkeepers; but Cethegus was also trying to arrange his own rescue (Sal. *Cat.* 50.2; App. *B. Civ.* 2.5). Then Silanus, influenced by Caesar's speech, said that he would support Nero's proposal (Sal. *Cat.* 50.4).[16] In a bizarre attempt to conceal his change of mind, he claimed that when he had used the word *supplicium* he had in fact meant imprisonment, not execution (Plut. *Cic.* 21.3; *Cat. Min.* 22.5; Suet. *Jul.* 14.1).

The first senator to speak against Caesar's proposal was Quintus Lutatius Catulus, the consul of 78 and friend of Catiline (but not of course a conspirator). Earlier in the debate, he had supported Silanus' original proposal (Cic. *Att.* 12.21.1). Now, he made clear that (unlike Silanus) he had not changed his mind and still favored execution (Plut. *Cic.* 21.3; *Caes.* 8.1). Eventually, it was the turn of Marcus Porcius Cato to speak (Sal. *Cat.* 52.1; Plut. *Cic.* 21.3; *Cat. Min.* 23.1). He was a tribune-elect and "among the last to be asked for his opinion" (Vell. 2.35.3).[17] His speech is not mentioned in the *Fourth Catilinarian*, but Plutarch gives an account of its content. It was angry and passionate, he says: Cato reproached his brother-in-law Silanus for changing his mind and violently attacked Caesar (Plut. *Cat. Min.* 23.1–2; cf. *Cic.* 21.3; *Caes.* 8.1; App. *B. Civ.* 2.6). In spite of his popular pose and humane sentiments, Cato maintained, Caesar was undermining the city and seeking to intimidate the senate, when in fact it was he himself who had most cause to be afraid. His past record was deeply suspect, and now he was attempting to save Rome's enemies. He felt nothing for his country in its hour of danger, but was instead weeping for men who ought never to have been born, and was complaining at the prospect of the city being freed from danger by their deaths. Another detail that is known of the speech is that in it Cato praised Cicero to the skies (Cic. *Att.* 12.21.1; Vell. 2.35.4). At some point in the proceedings, Cato

---

[16] Ryan (1998: 317–18) argues that Silanus actually changed his mind because he thought that his proposal would be defeated and feared embarrassment.

[17] Ryan (1998: 116–19) rejects the suggestion of Taylor and Scott (1969: 554–55) that Cato's status as a priest (Plut. *Cat. Min.* 4.1) gave him the right to speak with the former praetors.

happened to see a small writing tablet being brought in to Caesar from outside, and he accused him of receiving information from the conspirators and challenged him to read out what was written on the tablet. Instead, Caesar handed the message to Cato; it was a love letter from Cato's half-sister Servilia. Cato threw it back at Caesar and continued with his speech (Plut. *Cat. Min.* 24.1–2; *Brut.* 5.2–3).

Sallust gives us his own version of Cato's speech at *Bellum Catilinae* 52. It differs from Plutarch's account in omitting the criticism of Silanus and the invective against Caesar, and in containing a heavy emphasis on contemporary extravagance and greed (which are central themes of Sallust's work). In this version, Cato talks about the intentions of the conspirators, the danger from Catiline and his army, and the risk to the senators' own lives and property. He points out that in describing death as a release, Caesar has not taken into account the punishment to be expected in the underworld, and there is a brief hint (but no more than that) that Caesar may have his own private reason for being unafraid of the conspirators. He assures the senate that decisive action will demoralize Catiline's army and that weakness will embolden it, and he pours scorn on the idea of showing mercy to men such as Lentulus and Cethegus. In the final words of the speech, he delivers his verdict: "Punishment must be imposed according to the custom of our ancestors" (*more maiorum supplicium sumundum*, *Cat.* 52.36).

As soon as Cato had sat down, all the former consuls and a large number of others praised his proposal and accused each other of faint-heartedness (Sal. *Cat.* 53.1). Caesar, however, rose to speak again. Cato had not only proposed execution but had adopted his suggestion of confiscation of property, and Caesar now argued that it was wrong that the humane element of his proposal should be rejected but the most severe element accepted (Plut. *Cic.* 21.4). He therefore proposed that the property of the men should not be confiscated. This of course made a mockery of his claim to have wanted the conspirators to be punished with the strictest penalties available (Cic. *Cat.* 4.7). He came under violent attack and appealed to the tribunes for help, but they ignored him, and so he left the meeting, being threatened by the equestrians with swords once he was outside the temple (Sal. *Cat.* 49.4; Plut. *Caes.* 8.2; Suet. *Jul.* 14.2). Cicero put the proposal for execution to the senate in Cato's wording but left out the clause about confiscation of property, and the decree was passed (Sal. *Cat.* 53.1; Plut. *Cic.* 21.3–4; *Cat. Min.* 23.3). Even Cethegus' brother is said to have voted for execution (Ampelius 31).

What I have done so far in this chapter is to take what I think are the delivered passages out of the *Fourth Catilinarian* and place them in their original historical context. It remains now to examine a different text, the published *Fourth Catilinarian*, which is an imaginative fiction[18] set within the same historical context that I have described. The speech can be analyzed as either, on Approach A, a speech delivered by Cicero to the senate on 5 December 63 or, on Approach B, a self-justifying production of 60.[19] But it is important to understand that in analyzing it on Approach A we are not analyzing a real, historical speech but an imaginary one—a speech comparable, for example, to the ones that Sallust puts into the mouths of Caesar and Cato. Indeed, Cicero fills the speech with self-justification in exactly the same way that Sallust fills Cato's one with his own views on contemporary morality. The context is real, but the speech (except for the original passages) is not.

The *Fourth Catilinarian*, then, on Approach A, is a speech delivered by Cicero to the senate at some point during the debate on the arrested Catilinarian conspirators on 5 December 63. We are told by Plutarch (the information appears in no other source) that the original speech was an intervention made after Caesar's speech and before the second speech of Silanus and the speeches of Catulus and Cato. Plutarch writes: "When he [Cicero] himself rose, he tried his hand in each direction, in some ways advocating the former proposal [i.e., that of Silanus], in others Caesar's" (*Cic.* 21.2, tr. J. L. Moles). That does sound like a description of §§ 7–11a of our

---

[18] Cf. Lintott 2008: 17 ("*In Catilinam* 4 as a whole is fiction"), 147 ("The *Fourth Catilinarian . . .* may be largely a fiction").

[19] Approaches A and B are articulated at pp. 87–89.

speech.[20] Cicero's original readers, however, did not have Plutarch to guide them, and it is not immediately obvious from the speech itself at which point in the debate the speech is to be imagined as having been delivered. There is much in it that has the character of a final summing-up: the senators have given their views, and Cicero as the convener gives a summary of the two main proposals before asking the senators to choose between them. In this scenario, Cato would have given his speech, but Cicero would not mention it, because the proposal for execution had originally been put forward by Silanus, who spoke before Cato and was greatly senior to him; and perhaps Cicero would have wished in any case to avoid publicizing Cato's contribution, which had been so much more memorable than his own. This scenario seems superficially so attractive that David Stockton, overlooking the evidence of Plutarch, believed that the *Fourth Catilinarian* is actually the consul's final summing-up.[21] However, the speech also contains the words (from the original *relatio*) "Nevertheless I have chosen to refer the matter to you, conscript fathers, as if it were still an open question: I want you to give your verdict on what has been done and decree the punishment. I shall state in advance the points that it is appropriate for the consul to make" (6). That shows that not only has the debate not yet come to an end, but it has not even started. And yet, almost immediately after reading those words, Cicero's readers would find themselves in mid-debate, with proposals by Silanus and Caesar having already been put forward (7). This looks very much like carelessness on Cicero's part—the same carelessness that has resulted in the speech having two alternative endings (§§ 18 and 24). We have to conclude, therefore, that Cicero was not particularly concerned to make his speech appear authentic, by helping his readers to situate it within a precise context within the debate.[22] When considering the speech

---

[20] Lintott 2013: 161.

[21] Stockton 1971: 135, 342. Winterbottom (1982: 69 n. 20) also inclines to this view.

[22] It seems likely that Cicero's original readers were less concerned with the historical authenticity of his published speeches than modern readers are. Cf. the remarks of Hutchinson (2010: 104–6) on another fictional speech of Cicero's, *Pro Milone*.

as a whole, readers will find it easiest to treat it as an intervention and suspend their critical faculties when reading § 6. But Cicero seems to have been more concerned that there should exist a significant and substantial speech by himself from the celebrated 5 December debate than that an accurate version of his intervention be transmitted to posterity. The *Fourth Catilinarian* is also required to serve as the grand finale to the *Catilinarians*, and not as a historically informative coda. It is required, especially, to drive home the message of self-justification that runs through all the *Catilinarians*. It is at this point that Approach A gives way to Approach B. We can treat the speech as Cicero's intervention in the Catilinarian debate; but once we start to do so, the perspective of 60 BC, in which Cicero hands down to us the authorized version of his consulship, quickly takes over. But let us review the speech as a whole and see how the application of Approaches A and B works in practice.

The *Fourth Catilinarian*, like the *Second* and *Third*, is a deliberative speech: in it, Cicero deliberates about a course of action. However, Michael Winterbottom has argued that the recasting of the speech in 60, involving a shifting of the focus from the conspirators to Cicero himself, has moved the speech in the direction of forensic oratory: the speech has changed from being *In Catilinam* to being *Pro Cicerone*—it has become a defense of Cicero.[23] Winterbottom believes, as I do, that §§ 1–3 and 19–24 are "hardly conceivable in the original senatorial speech," and he points out that in these sections Cicero's emotional reference to "the grief of my dear beloved brother who is with us" (3) and, at the end of the speech, his pitiful words "I commend my little son to you" (23) are topics more proper to forensic oratory than to deliberative. Whether considered as a real speech delivered to the senate or as a self-justifying production of 60, the speech is formally deliberative, but Winterbottom is right to draw attention to the forensic elements that arise as a consequence of its apologetic purpose.

---

[23] Winterbottom 1982: 61–62.

It is difficult to describe the rhetorical structure of the speech. Andrew R. Dyck, however, makes a good attempt.[24] He identifies §§ 1–6 as the *exordium* (introduction). Alternatively, one could separate off §§ 4–6, but it is not easy to see how else this part could be classified, since it is plainly the original *relatio* and does not entirely take on a different complexion when subsumed within the larger speech. §§ 7–8 are a recapitulation of the proposals of Silanus and Caesar; Dyck reasonably sees them as a *narratio* (narration). §§ 23–24 are obviously the *conclusio* (peroration): its beginning is signaled by the words *Quae cum ita sint* ("Since that is how the matter stands"); the same words introduce the *conclusio* of the original intervention at § 18). The core of the speech, §§ 9–22, is particularly difficult to assign labels to; it has something of the fluidity of the *First Catilinarian*. Dyck calls the more argumentative parts of it, §§ 11–19, *argumentatio* (argumentation) and the other parts *digressio* (digression; again, the term is not meant to suggest that Cicero has strayed from the point, but simply that the material does not conform to any of the standard parts of an ancient speech). The fact that Paul MacKendrick can class §§ 14–22 as *narratio* illustrates the degree to which the core of the speech defies structural analysis in conventional terms.[25] This is not surprising, in view of the patchwork quality of a speech made up of two original speeches and later additions. My own tentative analysis is as follows:

§§ 1–3, *exordium* (added later)

§§ 4–6 (original *relatio*)

§§ 7–8, *narratio* (original intervention)

§§ 9–11a (original intervention)

§§ 11b–13 (added later)

§§ 14–18 (original intervention, § 18 being its *conclusio*)

§§ 19–22 (§ 19 being a link passage intended to replace § 18; added later)

---

[24] Dyck 2008: 209–10.

[25] MacKendrick (1995: 93–94) proposes: 1–13, proem; 14–22, *narratio*; 23–24, *peroratio*.

§§ 23–24, *conclusio* (§ 24 being intended to replace § 18; added later)

The first sentence announces the subject of this fictional speech. The speech is not, as might have been expected, about the fate of the arrested men: in the *exordium*, they are not even mentioned. Instead, it is about the fate of Cicero (1):

> I see, conscript fathers, that the eyes and faces of all of you are turned in my direction: I see that you are concerned not just about the danger to yourselves and the country, but also, if that is averted, about the danger to me.

The senators are worried about Cicero, and at § 3 we learn that they have grouped themselves around him and are in tears. In §§ 1–3, he keeps repeating the same point. The senators should not be influenced by the danger to him because he will gladly endure every kind of suffering, pain, and torture if this will bring safety to the senate and Roman people (1). He has been the subject of repeated assassination attempts, but he is willing to give his life for the rescue of the senate and Roman people and of all Italy (2). The senate, therefore, should vote in the way that will protect Rome, without worrying about him. He is ready to die. He feels concern for his family, but, again, he is willing to die to save them (3). The message that is being hammered home is that he is willing to sacrifice himself for Rome and its people. On Approach A, the aim is to ensure that the senators are not deterred from voting for execution by the fear that Cicero may find himself in trouble for it afterwards. But it is a little difficult to imagine that in reality this factor would have played such an important part in their decision. On Approach B, the passage has a more believable aim. Cicero has come under heavy and persistent public criticism for executing the conspirators and has been called a *rex* ("king," "tyrant"), and he therefore wants to argue that his actions were done for the benefit of Rome rather than himself, that they did save Rome, and that he deserves praise for them, not blame.

The *exordium* is unusual. Normally, Cicero's *exordia* touch upon all the major themes of the speech, avoid repetition, and contain no argument. This *exordium* only covers one theme of the speech, makes the same point four times, and contains what appears to be a conclusion at the beginning of § 3: "Therefore, conscript fathers [*Qua re, patres conscripti*], consider your own interests, take thought for your country." But this departure from convention serves to give an impression of spontaneity: the speech is to be seen as not having been worked out in advance. The unconventional structure of the speech can also be defended on the same grounds. It is clear from the end of the *Second Philippic* that Cicero did want the speech to be seen as having actually been delivered. In this *exordium* he writes: "For a man of courage, death cannot be shameful; for a man who has reached the consulship, it cannot be untimely; and for a wise man, it cannot be pitiable" (3). At *Philippic* 2.119 he famously recalls those words:

> If nearly twenty years ago in this very temple I declared that death could not be untimely for a man who had reached the consulship, with how much more truth could I now say "for an old man"?

In 44 BC, then, Cicero told his readers that he had actually delivered those words from the *Fourth Catilinarian* in the Temple of Concord. Few in the senate of 44 would have been members of that body for long enough to be able to contradict him. Ironically, however, the *Second Philippic* was not delivered either: like the *Fourth Catilinarian*, it is a fictional speech set within a real historical context. One can only admire the ingenuity and freedom with which Cicero rewrites history in both these speeches.

The next section, §§ 4–6, was originally the freestanding *relatio* but in the fictional speech is an integral part of Cicero's intervention. To maintain the illusion that Cicero is speaking in mid-debate, the reader has to avoid thinking too deeply about sentences such as "I shall state in advance the points that it is appropriate for the consul to make" (§ 6). The beginning of § 4 reduces the awkwardness by linking the section to what precedes, although this is done with the same formula that was used at the start of § 3, and so there is some sense of piling up: "Therefore, conscript fathers [*Qua re, patres conscripti*], apply yourselves to the security of the country." The aim of this section is straightforward. On Approach A, Cicero wants to emphasize the seriousness of the men's crimes, their clear guilt, and the prior acknowledgment of that guilt by the senate, and he wants to ensure that the men's punishment is decided before the end of the meeting. The instruction "You must make up your minds before nightfall" (6) adds urgency and drama. On Approach B, Cicero justifies the executions and his own authorization of them: the men were guilty of the most serious crimes and were therefore rightly executed; Lentulus was no longer a magistrate when he was executed, and therefore Cicero did not commit sacrilege;[26] and it was the senate, not Cicero, which decreed the punishment. This is in line with his general policy of claiming the credit for saving Rome but shifting to the senate the blame for the action taken.[27]

At § 7 we move on to the original intervention. The beginning of it is the *narratio* of the speech (§§ 7–8). It is a conventional *narratio* in that Cicero narrates the events that are the reason for his speech in a factual, ostensibly neutral way, but one intended to dispose his audience subtly to his own point of view. He wants to appear as the impartial moderator of the debate, but also to direct its outcome. He therefore discusses both proposals, but he concentrates more on the one that he wants his audience to reject, that of Caesar, listing the reasons why it is impractical, but claiming that the difficulties can be overcome. Hesitation is implied by *ut spero*: "I shall do as you direct and shall manage, *I trust*, to find someone who does not consider himself honor-bound to refuse to carry out your wishes" (8). Evidently the chief magistrates of some of the Italian towns, good people that they are, will consider it a matter of honor (*dignitas*) not to comply with Caesar's proposal. The more Cicero says about the proposal, the more he hopes the senators will become inclined

---

[26] See pp. 72–73.
[27] See pp. 188–189.

to reject it. By repeating Caesar's argument that imprisonment is a more severe punishment than execution, he reminds them of its absurdity (7). The *narratio*, on Approach A, aims simply to turn the senate away from Caesar's proposal. On Approach B, the passage shows at least that Cicero, as a conscientious moderator, gave Caesar's proposal due consideration and did not dismiss it out of hand. It also helps, to some extent, to justify the executions, since Silanus' proposal is presented entirely positively as logical, appropriate, and justified by many precedents (7).

The next section is §§ 9–11a, also from the original intervention. In it, Cicero attempts to answer an objection to execution, that it will draw fury from the *populares* politicians (such as Nepos and Bestia, who are not named). It is the politicians rather than the people that he expresses concern about, although obviously the tribunes of the plebs had the means to stir up the people. The way he deals with this is to draw a distinction between true *populares*, of whom he claims to approve ("the truly popular spirit that has the people's interests at heart"), and demagogues, who are "fickle" (*levitatem*, 9). He is careful to put Caesar, who was influential and needed to be kept on the side of the senate, into the former category, and he goes out of his way to exclude Lentulus from it, on the grounds that a man who has plotted to massacre the Roman people cannot be considered a *popularis*. If Crassus is the absent senator referred to at § 10, then what Cicero does is to place him in the former category as well, but give him notice that his continued support for the senate is expected. Cicero declares that Caesar recognizes that "someone who is an enemy of the state cannot conceivably be viewed as a citizen" (10). Here too he is constructing categories (a rhetorical ploy used throughout his speeches; cf. *Cat.* 2.18–24) and consigning the arrested men to the one that does not enjoy the protection of the law, while maintaining that this is the position of a true *popularis*. What this rather complicated argument does is give the impression that execution is not vulnerable to objections from *populares*: although Caesar opposes execution, he does so only because he regards life imprisonment as more severe, and he does not object to execution in principle. And anyone who does object to execution in principle cannot by definition be a true friend of the people: they will fall (like Nepos and Bestia) into the wrong category. On Approach A, the passage seeks to neutralize the opposition to execution of a powerful *popularis*, Caesar, and to dismiss the opposition of false *populares* (Nepos and Bestia). On Approach B, it counters objections made against the executions after they have taken place and implies that Cicero's attackers—that is, in 60 BC, Clodius—are demagogues who do not truly represent the people's interests.

§§ 11b–13 appear to be a later insertion into the original intervention. The passage consists of further argument—not needed on 5 December, but needed subsequently—that executing the conspirators would be neither cruel nor excessive, but an act of mercy (toward the *patria*), and that sparing them would be an act of cruelty (toward the *patria*). The argument has the same paradoxical quality as Caesar's argument that life imprisonment would be a more severe penalty than execution. It fits neatly into its context, because it follows on from the remark at § 10 that "Caesar himself is the mildest and gentlest of men" (*homo mitissimus atque lenissimus*).[28] But immediately afterwards Cicero grants himself that distinction: "For who has a milder nature than I?" (*quis enim est me mitior?*, 11). This intrusion of the *lenitas* theme is one sign that the passage was added in 60: the heavy and sustained emphasis on mildness, humanity, compassion, mercy, and especially lenience was not appropriate to the time of the debate (that is, before the conspirators had been executed and well before Cicero had begun to be criticized), but was entirely appropriate to the situation in which Cicero found himself in the following years (see pp. 69–71). But another sign is the extraordinary vividness and extravagance of the oratory at §§ 11–12:

---

[28] Hutchinson (1995: 488) points out that *atque* + a consonant (*atque*, "and," is normally followed by a vowel) is a stylistic feature found much more often in the *Fourth Catilinarian* (seventeen times) than in any other work of Cicero, and he infers that "Cicero must be seeking to enhance the momentousness of the situation" in this speech.

I seem to see this city, the light of the world and the citadel of every nation, suddenly being burnt to the ground. I see in my mind's eye pitiful heaps of citizens unburied, in a country that has itself been buried. There appears before my eyes a vision of Cethegus, crazily raving over your slaughter. And when I imagine Lentulus ruling over us as king [*regnantem Lentulum*], as he told us himself that prophecies had given him reason to hope, and Gabinius attending him as his vizier, and Catiline having arrived with his army, I cannot help but shudder at the thought of mothers weeping, girls and boys running for their lives, and Vestal virgins being violated [*vexationem virginum Vestalium*].

Few passages in Cicero are quite so visual as this one. Its aim (on Approach A) is to whip up the feelings of the senators to make them vote for execution. But that was not what Cicero, as the moderator of the debate, needed to do; his task was to summarize the two proposals that had been made in an ostensibly neutral fashion and ask the senate not to waste time in coming to a decision between them. The parts of the speech that were actually delivered do precisely that. Compare this passage with, for example, the measured approach taken at § 6: "You can see the magnitude of the crime that has been reported to you." That is the authentic voice of a moderator: there was no need to go into details. Our passage undermines the delivered parts of the speech by destroying the impression of neutrality and potentially prolonging the debate. But its primary function (on Approach B) is to justify the executions by presenting the most horrifying picture possible of what would have happened if the conspiracy had not been suppressed. In addition, the passage seeks to counter the accusation made against Cicero from 62 BC that he was a *rex*: on the contrary, he asserts, it was Lentulus who, on his own admission, aspired to be a king. As Cicero declares in *Pro Sulla* in 62 BC: "In that magistracy [his consulship], I did not start a tyranny [*regnum*], but stopped one" (*Sul.* 21;

cf. 21–35, 48).[29] And he has a further aim. His original intervention was not a major speech, or a memorable one, and yet he wanted to be remembered as a commanding figure in the debate. Seventeen years later, he told Atticus that he was annoyed because Brutus had praised him merely for having referred the question of the arrested men to the senate (*Att.* 12.21.1). Our passage helps to increase the apparent significance of his contribution, while also seeking to ensure that the *Fourth Catilinarian* does not fall too far behind the first three speeches in oratorical power.

The next section, §§ 14–18, is the last part of the original intervention, and § 18, with its personification of the *patria*, is its *conclusio*. Cicero has everything under control and has "sufficient forces [*satis praesidi*] to implement whatever decision you come to today" (14)—by which he means essentially (since this section should be seen as following on from § 11a) that he has the capability, if the senate so decrees, to execute the arrested men. (At § 11a he said that he would tell the people that execution was "much more lenient" than life imprisonment.) The rest of the passage proclaims the unity of all sections of society in Rome, from the equestrians down to the freedmen and slaves. If this unity can be made permanent (by a vote for execution, he implies), then Rome's future will be transformed: "If we can make this national unity, forged in my consulship, permanent, then I can promise you that no internal civil disturbance will ever again affect any part of our national life" (15). (The fact that Cicero's hopes quickly proved in vain helps to confirm that this passage is original.) "All the orders are of one mind—in head, heart, determination, courage, and voice—to save our country" (18). On Approach A, Cicero is trying to bring the senate's vote into alignment with what he claims is the universal view of the equestrians and the rest of Rome, and to make it unanimous for execution. On Approach B, he is claiming that he had universal support on 5 December 63 for the action that he took on that day.

---

[29] See further Berry (1996): 177–78.

The rest of the speech (§§ 19–24) is all later addition. It is closely connected with the *exordium*, and was presumably written at the same time as it: §§ 1–3 announce that the speech will be about Cicero (who is willing to sacrifice himself for Rome), and accordingly §§ 19–24 are concerned exclusively with him. § 19 is a link passage, but it links to § 17, § 18 being the original *conclusio* that was not suppressed. Curiously, § 19 begins: "You have a leader who is thinking of you and not of himself" (*habetis ducem memorem vestri, oblitum sui*).[30] That statement follows from the theme of self-sacrifice in §§ 1–3 but will be contradicted by everything that follows: Cicero is thinking, and speaking, primarily of himself. The statement replaces the following sentence from § 18: "You have a consul [*habetis consulem*] who has been allowed to escape from a great many dangers and plots and from the jaws of death not for the sake of his own life, but to ensure your safety." Similarly, the sentence from § 18 about all the orders being of one mind is replaced by "You have a situation in which all the orders, all men, and the entire Roman people . . . are of one and the same mind."

§§ 20–22 is the section following the link passage and begins: "Now before I ask you once again for your view, I should like to say a word about myself." The reader is expected to believe that Cicero himself is a new topic not so far considered in the speech. By this means he gives himself permission to turn aside from the issue facing the senate, the punishment of the arrested men, and devote himself to his *apologia*. In Winterbottom's terms (p. 175), the speech now switches from *In Catilinam* to *Pro Cicerone*. This section is the culmination not so much of the *Fourth Catilinarian* as of the set of four speeches. Its primary subject is Cicero's achievement and his place in history.

In § 20, Cicero provides more detail about his possible self-sacrifice. There are a great many conspirators (he seems no longer

---

[30] Lintott (2008: 148) points out that the emphasis on Cicero's leadership in what follows "seems hardly appropriate on 5 December 63, especially as Cicero was seeking at the time to underplay his own leadership by comparison with the authority of the senate."

to be thinking about the arrested men), and they are his personal enemies, but they are weak (he seems to have forgotten that Catiline is supposed to be marching on Rome). "If," however, "that gang should ever again be stirred up by the rage and criminality of some individual" (writing in 60, he means Clodius) and should succeed in gaining control of Rome, then even if he should be threatened with assassination, he will not regret the action that he took against the conspirators, considering the unprecedented honors that the senate has voted him for saving the state. On Approach A, the aim must logically be the same as that of the *exordium*, to ensure that the senators are not deterred from voting for execution by fear that this will place Cicero in danger. But it is hard to accept it as that, because he does not go on to say here, as he does at § 3, "Stop sparing me trouble and worrying on my behalf" (or something to that effect). In any case, the sense that he is intervening in a debate is no longer strongly felt. Instead, the passage, and what follows, ceases to be an argument and becomes (on Approach B) a personal statement.

The oratory of this part of the speech rises to the same level as that of an earlier added portion, §§ 11–12. Cicero provides a list of the greatest generals in Roman history and places himself at the end of it (21):

> Let Scipio have his fame, since by his intelligence and courage he forced Hannibal to leave Italy and return to Africa; let the second Africanus be showered with the highest praise for destroying the two cities most hostile to this empire of ours, Carthage and Numantia; let Paullus be judged outstanding, since his triumph was adorned by the most noble and once the most powerful of kings, Perseus; let Marius have everlasting glory for twice liberating Italy from occupation and the prospect of slavery; and let Pompeius be rated higher than all of these, since his achievements and merits are bounded by the same borders and limits as the course of the sun. But amid the praise due to these men there will surely be some space left for my own glory—unless perhaps it is a greater achievement to open up provinces for us to go

out to than to ensure that those who have gone out to them have a country to which they can return in triumph.

The statement that Pompey should be rated higher than his predecessors makes it clear that this is an escalating list—with Cicero at the top. The words "there will surely be some space left for my own glory" provide a note of modesty, but this is followed immediately by the suggestion, which Cicero surely intends the reader to accept, that his own achievement—the saving of Rome from annihilation—in fact surpasses the achievements of Pompey and hence those of all the generals listed. In addition, readers (but not Cicero's audience in 63) might recall that at some point after he had returned to Rome at the end of 62, Pompey had publicly complimented Cicero by declaring that "he [Pompey] would have brought home his third triumph in vain were it not for the fact that my [Cicero's] service to the state had ensured that there *was* a home to which he could bring it" (Cic. *Off.* 1.78). In § 22 Cicero continues the comparison with Pompey in a way that suggests that his own task, and therefore his achievement, is greater, because he has to deal with an ongoing threat: Pompey will face no further trouble from the foreign enemies he has defeated in the east, but Cicero will forever be in danger from citizen traitors. "It is obvious to me, therefore, that the war that I have undertaken against citizen traitors must be unending [*aeternum bellum*]." But if the bond between the senate, the equestrians, and the loyal citizens holds strong, he argues, that war will easily be repelled by him and those who stand with him (*a me atque a meis*). The use of categories is strong again here: for Cicero, there are two mutually exclusive classes of citizen, namely, traitors (*perditi cives, hostes patriae*) and the loyal (*boni omnes*). There is no suggestion in §§ 21–22 of self-sacrifice; on the contrary, Cicero now anticipates victory. When this section is considered as an intervention in the debate (Approach A), it serves, like § 20, little obvious purpose. The best that can be said for it is that it shows Cicero's concern in the debate to secure his own place in history. On the other hand, the length of the passage impedes another of Cicero's aims, that of bringing the session to a close before nightfall.

When considered as a production of 60 (Approach B), however, this section makes a powerful case, first, for recognizing Cicero's suppression of the conspiracy (including his execution of five of the conspirators) as a service to Rome of the very highest order and, secondly, for supporting him in his continuing battles against his enemies, who are by his definition Rome's enemies too. The passage is not merely an *apologia* but a call to arms—against Clodius and against any other citizen traitors whom Cicero should happen to identify at any point in the future. In addition, it trumpets his achievement not just to his contemporaries but to posterity.

The *conclusio*, as is normal in Cicero, has a major section (although this one is brief, § 23) and then a quieter coda (§ 24). The major section continues the personal theme and recapitulates both the *exordium* and §§ 20–22. Cicero returns to the theme of self-sacrifice, but this is initially presented as a voluntary forfeiture not of his life but of the customary rewards of high office—a military command, a province, and a triumph. He declares that he asks for no reward for his diligence in saving Rome except that the senate keep in mind this moment and his whole consulship; in other words, he asks the senate to back him up in the future, when people will surely remember the illegal executions but forget the reason why they were necessary. But if the senate does not do this (the possibility is implied rather than stated) and the violence of traitors (*vis improborum*) prevails (and, we understand, Cicero is assassinated, or perhaps driven into exile—at any rate, removed from the political scene), then he commends "my little son" to the senate (Marcus was two years old at the time of the debate). If the senate will only remember that Cicero saved Rome, then young Marcus will surely receive the protection necessary to ensure not just his survival but his standing in the state (i.e., in due course, the consulship).[31] This recalls the reference to self-sacrifice in the last sentence of the *exordium*: "Even if I myself should meet a violent end, at least my family and you may all be safe, instead of both them and us dying together

---

[31] Berry 2006: 317 (cf. *Off.* 1.78); Dyck 2008: 239. Marcus did become consul, in 30 BC.

amid the destruction of our country" (3). This section shows Cicero asking the senate to stand by him both in the future, if he is called upon to execute the arrested men (Approach A), and in the present, since the men were executed and Cicero is being attacked for it (Approach B). But memory as well as time is a dominating idea in the passage: Cicero is concerned (on both approaches) not just with his personal safety but with his place in history. That is something that ultimately he secured not by addressing the senate and the people but by writing and publishing the *Catilinarians*.

The coda (§ 24) returns to the immediate matter in hand. It contains strong verbal echoes of the original *conclusio* at § 18. Cicero asks the senate to make its decree "diligently, as you have begun to do, and courageously [*fortiter*]." If one presses the meaning of that, he says that the senate has been debating the matter conscientiously but has not yet found the courage to vote for execution. It is Cato who will later inject into it the required dose of courage, although Cicero's readers may not necessarily know that, and Cicero does not tell them. The speech ends: "You have a consul [*habetis . . . consulem*, repeated from § 18] who will not hesitate to obey your decrees, and who will defend your decisions and answer for them personally for the rest of his days." He does not need to spell out that this places a strong moral obligation on the senate to protect him when he comes under attack in the future for executing the conspirators. But his words neatly transfer the responsibility for the executions from himself to the senate. The job of the senate was to advise, and the job of the consul was to decide and to act (within the constraints of the law); this is tacitly acknowledged by Cicero when he undertakes at §§ 7–8 to do as the senate directs ("But if that is what you want, go ahead and decree it: I shall do as you direct"). Talk of "obeying" (*parere*) the senate was misleading; and yet this was to become a constant refrain of Cicero's whenever he found himself under attack for the executions ("I take it you mean my consulship, in which I gave no orders but on the contrary obeyed the conscript fathers and all loyal citizens," *Sul.* 21; "What terrible offense did I commit on that day . . . when I obeyed you?," *Sest.* 145; "I obeyed the senate: although that vital and conscientious *relatio* was the work of the consul, the verdict and the punishment were the work of the senate," *Pis.* 14; cf. "The arrest of the guilty men was my doing, their punishment the senate's," *Phil.* 2.18).[32] (The original *conclusio* at § 18 contains nothing of this evasion of responsibility.) The speech therefore ends pointedly as *Pro Cicerone*. The final image of the *Catilinarians*, of a consul who was only obeying orders, is an explicit indication of the weakness that prompted Cicero to write and publish the speeches.

This analysis of the *Fourth Catilinarian* has identified five principal aims of the fictional speech (i.e., the *Fourth Catilinarian* considered on Approach A as a unified, single speech delivered by Cicero before the senate in a real historical context on 5 December 63). First, Cicero wishes to emphasize the seriousness of the conspirators' crimes and the fact that the senate has already acknowledged the men's guilt (4–6, 11b–13). Secondly, and most importantly of all, he wishes to persuade the senators to vote for execution. There is more persuasion for execution than may appear at first sight. Since Cicero as the moderator of the debate must appear to be neutral, much of this persuasion has to be covert. But it pervades most of the speech. He whips up the senators' feelings of anger and outrage (11b–13). He wants to convince them that a vote for execution will be universally approved by all classes of society (14–19). He wants them to dismiss any concern that executing the conspirators will place him in danger (1–3, 20). Most especially, he wants to put them off Caesar's proposal (7–8) and to neutralize the opposition to execution from Caesar and other *populares* (9–11a). In a word, he aims to persuade the senate to vote for execution, but without actually saying so. His third aim is to ensure that a decision is taken before the end of the meeting (6, 18). Fourthly, he wishes to put moral pressure on the senate to stand by him and protect his family in the future, if the conspirators are executed (3, 23). Finally, he wishes to secure his place in history as the man who saved Rome from

---

[32] Elsewhere, however, he talks merely about following the advice (*consilium*) of the senate: *Pis.* 7; *Phil.* 2.11. See further Berry 1996: 178.

the conspiracy (20–23). The first three aims may be classed as *In Catilinam*, the last two as *Pro Cicerone*.

When considered as a production of 60 (Approach B), the overriding aim of the speech is to justify Cicero's actions as consul and to rebut the accusation that he acted as a *rex*. That is why the *exordium* indicates that the speech is not about the arrested men but about Cicero. He wishes above all to convince his readers and posterity that he acted correctly during the debate and that he was correct to execute the conspirators (4–6, 9–13). During the debate he did not put forward his own view but acted as a conscientious, impartial moderator and servant of the senate (7–8, 24). All the senators, even Caesar, agreed that the most severe punishment should be chosen; the only dispute was which punishment was the most severe (7–11a). The senate made its decision, and Cicero, whatever his private view may have been, implemented it (24). That decision enjoyed universal support (14–19). The consul was, and still is, prepared to sacrifice his career and even his life for Rome (1–3, 20): he is a selfless Roman acting for the good of the entire community (the opposite of Catiline, although Cicero does not make the point; he does not need to, since Catiline is dead). His actions saved Rome, Italy, and the empire (2, 4, 21–22). In view of this, the senate owes him and his family their protection and support for as long as he lives (3, 23). Cicero wished in addition to persuade his readers and posterity that he had played a major part in the debate on 5 December, by making an important speech that guided the senate at a moment of dangerous indecision. To do this, two separate original speeches were combined into one, the second speech was filled out, and a new beginning and ending were added. The added parts were all about Cicero; they contained grander oratory than the original parts; and they brought the resulting speech closer to the length of the first three *Catilinarians*. This allowed the speech to serve as an impressive finale to the set of speeches against Catiline. But this last speech, on Approach B, is not concerned with Catiline or the conspirators; it is exclusively *Pro Cicerone*.

It remains to judge the success of the speech. For each of the first three *Catilinarians*, I have attempted to assess the effect of the speech on its original audience and the effect of the published version on its readership in 60 and on posterity. Regarding the original audience, the *First Catilinarian* seems to have been received with approval by the senate and was considered a success by Sallust (*Cat.* 31.6, 31.8). The *Second* did not cause the people to change their minds about Catiline but may have persuaded many of them not to join him. The *Third* did little more than celebrate a victory already achieved by action, not speech. As for the *Fourth*, it had no effect, because it was never delivered in its published form: it is a fiction. At the meeting of the senate on 5 December, it was Cato, not Cicero, who turned the debate around. Cicero's original intervention, which is ignored by Sallust, was essentially a covert attempt to put the senate off Caesar's proposal, and it failed: the senators who gave their views immediately afterwards backed Caesar (Plut. *Cic.* 21.2).[33] Cicero considered that the fifth of December represented an immense personal success: on 15 March 60 he reminded Atticus of "the splendid and immortal glory of the famous nones of December" (*Att.* 1.19.6). Then in 59, at the trial of Flaccus, he exclaimed: "O the famous nones of December, what a day you were when I was consul! A day that I can truly call the birthday of this city, or at least the day of its salvation" (*Flac.* 102). But it was a personal success because it was the day on which the conspiracy in Rome was stopped in its tracks—as a result of Cicero's success in tricking the leading conspirators into incriminating themselves by writing letters (an achievement he never mentions)—not because of any oratorical triumph or feat of persuasion.

The effect of the published versions of all four speeches on their readership in 60 is entirely unknown. As for their effect on posterity, this is difficult to assess for each speech individually. Overall, the

---

[33] Cf. Syme 1964: 106 ("The *Fourth Catilinarian* . . . was anything but a decisive contribution to the debate"), 109 ("Cicero's intervention . . . was cautious and ambiguous, as was proper in a presiding magistrate. It led to nothing. The oration which he published in 60 reflects subsequent events and attitudes"); Price 1998: 128 ("The *Fourth Catilinarian* was also [in addition to the *First*] a failure in that, as all other sources attest, Cicero's contribution had surprisingly little influence in the Senate debate"). For a contrary view, see Dyck (2008: 13), who finds success in all four speeches.

speeches have been notably successful in persuading posterity that Catiline and his associates were bad men, that their intentions were selfish and harmful to the state, that Cicero was right to oppose them, and that his suppression of the conspiracy was expertly managed and was a great achievement. They have also been quite successful in persuading posterity that the conspiracy was more important than it was (see pp. xxiii–xxv). But they have not been successful in reducing the controversy surrounding the illegal executions; indeed, Cicero was exiled because of this. The *First Catilinarian* has attracted the most attention, mainly because it was the only speech of the four to have been delivered in Catiline's presence. This gives it a frisson that is not present in the other speeches to the same extent. It is not clear that the *Fourth Catilinarian* has had much effect on posterity independently of the other speeches. The speech is in many ways unsatisfactory: it is not the speech that was delivered, it is too long to be entirely convincing as an intervention in a debate that Cicero wanted to be concluded quickly, it contains separate speeches that patently come from different points in the debate, it has two *conclusiones* that share similar phrasing, it contains allusions to events that occurred after its dramatic date, and it is based on a speech that failed in its aim. As a later fiction, the speech lacks the sense of authenticity that is found in the other three speeches. Even so, it is in some ways impressive—for example, in the way Cicero comments on Caesar and attempts, by applying lukewarm praise with exquisite politeness, to undermine his proposal. And just as in the *First Catilinarian* the reader is fascinated by the person of Catiline, present in the temple and listening to what will be the most famous speech in Latin literature being delivered against him, so in the *Fourth* there is inevitably a gruesome fascination that arises from the fact that the author of the speech is seeking to have five men illegally killed in cold blood before the day is out. That is not of course how Cicero would have wanted his readers to react to the speech, but it is principally that which makes the speech interesting to posterity. The conspirators will receive no mercy—but neither, in his lifetime at least, will Cicero.

Cicero in the *Catilinarians*, together with Sallust in his *Bellum Catilinae* two decades later, created a pair of characters, Catiline and Cicero himself, a cast of supporting characters, and a narrative that would inspire creative artists over many centuries, down to our own time. This long afterlife of Catiline will be the subject of our final chapter.

· 6 ·

Catiline in the Underworld
and Afterwards

During the debate in the senate on 5 December 63 BC, Caesar and Cato are said to have deliberated on what would happen to the Catilinarian conspirators after their deaths. Caesar's view was that "the immortal gods have not ordained death as a punishment, but as a natural and inevitable end or as a release from pain or misfortune," and that was allegedly one of the reasons why he proposed imprisonment for the arrested men rather than execution (Cic. *Cat.* 4.7; cf. "Death constitutes, not torture, but a rest from affliction: it dissipates all the maladies of mortals, and beyond it there is no place for either worry or joy," spoken by Caesar, Sal. *Cat.* 51.20). But Cato then pointed out that Caesar's view implied a rejection of the tradition that wicked men are sent to the underworld after their deaths, where they "dwell in places that are rotten, neglected, foul, and fearful" (Sal. *Cat.* 52.13). If one accepted that tradition, then execution was an appropriate punishment for the conspirators and not an escape. The final destination of the five executed men is unknown, but Catiline himself did descend to the underworld after his death—at least according to Virgil. In Book 8 of the *Aeneid*, Virgil has been describing the scenes from Roman history that Vulcan has depicted on the shield he has made for Aeneas, and he continues (8.666–70):

> Away from these he adds
> The abode of Tartarus, the tall portals of Dis,
> The punishment of crime, and you, Catiline, clinging

Cicero's Catilinarians. D. H. Berry, Oxford University Press (2020). © Oxford University Press.
DOI: 10.1093/oso/9780195326468.001.0001

To an overhanging cliff, and trembling before the faces of
the Furies—
And, far apart, the virtuous, with Cato giving them laws.[1]

Catiline also appears in Tartarus (a part of the underworld) in
Book 6, although his presence there was not detected until 1992.[2]
Aeneas observes Tartarus (from a safe distance, because he is one of
the virtuous), and his guide, the Sibyl, describes the sinners who are
being punished there. She draws his attention to a series of mythological characters (6.580–607), then Sextus Pompeius (612–13), then
some more mythological characters (616–20), then Mark Antony
(621–22), and finally Catiline (623–24):

This one forced his daughter's wedding chamber and a for-
bidden marriage:
All dared a monstrous sin, and what they dared attained.

The reference is to the claim made first by Cicero in *In toga candida* and then by Lucius Lucceius in his prosecution of Catiline in
64 that Catiline's wife (Orestilla, or an earlier wife) was his own
illegitimate daughter (Asc. 91–92 C). An allusion of a similar kind
had already been made by Catullus in his denunciation of modern
corruption at the end of Poem 64 (397–98, 401–2):

But after the earth was stained with crime unspeakable
And everyone banished justice from their lustful hearts . . .
The father prayed for the death of his youthful son
So as to possess without hindrance the bloom of a fresh bride.

---

[1] S. J. Harrison (1997: 74) sees these lines as an allusion to Sallust's *Bellum Catilinae*, but
Virgil is perhaps thinking in the first instance of Catiline and Cato themselves, that is,
as actual people. Born in Mantua in 70 BC, the poet no doubt remembered the alarm
caused by Catiline's movements in the area.

[2] It was detected by the present writer: Berry 1992. The identification has been accepted
by Muse 2007: 592 n. 25; Woodman 2007: xviii; Horsfall 2013: 432, "We should not
have had to wait until Berry, *cit.*, to learn (which we now do, with gratitude) the identity of the obvious candidate, Catiline."

Catullus, writing within a decade of the Catilinarian conspiracy (and before Sallust), seems to be referring to the allegation that Catiline murdered his son in order to remove an obstacle to his marriage to Aurelia Orestilla (Sal. *Cat.* 15.2; cf. Cic. *Cat.* 1.14).[3]

A third indication of Virgil's interest in Catiline is provided by his account of the ship race in Book 5. Games are held to commemorate the first anniversary of the death of Aeneas' father, Anchises, and a race takes place between four of Aeneas' ships. One of these is the *Centaur*, captained by Sergestus, "from whom the Sergian house takes its name" (5.121). Virgil does not need to explain that the most notorious Sergius in Roman history was Lucius Sergius Catilina. In the race, Sergestus, his spirit raging (*furens animi*, 202), recklessly steers the *Centaur* onto the rocks and damages it, and then returns to the shore in last place, "without honor" (272). So did Catiline, through his reckless ambition, damage the ship of state.[4]

Catiline makes further appearances in Roman poetry. In Cornelius Severus, an epic poet from the reigns of Augustus and Tiberius, the severed head of Cicero lying on the rostra prompts the onlookers to recall the consul's "mighty deeds, the bands of conspirators, the detection of criminal compacts and the blotting out of aristocratic wickedness; they remember too Cethegus' punishment and Catiline cast down from his abominable ambitions" (fr. 219.4–7; tr. Adrian S. Hollis). These lines contain faint echoes of the first three *Catilinarians*.[5] There are echoes of the *First* and *Third Catilinarians* in Seneca's *Medea* (probably from the reign of Claudius): Creon, the king of Corinth, orders Medea into exile, telling her to "purge the kingdom" and to "free the citizens from fear" (*purga regna . . . libera cives metu*, *Med.* 269–70; cf. *purga urbem*, "purge the city," *Cat.* 1.10; *libera rem publicam metu*, "free the country from fear," *Cat.* 1.20).[6] Similarly, in Seneca's *Phoenissae* (probably

---

[3] Quinn 1970: 350.
[4] For a full analysis of the parallels between Sergestus and Catiline in this passage, see Muse 2007: esp. 591–96.
[5] Hollis 2007: 360–61.
[6] Keeline 2018: 153–54.

from the reign of Nero), Jocasta urges her son Polynices to go into exile rather than attack his native Thebes, telling him to "free your country from fear" (*libera patriam metu, Phoen.* 642).[7] A successor of Severus, the epic poet Lucan (in the reign of Nero), follows Virgil in placing Catiline in Tartarus. Before Pharsalus, Pompey's son Sextus consults a Thessalian witch about the outcome of the coming battle. She reanimates an unburied Pompeian soldier, who recounts how in Tartarus Catiline, having broken his chains, is exulting at the Civil War and the impending slaughter (Luc. 6.793–94).[8] In Silius Italicus' *Punica*, an epic on the Second Punic War written under the Flavian emperors, there is an echo of the opening of the *First Catilinarian*: at Carthage, Gestar, the advocate of war, denounces Hanno, the advocate of peace, and expresses his outrage that a man who has not yet taken up arms but is nevertheless an open enemy should be sitting in the senate (Sil. 2.330–32). The satirist Juvenal, writing in the early second century, explores the contrast between the aristocrats Catiline and Cethegus, who plotted to set Rome on fire, and the new man Cicero, who saved the city without engulfing Rome in civil war (Juv. 8.231–44, quoted on p. 1).[9]

Historians and biographers, of course, included the Catilinarian conspiracy in their narratives, using as sources the *Catilinarians* (and related speeches such as *In toga candida*, *Pro Murena*, *Pro Sulla*, and *Pro Caelio*), Cicero's prose account of his consulship in Greek, and Sallust's *Bellum Catilinae*.[10] Should Sallust's monograph itself be thought of as the beginning of the reception of the *Catilinarians*? His account does not appear to be primarily based on the speeches of Cicero:[11] he has too much information that is not in Cicero (his

---

[7] Ginsberg 2016: 484–88.

[8] There are further references to Catiline at Luc. 2.541–43 (Pompey compares Caesar to Catiline, Lentulus, and Cethegus) and 7.62–64 (under Cicero's civilian jurisdiction, Catiline trembled before the peace-bringing axes).

[9] Juvenal has further references to Catiline and Cethegus at 2.27, to Lentulus, Cethegus, and Catiline at 10.286–88, and to Catiline at 14.41–42.

[10] See Levick 2015: 115–19.

[11] Dyck (2008: 13), citing Syme (1964: 73), states that the *Catilinarians* were "a main source" for Sallust. But Syme says merely that "the main sources of Sallust were probably the writings of Cicero." Ramsey (2007b: 9) states that "the influence of the four

account complements Cicero's rather than duplicating it), and in his narration of the events leading up to the arrest of the conspirators he reveals a detail that Cicero never admits, that Cicero had instructed the envoys of the Allobroges to trick the conspirators into incriminating themselves in writing (*Cat.* 41.5, 44.1).[12] The events that Sallust describes were sufficiently recent for him not to have had to depend on Cicero's speeches, although he will naturally have read them (he takes the words *quo usque tandem* from *In Catilinam* 1.1 and puts them back into Catiline's mouth at *Bellum Catilinae* 20.9,[13] and he takes details[14] from the related speeches of Cicero just mentioned). He is likely to have relied to a large extent on oral sources (see *Cat.* 14.7, 17.7, 19.4–5, 22.1–3, 48.7–8), and he even names one of them: he mentions that he heard Crassus complain that Cicero had tried to incriminate him in the conspiracy (*Cat.* 48.9). His perspective is different from Cicero's: Cicero's *Catilinarians* are primarily about Cicero himself, but Sallust is not concerned with defending or enhancing Cicero's reputation (although he does believe that he managed the Catilinarian crisis well: see *Cat.* 31.6, 43.1). Instead, he is interested in Catiline, Caesar, and Cato, all men who provided richer material for moral analysis than Cicero did. In addition, Caesar and Cato, unlike Cicero, were interesting for their later careers: Caesar for his conquests, dictatorship, and assassination and Cato for his part in the Civil War and his heroic suicide. Nevertheless, Cicero's descriptions of Catiline's character (*Cat.* 3.16–17; *Cael.* 12–14) have certainly made a contribution to Sallust's portrait (*Cat.* 5.1–8).[15] Sallust's *Bellum Catilinae*, then, is part of the reception of the *Catilinarians* only to a limited extent. To a greater extent, he is independent of Cicero, and each author has had a considerable influence on posterity—outside the

---

Catilinarians may be detected here and there in Sallust." The question deserves further investigation.

[12] See pp. 138–149.
[13] See pp. 92–93.
[14] See Ramsey 2007b: 9.
[15] See pp. 8–9.

rhetorical schools, Sallust more so than Cicero. But the reception of the *Catilinarians* and that of the *Bellum Catilinae* are not always easy to separate. In what follows, I will comment on both but will focus more particularly on the *Catilinarians*.

A generation after Sallust, the influence of Catiline and the *Catilinarians* finds its way into the great history of Livy. Livy's account of the sedition of Marcus Manlius Capitolinus in 385–384 BC mirrors the rising of Catiline, with Manlius, a patrician, appealing to the plebeians, campaigning against debt, making speeches at his house and at night, having the emergency decree (anachronistically) passed against him, being accused by the senate of plotting to seize power, and ultimately being tried and executed by being thrown from the Tarpeian rock (Liv. 6.11–20).[16] Livy even gives Manlius a speech in which he echoes the words of Catiline famously thrown back at him by Cicero (*Cat.* 1.1) and then put into Catiline's mouth by Sallust (*Cat.* 20.9): "How long, I ask you, will you remain ignorant of your own strength?" (*Quo usque tandem ignorabitis vires vestras?*, 6.18.5) and "How long are you going to look to me?" (*Quo usque me circumspectabitis?*, 6.18.8).[17] At a later point in his history (39.8–19), Livy describes the senate's suppression of the Bacchanalian conspiracy in 186 BC, and it has only recently been pointed out that here too his account mirrors the suppression of the Catilinarian conspiracy.[18] In the Bacchanalian conspiracy, a consul (Spurius Postumius Albinus) is informed of secret meetings of conspirators by a woman (Hispala Faecenia) who has a male lover (Publius Aebutius); he takes the matter to the senate; the senate pass a vote of thanks to him; he orders various lesser magistrates to apprehend those responsible and keep them under house arrest; he makes an address to the people and has the senate's decrees read out to them; rewards are voted to the

---

[16] See Oakley 1997: 481–84; Nousek 2010: 158–59.
[17] See Oakley 1997: 545–46 (*quo usque tandem*), 548–49 (further allusions in the passage to the *Catilinarians*).
[18] Nousek 2010 (cf. Briscoe 2008: 250). Livy refers to the Bacchanalian affair as a "conspiracy" (*coniuratio*) fourteen times: Nousek 2010: 160 n. 17.

informers; and the conspirators are tracked down and punished by imprisonment (apparently permanent)[19] or execution. One of the ringleaders, Minius Cerrinius, is sent to an Italian town, Ardea, for imprisonment (39.17.6, 19.2)—a precedent for Caesar's proposal on 5 December 63 BC. In the consul's address to the people, there are echoes of the *Catilinarians*.[20] For example, at 39.15.9, the consul divides the conspirators into two types, recalling Cicero's categorization of Catiline's supporters into six types at *In Catilinam* 2.18–23 (Livy's two types are women, who are "the source of this evil," and "males closely resembling women, who submit to and inflict sexual abuse [*stuprati et constupratores*]"). Livy took Catiline as a model for his portrait of Hannibal at 21.4.5–10, but in this case the influence is primarily from Sallust (*Cat.* 5.1–8).[21] Likewise, Sallust's Catiline has provided a model for Tacitus' portrait of Tiberius' "partner in toil" (*socius laborum*), the conspirator Sejanus, at *Annals* 4.1.2–3.[22] In the collection of imperial biographies from late antiquity known as the *Historia Augusta*, Avidius Cassius and Clodius Albinus, usurpers under Marcus Aurelius and Septimius Severus, respectively, are both said to have been described as Catilines (Scriptores Historiae Augustae, *Avid. Cass.* 3.5, "nor were there lacking people who called him a Catiline"; *Clod.* 13.2, "Not wrongly was he called the Catiline of his age"). In each case, the point of comparison is that the usurper combined contradictory qualities. This characterization ultimately goes back to *Pro Caelio* 12–14, but Sallust is the immediate source: Sallust's Catiline has a "versatile mind" (*animus . . . varius*, *Cat.* 5.4), while Albinus is "versatile in his pleasures" (*in luxurie varius*, *Clod.* 13.1).[23]

Among Christian writers, there is no evidence that Lactantius knew any speeches of Cicero besides the *Verrines*, the *Fourth*

---

[19] Briscoe 2008: 283–84.
[20] Nousek 2010: 163–65.
[21] Clauss 1997: esp. 169–82; cf. Levene 2010: 99–104.
[22] Martin 1969: 135–36; Martin and Woodman 1989: 84–85, Woodman 2018: 4–9, 59, 66–67.
[23] Wiedemann 1979.

Catilinarian, and perhaps *Pro Marcello*.[24] Augustine, on the other hand, knew the *Verrines*, the *Catilinarians*, *Pro Marcello*, and at least a further seven speeches.[25] He quotes the *Catilinarians* more frequently than any of the others, although he quotes Sallust's *Bellum Catilinae* more often still.[26] Jerome knew the *Verrines*, *Catilinarians*, and *Philippics* and at least fourteen or fifteen other speeches, including some that are now lost.[27] In his writings, five quotations or echoes of the *Catilinarians* have so far been found.[28] The Old Testament is a surprising place to come across an echo of Cicero, but in his Vulgate translation of the Book of Judges Jerome writes (20.25), "The sons of Benjamin . . . raved against them [the sons of Israel] with such slaughter [*tanta in illos caede bacchati sunt*] that they destroyed eighteen thousand men." The word "raved" does not occur in Jerome's Hebrew source, and the collocation of "rave" and "slaughter" occurs nowhere else in classical or patristic literature except at *In Catilinam* 4.11: "There appears before my eyes a vision of Cethegus, crazily raving over your slaughter [*in vestra caede bacchantis*]."[29] In the Nova Vulgata, the official Latin translation of the Bible published by the See of Rome in 1979, the words "raved against them with such slaughter that" are omitted, presumably as being an addition of Jerome's.

From the early empire to late antiquity, the speeches and rhetorical treatises of Cicero formed the basis for the teaching of rhetoric. Nearly half of the citations in Quintilian's *Institutio Oratoria* are to Cicero, and they include twenty-four references to the *Catilinarians* (all but four of them to the *First Catilinarian*). The *Catilinarians*, with the *Verrines*, represented the Ciceronian syllabus of the provincial schools in the later Roman empire.[30] The statuette from Fendeille of a grammarian, discussed in chapter 2 (pp. 62–63), shows that the

---

[24] Ogilvie 1978: 71–72.
[25] Hagendahl 1967: 479–81.
[26] Hagendahl 1967: 43–47, 481–85 (*Catilinarians*); 226–39, 631–49 (*Bellum Catilinae*).
[27] Hagendahl 1958: 285.
[28] Hagendahl 1958: 176, 287; Adkin 1992: 419–20; Adkin 2003: 94–95.
[29] Adkin 2003: 94–95.
[30] Rouse and Reeve 1983: 55, 61.

First Catilinarian was taught to school pupils in southern Gaul at the end of the fourth century or in the first half of the fifth. At the same time (fourth to fifth centuries), the *Catilinarians* were being taught to Greeks in Egypt, on the evidence of four papyri (or groups of papyri) containing parts of the first three speeches; in three of these papyri (or groups), Cicero's words are accompanied by Greek translations.[31] There has survived in some fifteenth-century manuscripts an invective against Catiline entitled *Declamatio in L. Sergium Catilinam*, spoken as if by Cicero in an imaginary prosecution of Catiline on the day after the meeting at Laeca's house.[32] Hortensius is cast as Catiline's advocate. The speech, which is not mentioned by any ancient author, is sometimes referred to as the *Fifth Catilinarian*, although its dramatic date precedes the *Second, Third,* and *Fourth Catilinarians*. In 1452 Poggio Bracciolini, even before seeing it, doubted that it could be by Cicero, because Cicero refers at *Ad Atticum* 2.1.3 to four speeches against Catiline, not five (*Fam.* 2.4.10, =3.142–43 Harth). Consisting essentially of twenty-two pages of outrage at Catiline's criminality and vices, the *Declamatio* draws heavily on the *Catilinarians* and many other speeches of Cicero, and also on Sallust. Clearly a rhetorical exercise, as its title implies, it is thought by its most recent editor to be likely to date from late antiquity, perhaps from the fourth or fifth century.[33]

From the eleventh or twelfth century, a second *Fifth Catilinarian*, the *Quinta Catilinaria*, and a reply to it as if by Catiline, the *Responsio Catiline* (*sic*), have come down to us.[34] Both speeches are short and simply expressed. In this *Fifth Catilinarian*, Cicero accuses Catiline before the senate and urges it to expel him from Rome. His theology is brought up to date: Catiline is "hostile to God and

---

[31] Internullo 2011–12; Sánchez-Ostiz 2013; Internullo 2016 (which bring Maslowski 2003: x–xiv, I up to date).

[32] It has been edited by Zimmerer 1888; Kristoferson 1928; Schurgacz 2004 (with German translation). There is also an Italian translation by De Marco 1967. See further Clift 1945: 98–99; Sallmann 1997: 280–81.

[33] Schurgacz 2004; 184–92.

[34] Edited by De Marco 1991; translated into Italian by De Marco 1967. See further Clift 1945: 99.

mankind" (*Deo hominibusque infestus*, 2). The speech draws heavily on the *Catilinarians* and on Sallust. In the *Responsio*, which draws on a range of rhetorical treatises but not on the *Catilinarians*, Catiline assures the senate of his innocence. The tradition of writing speeches based on the opposition of Cicero and Catiline continued into the Renaissance with Buonaccorso da Montemagno's *Oratio L. Catilinae in M. Ciceronem* (c. 1417), a speech in which Catiline again defends himself before the senate against Cicero's calumnies.[35] This speech is notably more elegant and accomplished than its predecessors in the genre. It expands on the points made by Catiline in his reply to the Cicero's *First Catilinarian* at Sallust, *Bellum Catilinae* 31.7, and this time appeal is made to the gods, plural. Buonaccorso, a native of Pistoia (Pistoria), was a judge in Florence, where the relative claims of aristocracy and meritocracy were a subject of vigorous debate (Florence was a republic under threat from the Duchy of Milan). In the *Oratio*, Catiline is made to put forward the claims of noble birth. Later, in 1428, Buonaccorso followed up his Catilinarian oration with a *De nobilitate tractatus*, in which the theme of nobility is explored further through opposing speeches from two historical Roman characters.[36]

Catiline had in fact been prominent in the literary culture of Florence for two centuries, since his appearance in the *Gesta Florentinorum* of Sanzanome (completed by 1231).[37] The historical Catiline, after leaving Rome, had marshaled his army at Faesulae (Fiesole) and had been defeated and killed at Pistoria, some twenty-one miles to the northwest. Florence, which lies below Fiesole and three miles to the south of it, was for several centuries a rival of

---

[35] Edited by Casotti 1718: 98–141; Glei and Köhler 2002. See further Clift 1945: 99; Glei 2002.

[36] Glei 2002: 170–71. The *De nobilitate* is edited by Casotti 1718: 2–97.

[37] Patricia J. Osmond has shed much light on this complex and interesting topic. This and the next three paragraphs are mostly summarized from Osmond 2000. Osmond's paper includes illustrations from an early fourteenth-century Bolognese manuscript showing Cicero denouncing Catiline in the senate, along with the battle of Pistoria and the death of Catiline (Osmond 2000: 17, 20). A previous paper contains an illustration of the oath of Catiline from the same manuscript (Osmond 1995: 140).

that city before finally destroying it in 1125. Catiline's rising, his flight to Fiesole, and his death at Pistoia feature in numerous works of Florentine historiography such as the *Chronica de origine civitatis* (c. 1228), Giovanni Villani's *Nuova cronica* (first half of the fourteenth century), the *Libro fiesolano* (early fourteenth century), and Leonardo Bruni's *Historiae florentini populi* (c. 1418). The traditions recorded in these works are still alive today in the topography of Pistoia, where a Torre di Catilina (a ninth-century tower) in the Via Tomba di Catilina marks the spot where Catiline was believed to have been buried.

In the *Chronica de origine civitatis*, Catiline's death at Pistoia inaugurates a period of hostility between Rome and Fiesole. After a party from Fiesole kill the Roman commander Florinus in a nocturnal attack, the new commander, Caesar, retaliates by destroying the city and founding Florentia (Florence) on the spot where Florinus had died. The Romans were thus represented as the predecessors of the Florentines, and Rome's enemy Catiline and his followers as the predecessors of the Fiesolans. For the people of thirteenth-century Florence, the story provided an explanation of both the origin of their city and its long struggle against Fiesole, while also helping to justify the extension of Florence's power over the other cities of Tuscany. From the second half of the century, other writers, including Brunetto Latini in his *Li livres dou tresor* and Dante in his *Convivio* (4.5.19), represented the eloquent and wise Cicero and the virtuous Cato as embodying the civic values of republican Rome, and hence of Florence, and Catiline as embodying the dangers of party strife.[38] All these themes were reprised by Villani in his *Nuova cronica* (Cicero is again characterized by eloquence and wisdom), but the figure of Catiline was now used to stigmatize the lower-class immigrants of Florence as troublemakers and revolutionaries.

---

[38] On Latini's attitude to Cicero and Catiline and his self-identification with Cicero, see Milner 2005: 172–75.

The *Libro fiesolano* marks the beginning of the romantic, chivalric tradition of Catiline. Villani's chronicle includes a cautious reference to Uberto Cesare, the fictional son of Catiline and supposed ancestor of the Uberti of Florence. In the *Libro fiesolano*, on the other hand, Catiline survives the battle of Pistoria, becomes the leader of Fiesole against the Romans, is besieged there for eight years, escapes, and is then defeated at Pistoia a second time and finally killed. His son Uberto Cesare marries a woman of Fiesole, becomes the ruler of Florence, and fathers sixteen children. The book ends with a genealogy. In accounts of the second half of the fourteenth century, including Ricordano Malispini's *Storia fiorentina*, the stories surrounding Catiline become even more colorful. Appearing now as a knight, he falls in love with Queen Belisea, the widow of Florinus, and kills her kidnapper, the knight Pravus, before carrying her off himself to his palace at Fiesole; and then he attempts to rescue her daughter Teverina from another kidnapper, the knight Centurione.[39] He lays siege to the castle where Teverina is being held prisoner but is forced to return to Fiesole to defend it from a renewed attack by Caesar. Belisea, however, persuades him to reveal to her the secret of Fiesole's defense (a hidden water supply) and betrays the city to Caesar. Catiline flees to Pistoia and is defeated and killed—or, in a further version, he escapes to another castle and is killed fighting against Attila.

At the beginning of the fifteenth century, Leonardo Bruni used the Latin sources, Cicero's *Catilinarians* and Sallust's *Bellum Catilinae*, to bring Catiline's story back to its historical origins (his *Historiae florentini populi* was exactly contemporary with Buonaccorso da Montemagno's *Oratio*). But it was now used to teach civic lessons: the fate of Catiline was held up as an example of what happens to those who attack their country, while Cicero, the "father

---

[39] Osmond 2000: 25 n. 50 suggests that Pravus may be a corruption of Petreius, the legate of Antonius who defeated Catiline at Pistoria. I suggest that Centurione is likely to refer to Catiline's supporter Manlius, the former Sullan centurion ("Manlius, the centurion who has set up a military camp in the territory of Faesulae," Cic. *Cat.* 2.14; cf. Asc. 50 C; Dio 37.30.5).

of his country," was presented as a model of patriotic duty. The Florentines, Bruni argued, had followed Rome's example, and as a result the virtues of hard work, frugality, and public service that had made Rome great had caused Florence to grow and prosper also. This analysis appealed to the merchant and banking families who now governed Florence and who saw themselves as following the Ciceronian example of duty and service to the republic.

From the Italian Renaissance to the English Renaissance is a large jump,[40] but Catiline's next significant appearance is in the play by Ben Jonson *Catiline His Conspiracy* produced in 1611. Catiline seems to have been a familiar figure on the London stage by this time: he had already been the subject of a play (now lost) by Stephen Gosson, *Catiline's Conspiracies*, produced between 1576 and 1579, and there is a record of sums paid in 1598 to Robert Wilson and Henry Chettle for a play called (with different spellings) *Catiline* or *Catiline's Conspiracy*.[41] These earlier productions should caution us against interpreting Jonson's play too closely as a response to the Gunpowder Plot of 1605.[42] An analogy with Catiline came readily, however, to the translators of the King James Bible (also published in 1611) when in their preface they set out to demonstrate the error of Roman Catholics who burned translations of the Bible: given that the city of Rome (like a translation of the divine word) was imperfect, "was Catiline therefore an honest man, or a good patriot, that sought to bring it to a combustion?"

Jonson's play, produced in the same year as Shakespeare's *Cymbeline*, follows in some respects the forms of Senecan drama. It opens with a soliloquy from the ghost of Sulla, which has come up from the underworld to visit Catiline in his study and urge him to pursue "the ruin of thy country" (1.1.45; the idea of Sulla's ghost

---

[40] From this point, this survey will be more selective. For an exhaustive list of novels, plays, operas, works of art, and films about Catiline produced between 1576–79 and 1965, see Criniti 1971: 61–68 (cf. Osmond and Ulery 2003: 215). On the plays and operas, see Speck 1906 (with the list at 99); Stinchcomb 1934.

[41] Ewbank 2012: 12.

[42] See Ewbank 2012: 14.

is likely to have been suggested by Lucan 1.580–81). At the end of each of the first four acts there is a chorus of Roman citizens that comments on the action and articulates a conception (derived from Sallust) of a previously virtuous Rome being destroyed by ambition and avarice. Then at the end of the play there is a messenger speech from the legate Petreius, who, entering the senate only moments after the conspirators have been led away to their execution, gives an account of the battle of Pistoria and Catiline's "brave bad death" (the words of Cato, 5.5.268). Aside from these Senecan touches, however, the play has much in common with the plays of Shakespeare.[43]

The premature announcement of Catiline's death is one of three modifications that Jonson has made to the chronology. In the play, there is only one consular election: Cicero and Antonius are elected and become consuls at once, and Catiline starts his conspiracy immediately, without standing for the consulship a second time. Moreover, the emergency decree is passed not in response to Manlius' uprising in October 63 BC but in response to the accusations made against Catiline in the senate in the *First Catilinarian*. This gives the *First Catilinarian* a successful result that it did not have in reality. The scene in which Sulla's ghost appears is obviously invented, but most of the other scenes have at least some historical basis. Especially interesting to readers of the *Catilinarians*, perhaps, are the scenes in which Cicero is shown operating in secret, and successfully, against the conspirators—operations about which Cicero himself maintained a lifelong silence. In act 2, scene 1, the conspirator Curius reveals the existence of the conspiracy to his mistress Fulvia, and in act 3, scene 2, Cicero and Fulvia persuade Curius to gather information about the conspirators and pass it back to Cicero. In act 4, scene 1, Cicero meets the envoys of the Allobroges in the street and sends them to their patron, Fabius Sanga, and then in act 4, scene 4, Sanga brings the envoys to Cicero's house, where Cicero tells them to play along with the conspirators

---

[43] For a comparison, see Hunt 2016.

and ask them for letters to show to their people in Gaul. Except for the scene in the street, all these scenes derive from Sallust (*Cat.* 23.1–4, 26.3, 28.2, 41.4–5). In act 5, scene 1, Petreius gives an address to his troops before the battle of Pistoria. Jonson has taken this from the *De coniuratione L. Catilinae* of Constantius Felicius Durantinus (1518), who appears to have invented it;[44] but, even so, in Sallust's account, Petreius is shown giving encouragement to his men (*Cat.* 59.5–6). A few liberties are taken with the history, but they are minor. Cethegus' collection of weapons is not just removed from his house but is displayed in the senate, and Cicero orders the execution of the arrested conspirators without an explicit senatorial decree. Unlike modern scholars, Jonson has no interest in the legal and constitutional questions surrounding the executions. For him, Catiline and his followers are wicked and Cicero virtuous, and there are no other considerations.

Overall, the play is notable for its extraordinary historical accuracy and its historical detail.[45] Jonson was a learned classical scholar and studied most or all of the sources that modern scholars use to reconstruct the history of the conspiracy. No sooner has the play opened than Sulla's ghost is combining the evidence of at least Cicero (*Cat.* 1.14), Sallust (*Cat.* 15.1–2), and Asconius (quoting Cicero's *In toga candida*, 91–92 C), and perhaps also Plutarch (*Cic.* 10.2), to give an account of Catiline's previous crimes (1.1.30–36):

Be still thy incests, murders, rapes before
Thy sense: thy forcing first a vestal nun;
Thy parricide, late, on thine own only son,
After his mother, to make empty way
For thy last wicked nuptials; worse than they
That blaze, that act of thy incestuous life,
Which got thee at once a daughter and a wife.

---

[44] Ewbank 2012: 19, 154. On Felicius, see Osmond and Ulery 1995; McLaughlin 2016: 80–81.

[45] Scanlon (1986: 19) even goes so far as to write: "That Sallust and Jonson told the truth and nothing but the truth can be plausibly argued for the events as they relate them."

Jonson's access to the sources was made easier by one of the books in his collection, an edition of Sallust published at Basel in 1564.[46] This presents the text of the *Bellum Catilinae* together with commentaries by nine scholars containing quotations from other ancient sources. Also included in the volume are *Pro Caelio* 12–14, the *Catilinarians*, the (medieval) *Fifth Catilinarian* and the *Responsio Catiline*, Buonaccorso da Montemagno's *Oratio L. Catilinae in M. Ciceronem*, the *Declamatio in L. Sergium Catilinam*, which at that time was thought to be a work by the Augustan rhetorician Marcus Porcius Latro,[47] and finally Constantius Felicius Durantinus's *De coniuratione L. Catilinae*, a history of the conspiracy that was intended to fill the perceived gaps in Sallust's account by giving greater credit to Cicero than Sallust does. The *Fifth Catilinarian*, the *Responsio*, and the *Oratio L. Catilinae in M. Ciceronem* are all assumed to be genuine speeches by Cicero and Catiline, even though the last of them was in fact written only a century and a half earlier; the roughness of style of the *Responsio* is accounted for by supposing that it was an extempore speech. Jonson's personal copy of this book is preserved in the library at Clare College, Cambridge, and contains vertical pencil markings, which some scholars believe to be by Jonson himself, beside certain passages; they cluster beside the sources for the passage just quoted.[48] Jonson's verses "That blaze, that act of thy incestuous life / Which got thee at once a daughter and a wife" are a translation of words from Cicero's *In toga candida* known only from Asconius (*cum ex eodem stupro tibi et uxorem et filiam invenisti*, ap. Asc. 91 C), and Jonson is not known to have consulted Asconius directly; but the passage from the *In toga candida* and Asconius' comments on it are included in the commentaries on Sallust, *Bellum Catilinae* 15.1–2, by two of the scholars in the Basel edition. Jonson provides translations of the ancient sources all through the play; each piece of evidence is fitted into its appropriate

---

[46] McPherson 1974: 84. Two hundred and six books owned by Jonson are known to exist.

[47] On these texts, see pp. 201–203.

[48] Ewbank 2012: 19–20.

place. Nothing that could be of use to him is omitted; he even includes, for example, Lentulus' plan to kidnap Pompey's children and keep them as hostages (3.3.153–55, from Plut. *Cic.* 18.1), a detail not often noticed by modern scholars.

One of the questions faced by both Sallust and Jonson was whether, and if so, how, to incorporate the speeches of Cicero. Sallust's solution was to omit them, except for a favorable reference to what was probably already the most famous one, the *First Catilinarian* (*Cat.* 31.6). They were much too long for him to insert into his narrative; they would have clashed with it in style; and they would have changed the focus of his work in a way that he did not want. For Jonson, on the other hand, Cicero was the focus of his play, and the *First Catilinarian* was such a well-known speech that he must have felt that he could hardly leave it out. In act 4, scene 2, the scene in which the senate meets in the Temple of Jupiter Stator immediately following the attempt to assassinate Cicero,[49] Jonson puts into Cicero's mouth a close but abridged translation of the *First Catilinarian*, amounting to no fewer than eleven pages in the Cambridge edition (4.2.116–402).[50] The speech begins:

> Whither at length wilt thou abuse our patience?
> Still shall thy fury mock us? To what licence
> Dares thy unbridled boldness run itself?

O tempora, o mores! (*Cat.* 1.2) is translated, a few lines later on, as "O age and manners!" (4.2.131). Jonson leaves out Cicero's historical parallels, many of the passages about individuals, and the first prosopopoeia. The second prosopopoeia is cut down to ten verses (329–38) and is put in the mouth of the "wise and sacred Senate" (328), not the *patria*. One-line interjections from Cato are used to divide the speech into its logical units. The result is a speech that is long, certainly, but coherent and easy to follow—arguably

---

[49] Jonson evidently does not share the view of some scholars that there was a twenty-four-hour delay before Cicero convened the senate (see p. 35 n. 61): he makes Cicero speak of the attempt on his life "not an hour yet since" (4.2.25).

[50] Ewbank 2012.

more so than the Ciceronian original. Jonson omits the *Second* and *Third Catilinarians* (although a part of Petreius' speech to his troops, 5.1.32–49, is loosely derived from *In Catilinam* 2.10 and 21–23 via Felicius). Then in act 5, scene 5, in the course of the debate in the senate on the captured conspirators, Caesar makes a speech of fifty lines and Cato one of forty-eight lines, both speeches being condensed versions of the ones in Sallust. Between these, Jonson gives Cicero a seventeen-line speech that neatly summarizes the *Fourth Catilinarian*, but in this speech Cicero makes no attempt at any kind of persuasion; he simply states the views of Silanus and Caesar and says he will carry out the senate's wishes, regardless of the danger to himself. The speech therefore has less point than the *Fourth Catilinarian*, but in its brevity it is more realistic.

At its first performance, Jonson's play was a failure. In a preface, "To the Reader in Ordinary," that is, to the common (unsophisticated) reader, he wrote: "You commend the first two acts, with the people, because they are the worst, and dislike the oration of Cicero, in regard you read some pieces of it at school and understand them not yet."[51] By 1635, however, the play had become popular, and it remained so for the rest of the century, apparently becoming the best loved play of Jonson, and more familiar even than the plays of Shakespeare.[52] In his diary for 11 December 1667, Samuel Pepys mentions that it was about to be performed for Charles II, and that the king had paid £500 for scarlet costumes for it. Even so, it fell from favor in the following century and has not been performed now for three hundred years. At the time of writing, the novels of Robert Harris set in the Ciceronian period—the Cicero trilogy, comprising *Imperium* (2006), *Lustrum* (2009, published in the United States in 2010 as *Conspirata*), and *Dictator* (2015)—have enjoyed enormous success, and have also been adapted for the stage by Mike Poulton under the title *Imperium: The Cicero Plays* (first performed in 2017). The popularity of Steven Saylor's detective

---

[51] Ewbank 2012: 26.
[52] Ewbank 2012: 5–6.

novel *Catilina's Riddle* (1998) likewise testifies to the public's enthusiasm for the world of Cicero and Catiline.[53] So perhaps the time is now ripe for a revival of Jonson's *Catiline* (the speech of Cicero could be shortened). Besides enjoying the exciting plot, modern audiences would appreciate the strong female characters, who appear prominently: Aurelia (Catiline's wife), Fulvia, and the conspirator Sempronia. Jonson, even more than Sallust, ensures that his story is not concerned only with men and their actions, and the play also offers a note of feminism that sounds unexpectedly contemporary to modern ears. In act 4, scene 5, Sempronia asks Lentulus why she should wait on the envoys of the Allobroges, when, unlike her, they are not scholars and know no Greek, and then goes on to declare (4.5.8–12):

> I do wonder much
> That states and commonwealths employ not women
> To be ambassadors sometimes! We should
> Do as good public service and could make
> As honourable spies.

Jonson's *Catiline* may have declined in popularity in the eighteenth century, but in England the *Catilinarians* remained one of the most familiar Latin texts. Scholarly interest in Cicero was given a boost by the publication in London in 1741 of the major two-volume biography of him by Conyers Middleton, in which Cicero's suppression of Catiline was recounted with glowing approval, and with lengthy paraphrases of the speeches.[54] A translation of the *Catilinarians* and other speeches of Cicero by the Scotsman William Guthrie was also published in London in the same year, and the work went through four editions, the last in 1778. Guthrie's translation of the opening of the *First Catilinarian* may be compared with that of Jonson:

---

[53] Other novels in English featuring Cicero and Catiline include Taylor Caldwell, *A Pillar of Iron: A Novel of Ancient Rome* (1965); John Maddox Roberts, *SPQR II: The Catiline Conspiracy* (1991); Colleen McCullough, *Caesar's Women* (1996).

[54] On Middleton, see Fox 2013: 331–35; Ingram 2015.

How far wilt thou, O *Catiline!* abuse our Patience? How long shall thy Madness outbrave our Justice? To what Extremities art thou resolved to push thy unbridled Insolence of Guilt?

Strangely, Guthrie did not translate *o tempora, o mores!*, although, a line further on, the words "mean and degenerate!" have perhaps been added in compensation ("Yet, mean and degenerate! the Traitor lives," translating *hic tamen vivit, Cat.* 1.2).

When William Caslon, an Englishman and a founder of metal type, first drew up his specimen sheet of typefaces in 1734, he used *Quo usque tandem* and other passages from the *First Catilinarian* to illustrate them, because, as William Blades, the nineteenth-century printer, explained, "all types show better in Latin than in English" (see Fig. 6.1).[55] After his death in 1766, Caslon's firm continued to use the same sheet, and on 4 July 1776 one of the typefaces on it was apparently selected by John Dunlap for the first printing of the US Declaration of Independence.[56] Two years later, when John Adams sailed across the Atlantic to seek French assistance against the British, he occupied himself on the voyage by helping his ten-year-old son John Quincy translate the *First Catilinarian*.[57]

Whatever differences Adams may have had with his French hosts, he was at one with them over their shared interest in Cicero, and especially the *Catilinarians.* The Catilinarian conspiracy had already been the subject of plays by Simon-Joseph Pellegrin (*Catilina*, 1742), Prosper Joliot de Crébillon (*Catilina*, 1748), and Voltaire (*Rome sauvée, ou Catilina*, 1750).[58] In the first two of these, scant attention is paid to the historical facts, and we seem to have returned to the world of medieval Florentine romance, if not chivalry. The theme of Pellegrin's play is Catiline's personal ambition and his manipulation of others to achieve power. But the plot revolves around the women. After banishing Catiline from Rome, Cicero offers him his

---

[55] Blades 1875: 7.
[56] Sherman 2012.
[57] Richard 2015: 126.
[58] See Speck 1906: 30–43; Stinchcomb 1934: 50–51.

FIGURE 6.1 William Caslon, specimen sheet of typefaces illustrated with quotations from Cicero's *First Catilinarian* (1734). From E. Chambers, *Cyclopaedia: Or, an Universal Dictionary of Arts and Sciences*, 2nd ed. (London, 1738).

daughter Tullia as a wife, in order to pacify him; and then he offers
her to the Gallic chief Arminius, to prevent him from lending his
army to Manlius. But Catiline's lover Sempronia also has plans for
Arminius and seeks to use him to promote her brother Lentulus'
bid for monarchy. Tullia is given a prominent part in Crébillon's play
also. Here, it is Cicero's rejection of Catiline's offer of marriage to
her that turns Catiline against him. Fulvia, on the other hand, is in
love with Catiline but is rejected by him, and therefore betrays the
conspiracy to Cicero—who is in love with her. Catiline is portrayed
as able and heroic. When he is defeated in battle, he dies a noble
death by suicide. Cicero is an unimpressive, cowardly figure and acts
throughout under the direction of Cato. On the government side,
only Crassus shows wisdom and insight.

Voltaire's play was a reaction to Crébillon's: he decided to set
the record straight, by removing the unhistorical love stories and
by making Cicero the hero and Catiline the villain (Middleton's
laudatory biography was probably one of his sources).[59] The title,
Rome sauvée, firmly makes his point of view clear. The play presents
Cicero as the ideal enlightenment philosopher—the ancient counterpart of Voltaire himself, who played the part of Cicero in the
first performances—and a statesman of irreproachable virtue, who,
although not of noble birth, saved the republic from the wicked and
fanatical Catiline. The motivations of the characters are political,
but even so, the play does not follow the history exactly: Catiline
is defeated in battle not by Antonius but by Caesar, who calculates
that he will first need to achieve military glory if he is to succeed
in imposing tyranny on the Romans. The play closes with a prayer
from Cicero that Caesar's great talents will always be used for the
benefit of his country, and never against it.

The speeches and philosophical treatises of Cicero inspired
many of the major figures during the American and French revolutions and in the years afterwards. In France, revolutionary orators,
educated in colleges in which Cicero's speeches and Sallust's *Bellum*

---

[59] Sharpe 2015: 339 (with 329–32 on the play generally).

Catilinae featured prominently in the curriculum, compared themselves to Cicero and denounced their opponents as Catilines.[60] On 19 April 1790, Mirabeau won public support for the deputies who had sworn the Tennis Court Oath (an oath not to separate until a new constitution was drawn up) by comparing them to Cicero, who on the last day of his consulship had sworn before the people that he had saved the state (Plut. *Cic.* 23.1–2).[61] Two years later, at a meeting of the National Convention on 29 October 1792, Louvet gave a speech modeled on the *Catilinarians* in which he made accusations against "Catiline" and his backer "Caesar" (understood to be Robespierre and Danton, respectively). Robespierre asked to be given a week to prepare his reply, and then on 5 November he defended himself before the Convention with a speech recalling Cicero's *Pro Sulla*.[62] The practice of referring to contemporaries not by their own names but by the names of Roman politicians of 63 BC became widespread. In his study of the influence of Cicero on the period, Gilbert Highet wrote, "In fact, one of the chief difficulties in reading the speeches made during the Revolution is to identify all the politicians who are so freely described as Catiline, Clodius, and Cicero."[63]

In the United States, politicians studied and imitated Ciceronian rhetoric, and the oratorical style of their speeches, despite the disapproval of Thomas Jefferson, proved popular with the public.[64] In 1794, at the height of the Whiskey Rebellion, Secretary of the Treasury Alexander Hamilton attacked the Whiskey rebels in a series of essays modeled on the *Catilinarians*: the rebels, he wrote, were attempting, like Catiline, to stir up popular discontent in order to seize power, but he, like Cicero, would foil their plans and save the republic.[65]

---

[60] Dubin 2016: 178. Dubin 2016 is a valuable study of the representation of the Catilinarian conspiracy in French revolutionary art.
[61] Blackman 2014.
[62] Zielinski 1929: 264–65; Highet 1949: 398; Berry 1996: 59.
[63] Highet 1949: 398.
[64] Richard 2015: 127–28.
[65] Richard 2015: 129.

At the end of the eighteenth century and through the nine-teenth, Catiline continued to be a popular subject with dramatists. In 1792, Salieri composed a "tragicomic" opera, *Catilina*, to a li-bretto by Giovanni Battista Casti.[66] This opera is based on *Rome sauvée*, but Cicero and Cato are turned into comic characters. Cicero is a fine speaker (in one aria, he is shown composing the *First Catilinarian*, which he later delivers) but a coward, and Rome is saved from Catiline not by him but by Fulvia, who serves both as Catiline's lover and as Cicero's daughter. The opera was intended to be performed at Vienna, but the production was postponed in-definitely upon the outbreak of war between Austria and France, and the work did not in fact receive its first performance until 16 April 1994, when it was put on at Darmstadt under the direction of Reinhard von der Thannen. In the meantime, an opera by Federico Cappellini, *Catilina*, had been performed at Verona in 1890, to a libretto by Pietro Emilio Francesconi, and another, *The Catiline Conspiracy*, by the Scottish composer Iain Hamilton, at Stirling in 1974. In the latter opera, the ghost of Sulla makes a reappearance. The theme of the opera is corruption through power, and com-parisons are suggested between the Catilinarian conspiracy and the Watergate scandal. A further setting of Casti's *Catilina*, composed by Serafino Amedeo De Ferrari in Amsterdam in 1852, has never been performed.[67]

The strangest of all the treatments of the Catiline story is per-haps the melodrama by Alexandre Dumas (the elder) and Auguste Maquet, *Catilina*, written and performed in Paris in October 1848, only months after the February revolution and the June Days up-rising.[68] The plot is based on the allegations that Catiline had sexual relations with a Vestal virgin (Sal. *Cat.* 15.1; Asc. 91 C), that he murdered his grown-up son in order to remove an obstacle to his marriage to Aurelia Orestilla (Sal. *Cat.* 15.2), and that, after binding his followers to him by an oath, he made them drink human blood

---

[66] See Speck 1906: 51–54.
[67] Criniti 1971: 67.
[68] See Speck 1906: 58–59; Stinchcomb 1934: 51–52.

mixed with wine (Sal. *Cat.* 22.1; in Jonson's play, Catiline is shown ordering a slave to be killed and his blood brought to him). The Vestal Marcia lives in Rome with the fifteen-year-old son she has borne to Catiline, who is called Charinus. Catiline becomes acquainted with Charinus unexpectedly, and the two men form a bond: when Cicero orders Catiline's execution, Charinus enables him to escape. At this point the consular election is held, and Fulvia tampers with the ballots, causing Catiline to lose to Cicero. Aurelia secretly kills Charinus, to prevent him from inheriting Catiline's property. The conspiracy is set in motion, and Catiline makes his followers drink human blood, only to discover that the blood is that of his son: Charinus is seen ascending to heaven with his throat cut. Catiline flees to Pistoia, where he is defeated and mortally wounded. Marcia covers him with her veil as he dies.

The revolutions of 1848 had a more pronounced influence, however, on two further plays, the *Catiline* of the Norwegian playwright Henrik Ibsen (written in January to March 1849 and published in Christiania, now Oslo, in April 1850) and the *Catilina* of the Austrian writer Ferdinand Kürnberger (written in 1851 and published in Hamburg in 1855). Kürnberger actually took part in the Austrian revolution of 1848 and was arrested for his participation in the Dresden uprising the following year. His Catiline is a popular hero who fights for freedom and justice in the face of the wickedness and corruption of contemporary Rome. In an inversion of history, he is made to prevent the assassination of Cicero, rather than commission it. Cicero, on the other hand, is once again depicted as a coward. Catiline is unsuccessful, and Rome will have to wait until Caesar for the revolution that will cure its ills.[69]

In the winter of 1848–49, the twenty-year-old Ibsen was working as a pharmacist's assistant in the small provincial town of Grimstad and in the evenings was studying the *Catilinarians* and Sallust's *Bellum Catilinae* in preparation for the matriculation examination for the Royal Frederick University at Christiania. Fired by

---

[69] See Speck 1906: 61–65.

the February revolution, the uprisings in Hungary and elsewhere, and the war over Schleswig—and irritated by the inward-looking community in which he lived—he wrote, quickly and at night, *Catiline*, his first play.[70] His reading of Cicero and Sallust persuaded him that Catiline had been ill-treated by history. As he explained later in 1875:[71]

> I did not at the time share the views of the two ancient Roman authors on Catiline's character and conduct and I am still inclined to believe that there must have been much that was great or significant about a man whom Cicero, the indefatigable spokesman of the majority, did not find it expedient to tackle until circumstances had so changed that he could attack him with impunity. One should also remember that there have been few people in history whose posthumous reputation has been more completely at the mercy of their adversaries than Catiline's was.

In Ibsen's play, Catiline is not the revolutionary hero that he is in Kürnberger, but is nevertheless (in the words of Manlius) a man "endowed with quite unusual gifts: / nobility of soul, unflinching courage,"[72] and a friend of the oppressed. At the end of act I, having sold his house to raise money to use for the purpose of bribery, he has a change of heart and gives the entire sum to an old soldier whose son has been imprisoned for debt. All the other politicians at Rome (including Catiline's fellow conspirators) are corrupt, and, conspirators apart, none of them—not even Cicero—appear in the play. This enables Ibsen to keep the focus exclusively on Catiline and present the reader, or audience member, with a psychological, rather than strictly historical, drama. As the play progresses, two forces, good and evil (both female), battle for Catiline's soul. Catiline is attracted to a Vestal virgin, Furia, who has

---

[70] There are translations by McFarlane and Orton 1970 and Laan 1992. For criticism, see esp. Johnston 1980: 29–49; Laan 1992: 77–108.

[71] Ibsen's preface to the second edition (1875), in McFarlane and Orton 1970: 110.

[72] McFarlane and Orton 1970: 44.

a mortal enemy; she asks him to swear that her enemy will be his mortal enemy too, and he swears it. But then she reveals that her enemy is the man who seduced her sister, Tullia, prompting her suicide, and Catiline realizes with horror that he has cursed himself. During their conversation, Furia has become stirred into a frenzy, in which she remains for the rest of the play, and she has let the sacred flame go out. As punishment, she is imprisoned in a subterranean vault, where she looks forward to descending to the underworld and being joined there by Catiline. But when the door opens, she discovers not Charon but Catiline's relation Curius, who is in love with her and has come to rescue her.

At the beginning of act 2, Furia rejoins Catiline, and for the rest of the play she goads him into taking over the leadership of the conspiracy and pressing on with it, knowing that it will lead to his death and eternal vilification ("Your name will be remembered / with dread and horror by posterity").[73] His wife Aurelia, on the other hand, repeatedly tries to persuade him to accompany her to Gaul, where they could enjoy a quiet pastoral life together. Catiline must choose between these two outcomes, and he opts for the evil one, exclaiming, "Away! Away! I've found myself at last!"[74] Furia induces Curius to betray Catiline, and then frightens the envoys of the Allobroges out of joining the conspiracy (the names of the envoys, Ambiorix and Ollovico, are those of Gallic leaders in Caesar's *Bellum Gallicum*).

Act 3 is set in Catiline's military camp. The ghost of Sulla appears and tells Catiline his fate: "Though thou shalt fall by thine own hand / yet shall another strike thee down."[75] Ibsen appears to have taken the idea of Sulla's ghost not from Jonson (apparently the young Ibsen knew no English)[76] but from the *Second Catilinarian*, where Cicero describes the third type of conspirator, the Sullan colonists: "Building as if they were aristocrats, delighting in coaches,

---

[73] McFarlane and Orton 1970: 67.
[74] McFarlane and Orton 1970: 69.
[75] McFarlane and Orton 1970: 89.
[76] Hurt 1972: 4; Aarseth 1994: 2. On Ibsen's English, see Laan 1992: 6.

litters, armies of servants, and sumptuous banquets, they have fallen so deeply into debt that, if they are ever to become solvent again, they would have to call up Sulla from the underworld [*Sulla sit iis ab inferis excitandus*]!" (2.20).[77]

Next, Curius arrives from Rome and informs Catiline that he is surrounded by enemies and that it was he who betrayed him, and he adds that Catiline's friends in the city are in prison and have perhaps been put to death. Catiline magnanimously forgives him. From this point, he is determined to die a hero's death. Furia eggs him on, while Aurelia tries to restrain him. The battle with the Roman army is fought, and Catiline reappears onstage, the only survivor. Furia taunts him with a wreath of poppies and reminds him of Tullia's death. Aurelia tries to embrace him, but he chases her offstage and mortally wounds her. Returning to the stage, he asks:[78]

> Is life then not an unabating struggle
> between the hostile forces in the soul?
> And in this struggle lies the soul's true life.

Furia seizes his dagger and stabs him in the chest. Catiline understands that his fate has been fulfilled and accepts that he is destined for the underworld:[79]

> Dash your waves now, murky Styx, against the shore
>   and swell
> high above your banks. Soon you shall carry Catiline
> off to gloomy Tartarus, towards his future home.

However, Aurelia reappears and begs him to choose the path to Elysium, not the one to Tartarus. He replies that although she will go to Elysium, Nemesis is taking him down into the dark. But then the dawn rises. The light pours into Catiline's soul, and he acknowledges the error of his ways. Aurelia's love has vanquished the powers

---

[77] Laan 1992: 54–55, 76.
[78] McFarlane and Orton 1970: 106.
[79] McFarlane and Orton 1970: 106.

of darkness, and he will dwell with her in the light. Husband and wife expire in each other's arms.

The play was rejected by the theatre in Christiania, but Ibsen had it published privately. Only about forty copies were sold in bookshops; most of the rest were sold to a dealer in waste paper.[80] Reviewers found the play immature and criticized the versification.[81] One of them pointed out that by killing Aurelia, Catiline forfeits our sympathy. One might add that it could already have been forfeited by his seduction of a Vestal virgin and her suicide. Another reviewer expressed the hope that the author would write more plays and "try his hand in the more rewarding field of Norwegian history."[82] Today the interest of the piece is usually considered to lie in the ways in which it foreshadows Ibsen's later plays—in the examination of the characters' psyche (Ibsen was a precursor of Sigmund Freud) and in the depiction of those characters' inner conflict, their self-realization, and their fulfillment of their destiny. In accordance with the theories later to be propounded by Freud, Catiline's life unfolds as it does because of an event that has taken place in his past, his seduction of Tullia. Ibsen reacted against Cicero's portrayal of Catiline, but, unlike Kürnberger, he did not choose to whitewash his character; instead, he used it to begin to work out his psychological theories and to present a picture of what might happen to a person when his soul becomes a battleground between the forces of good and evil, or, alternatively, between life and death.

On returning to his *Catiline* in 1874, Ibsen recorded what he felt about it:[83]

> I had almost forgotten the details of the work, but on re-reading it I found that it did contain a great deal I could still acknowledge, especially if one bears in mind that it was my first work. Much of what my later writings have been

---

[80] McFarlane and Orton 1970: 111, 583.
[81] Ibsen's preface to the second edition (1875), in McFarlane and Orton 1970: 111.
[82] McFarlane and Orton 1970: 582.
[83] Ibsen's preface to the second edition (1875), in McFarlane and Orton 1970: 111–12.

about—the clash of ability and aspirations, of will and possibility, at once the tragedy and the comedy of mankind and
of the individual—is already adumbrated here.

He revised the play and in the following year republished it.[84]
The name of Tullia, Furia's sister, was changed to Silvia. The other
changes were numerous but minor, and most were purely stylistic.[85] *Catiline* then finally received its first performance in 1881, in
Stockholm, but did not meet with success. The first performance in
Norway occurred as late as 1935, in Oslo. It was an unconventional
production: "Drunken Romans entered the stage to jazz music,
clad in togas and top hats, and Catiline and the conspirators wore
German steel helmets."[86] The play was subsequently performed in
England, in Croydon and London, in 1936, and then there were two
further productions in Norway, in 1972–73 and 1975–76. In every
case, it was the second edition of the play that was performed.[87]

From Ibsen's time down to our own, the *Catilinarians* have continued to hold their place in school and university curricula and
to fire the imaginations of many of those who read them. I shall
end with one example. One day in the early 1960s at Hot Springs
High School, Arkansas, a teacher, Elizabeth Buck, was reading the
Catilinarians with her Latin class. She decided that the class should
stage a mock trial of Catiline. One of the students, Bill Clinton,
raised his hand and said that he wanted to be Catiline's lawyer. In
the words of his biographer David Maraniss:[88]

> He put up a vigorous defense and became enraptured with
> the courtroom, where he had a captive audience susceptible
> to his powers of persuasion, a focus group for his budding
> rhetorical and political skills.

---

[84] Laan 1992 provides a translation of both versions.
[85] For a list, see McFarlane and Orton 1970: 581; with discussion, Laan 1992: 108–14.
[86] McFarlane and Orton 1970: 583.
[87] Laan 1992: 37.
[88] Maraniss 1995: 43.

Afterwards, Clinton told Mrs. Buck that the experience had made him realize that someday he would study law. Thus it was that the *Catilinarians* provided the United States with her forty-second President.

APPENDIX 1

A Catilinarian Chronology, 108–57 BC

108 or 106 BC	Catiline born.
106	Cicero born.
91–87	Social War; Cicero serves under Gnaeus Pompeius Strabo (89) and Sulla (88); Catiline serves under Strabo (?).
83–81	Catiline serves under Sulla, commits murders, and profits from proscriptions.
80	Cicero successfully defends Sextus Roscius (*Pro Roscio Amerino*).
80 or 79	Cicero successfully defends the freedom of a woman from Arretium; c. 80, marries Terentia.
79–77	Cicero studies in Greece, Rhodes, and Asia Minor; c. 78, Cicero's daughter Tullia born.
75	Cicero quaestor in western Sicily; Catiline quaestor (?).
73	Catiline prosecuted for sexual misconduct with Fabia, a Vestal virgin (first prosecution); acquitted.

71	Future conspirator Publius Cornelius Lentulus Sura and Gnaeus Aufidius Orestes consuls.
70	Gaius Antonius Hybrida and future conspirators Lentulus and Quintus Curius expelled from senate; Cicero successfully prosecutes Gaius Verres (*In Verrem*).
69	Cicero plebeian aedile.
68	Catiline praetor.
67–66	Catiline governor of Africa.
66	Cicero praetor in charge of extortion court; Antonius returns to senate as praetor; future conspirator Lucius Cassius Longinus also praetor; Cicero supports *lex Manilia* (*De imperio Cn. Pompei*); consuls-elect Publius Cornelius Sulla and future conspirator Publius Autronius Paetus convicted of electoral malpractice and expelled from senate; Catiline's candidature at supplementary election disallowed.
65	Lucius Aurelius Cotta and Lucius Manlius Torquatus consuls; Gaius Manilius convicted of violence or treason; Cicero's son Marcus born; Catiline prosecuted for extortion (second prosecution); acquitted.
mid-60s	Catiline marries Aurelia Orestilla.
64	Cicero's *In toga candida*; Catiline and Antonius attack Cicero's newness (Appendix 2, no. 1); Cicero and Antonius elected consuls for 63; Catiline not elected (first defeat); Catiline prosecuted for murder during Sullan proscriptions (third prosecution); acquitted.

63	January	Cicero and Antonius consuls; Lentulus returns to senate as praetor; Cicero defeats agrarian bill of Publius Servilius Rullus (*De lege agraria* 1–3).
	9 July	Cicero delivers a speech to the people on Lucius Roscius Otho, author of the *lex Roscia theatralis* of 67 (*De Othone*).
	July	Tribunician elections held; Cato, Quintus Metellus Nepos, and Lucius Calpurnius Bestia elected.
	during the campaign for the consular elections (July and August?)	Manlius comes to Rome to campaign for Catiline; concerns in senate about bribery; Cicero's *lex Tullia* passed.
	a few days before the consular elections (September?)	Cato threatens Catiline in senate with prosecution for electoral malpractice; Catiline replies (Appendix 2, no. 2); Catiline addresses supporters at his house (Appendix 2, no. 3).
	the day before the consular elections were due to be held	Cicero persuades senate to call off elections and instead to discuss Catiline's address to his supporters.
	next day (possibly 23 September, the day on which Augustus was born)	Cicero attacks Catiline in senate; he replies (Appendix 2, no. 4); senate declines to take further action.
	soon afterwards	Consular elections held; Cicero wearing a cuirass under his toga appears with a bodyguard; Decimus Junius Silanus and Lucius Licinius Murena elected consuls for 62; Catiline not elected (second defeat).

night of (18 or) 19 October	Crassus hands over to Cicero anonymous letters that have been delivered to him warning of a massacre in Rome.
next morning	Cicero convenes senate and has the letters read out by their addressees.
20 or 21 (or 22) October	Quintus Arrius reports news from Faesulae that Manlius is preparing an armed uprising; senate passes emergency decree (SCU).
27 October	Manlius, having heard of passing of emergency decree, is in open rebellion; Cicero organizes defense of Rome and Praeneste.
early November	Reports of slave revolts at Capua and in Apulia; government forces sent there and to Faesulae and Picenum; Lucius Aemilius Paullus gives notice of prosecution of Catiline for violence (fourth prosecution).
night of 6 November	Catiline addresses fellow conspirators at house of Marcus Porcius Laeca (Appendix 2, no. 5); assassination of Cicero planned.
early morning, 7 November	Cicero prevents assassins from entering his house.
7 (or 8) November	Cicero denounces Catiline in senate (*First Catilinarian*); Catiline offers to go into exile if senate will decree it (Appendix 2, no. 6); he replies to Cicero's speech, protesting his innocence (Appendix 2, no. 7).
that night	Catiline departs Rome, leaving behind letters, including one to Quintus Lutatius Catulus (Appendix 2, no. 8).
next day	Cicero informs the people of Catiline's departure (*Second Catilinarian*).

mid-November	News of Catiline's arrival in Manlius' camp reaches Rome; senate declares both men public enemies (*hostes*); Antonius sent against them; Cicero to defend city.
late November	Murena, prosecuted for electoral malpractice by Servius Sulpicius Rufus and Cato, is successfully defended by Hortensius, Crassus, and Cicero (*Pro Murena*); Cicero instructs Allobroges to obtain written evidence from the conspirators.
night of 2 December	Titus Volturcius and Allobroges arrested while leaving Rome with incriminating letters at the Mulvian Bridge.
3 December	Interrogation of Volturcius and Allobroges in senate; four conspirators (Lentulus, Gaius Cornelius Cethegus, Lucius Statilius, Publius Gabinius Capito) acknowledge their seals on captured letters and are put under house arrest; a fifth (Marcus Caeparius) is caught while escaping; decrees passed honoring Cicero; Catulus hails Cicero as "father of his country" (*parens patriae*); Cicero gives a report to the people (*Third Catilinarian*) and receives public support.
4 December	Lucius Tarquinius incriminates Crassus in senate but is disbelieved; senate votes rewards for Volturcius and Allobroges; conspirators declared to have acted against the state; attempts made to rescue conspirators.

	5 December	Senate debates punishment of five captured conspirators, and of a further four not yet apprehended; Cicero contributes (parts of *Fourth Catilinarian*); senate on Cato's motion votes for execution; Cicero executes five conspirators to popular acclaim.
	10 December	New tribunes take office; news of the executions causes seven thousand of Catiline's ten thousand men to desert.
	shortly before 29 December	Nepos criticizes Cicero in public meeting.
	29 December	Nepos and Bestia veto Cicero's retiring speech.
62	1 January	Silanus and Murena consuls.
	3 January and afterwards	Nepos again criticizes Cicero in public meeting; Cicero replies (*Contra contionem Q. Metelli*); senate grants Cicero immunity from prosecution; Cato persuades the people to vote Cicero the title "father of his country" (*pater patriae*); senate passes emergency decree (SCU) against Nepos, who flees to Pompey; Catiline's remaining three thousand men, including Manlius and Catiline himself, defeated and killed by army of Antonius, commanded by Marcus Petreius, at Pistoria; Catiline's head sent to Rome; coins struck to commemorate the "happy outcome."
	spring	Conspiracy crushed in central and southern Italy; Bestia criticizes Cicero; trial and conviction of remaining conspirators; public opinion turns against Cicero, who is accused of "cruelty" and "tyranny."

	summer	Cicero successfully defends alleged conspirator Publius Sulla (*Pro Sulla*).
61		Clodius criticizes Cicero; Clodius acquitted of sacrilege.
60		Publication of Cicero's "consular" speeches, including four speeches *In Catilinam*; publication of a prose account of his consulship in Greek and *Consulatus suus*.
59		Cicero defends Antonius unsuccessfully; funeral rites for Catiline.
58		Clodius tribune; Cicero exiled (March).
57		Cicero recalled (August); returns to Rome (September).

Catiline's Surviving Words

This appendix collects together all of Catiline's surviving words, whether they have come down to us in direct or merely in reported speech. The two orations that Sallust puts into the mouth of Catiline (*Cat.* 20.2–17, 58.1–21) are excluded because they are inventions.

1. Catiline's response to Cicero's *In toga candida*, in the senate. July (?) 64 BC. Malcovati 1976: 368 (no. I).

(i) Asconius 93–94 C:

> Huic orationi Ciceronis et Catilina et Antonius contumeliose responderunt, quod solum poterant, invecti in novitatem eius.

> Catiline and Antonius each made an insulting reply to this speech of Cicero's in the only way they could, by attacking his newness.

Cf. App. *B. Civ.* 2.2; *Scholia Bobiensia* 80.13–16 Stangl.

2. Catiline's response to Cato's threat to prosecute him for electoral malpractice, in the senate. A few days before the consular elections (September?), 63 BC.

(i) Cicero, *Pro Murena* 51:

> . . . praesertim cum idem ille in eodem ordine paucis diebus ante Catoni, fortissimo viro, iudicium minitanti ac denuntianti respondisset, si quod esset in suas fortunas incendium excitatum, id se non aqua sed ruina restincturum.

> . . . especially in view of the fact that, at a meeting of the senate only a few days before, he had told the valiant Cato, who was threatening him and announcing his intention of prosecuting him, that if his own fortunes should be set on fire, he would put out the flames not with water but by demolition.

Cf. Sal. *Cat.* 31.9: "*quoniam quidem circumventus . . . ab inimicis praeceps agor, incendium meum ruina restinguam*" ("Since I have been surrounded . . . and am being driven headlong by my enemies, I shall put out the fire besetting me by demolition");V. Max. 9.11.3; Flor. 2.12.7.

3. Catiline's address to his supporters, at a meeting held at his house. Shortly before the consular elections (September?), 63 BC. Malcovati 1976: 369 (no. II).

(i) Cicero, *Pro Murena* 50:

> Meministis enim, cum illius nefarii gladiatoris voces percrebruissent quas habuisse in contione domestica dicebatur, cum miserorum fidelem defensorem negasset inveniri posse nisi eum qui ipse miser esset; integrorum

et fortunatorum promissis saucios et miseros credere non oportere; qua re qui consumpta replere, erepta reciperare vellent, spectarent quid ipse deberet, quid possideret, quid auderet; minime timidum et valde calamitosum esse oportere eum qui esset futurus dux et signifer calamitosorum.

You will recall what that unspeakable gladiator was widely reported to have said at a meeting held at his house—that there could be no loyal defender of the poor who was not also poor himself; that people who were poor and in trouble should not trust the promises of the rich and trouble-free; that those who wished to recoup what they had spent and recover what they had forfeited should look at the size of his debts, the limits of his possessions, and the lengths to which he was prepared to go; and that the man who was going to be the leader and standard-bearer of the desperate should be the one who was the least afraid and most desperate himself.

4. Catiline's response on being invited by Cicero to justify no. 3 above, in the senate. On the day on which the consular elections were to have been held (23 September?), 63 BC. (For the date, cf. Suet. *Aug.* 5.1, 94.5.) Malcovati 1976: 369 (no. III).

(i) Cicero, *Pro Murena* 51:

Atque ille, ut semper fuit apertissimus, non se purgavit sed indicavit atque induit. tum enim dixit duo corpora esse rei publicae, unum debile infirmo capite, alterum firmum sine capite; huic, si ita de se meritum esset, caput se vivo non defuturum.

But he, forthright as ever, instead of attempting to clear his name, incriminated and trapped himself. He said that the state had two bodies, one feeble with a weak head, and the other one strong but with no head at all, and that this latter body, provided that it showed itself deserving of him, would never be without a head so long as he lived.

Cf. Plut. *Cic.* 14.4: "What . . . am I doing that is so terrible, if, when there are two bodies, one thin and wasted, but possessing a head, and the other headless, but big and strong, I myself put a head on the latter?"

5. Catiline's address to his fellow conspirators, at a meeting held at the house of Marcus Porcius Laeca. Night of 6 November 63 BC. Malcovati 1976: 370 (no. IV).

(i) Cicero, *In Catilinam* 1.9:

Fuisti igitur apud Laecam illa nocte, Catilina, distribuisti partes Italiae, statuisti quo quemque proficisci placeret, delegisti quos Romae relinqueres, quos tecum educeres, discripsisti urbis partis ad incendia, confirmasti te ipsum iam esse exiturum, dixisti paulum tibi esse etiam nunc morae, quod ego viverem.

So you were at Laeca's house that night, Catiline. You parceled out the regions of Italy. You decided where you wanted each man to go. You selected those you were going to leave behind in Rome and those you were going to take away with you. You designated the parts of the city to be burnt. You confirmed that you were on the point of leaving Rome yourself. You declared that you were experiencing a slight delay, because I was still alive.

Cf. Cic. *Sul.* 52; Sal. *Cat.* 27.3–4: *rursus intempesta nocte coniurationis principes convocat per M. Porcium Laecam, ibique multa de ignavia eorum questus docet se Manlium praemisisse ad eam multitudinem quam ad capiunda arma paraverat, item alios in alia loca opportuna qui initium belli facerent, seque ad exercitum proficisci cupere, si prius Ciceronem oppressisset: eum suis consiliis multum officere* ("At the dead of night, he again summoned the leaders of the conspiracy through the agency of Marcus Porcius Laeca, and there [at the house of Laeca], after many criticisms of their lack of spirit, he revealed to them that he had sent Manlius ahead to the body of men which he had prepared for taking up arms, and also other people to other strategic points to begin the war, and that he was eager himself to set off for the army, if he could first get rid of Cicero—because Cicero, he said, was a major stumbling block to his plans"); Dio 37.32.3–4: "He told them to assemble one night at a particular house where he . . . went to them and criticized them for their feebleness and lack of spirit. Then he went over in detail what would happen to them if they were caught and what they would gain if they were successful, and by this means encouraged and stirred them up so much that two of them promised to go to Cicero's house at dawn and murder him there."

6. Catiline's challenge to Cicero to put the question
   of his exile to the senate, in the senate (meeting in the
   Temple of Jupiter Stator). 7 (or 8) November 63 BC.

(i) Cicero, *In Catilinam* 1.13:

> Exire ex urbe iubet consul hostem. interrogas me, "num in exsilium?" non iubeo sed, si me consulis, suadeo.

> The consul orders a public enemy to get out of Rome. "Not into exile?" you enquire. That is not what I am ordering— but, if you ask my opinion, it is what I advise.

(ii) Cicero, *In Catilinam* 1.20:

> "Refer," inquis, "ad senatum"; id enim postulas et, si hic ordo placere sibi decreverit te ire in exsilium, obtemperaturum te esse dicis. non referam, id quod abhorret a meis moribus.

"Put the question to the senate," you say. That is what you demand; and if this order decrees that it wishes you to go into exile, you declare that you will obey. I am not going to put it to the senate; it runs counter to my practice to do so.

Cf. Cic. *Cat.* 1.16: *si hoc post hominum memoriam contigit nemini, vocis exspectas contumeliam, cum sis gravissimo iudicio taciturnitatis oppressus?* ("If no one else in history has ever been treated like that, do you really wait for the insult to be expressed in words, when you have been crushed by the strongest verdict—that of utter silence?").

7. Catiline's response to Cicero's *First Catilinarian*, in the senate (meeting in the Temple of Jupiter Stator). 7 (or 8) November 63 BC. Malcovati 1976: 370–71 (no.V).

(i) Sallust, *Bellum Catilinae* 31.7–8:

Sed ubi ille adsedit, Catilina, ut erat paratus ad dissimulanda omnia, demisso voltu, voce supplici postulare a patribus coepit ne quid de se temere crederent: ea familia ortum, ita se ab adulescentia vitam instituisse ut omnia bona in spe haberet; ne existumarent sibi, patricio homini, quoius ipsius atque maiorum pluruma beneficia in plebem Romanam essent, perdita re publica opus esse, quom eam servaret M. Tullius, inquilinus civis urbis Romae. ad hoc male dicta alia quom adderet, obstrepere omnes, hostem atque parricidam vocare.

But when he [Cicero] sat down, Catiline, prepared as he was to dissemble everything, with face downcast and suppliant voice began to demand of the fathers that they not believe rashly anything concerning him: he was sprung from such a family, and he had regulated his life from adolescence in such a way that he had good prospects in every respect; they should not reckon that, as a patrician whose own and whose ancestors' benefits to the Roman plebs were very numerous, he needed the destruction of the state—when it was being safeguarded by Marcus Tullius, a squatter citizen of the city of Rome. When he began to add other insults in addition, everyone heckled him and called him "public enemy" and "parricide."

Cf. App. *B. Civ.* 2.2.

8. Catiline's letter to Quintus Lutatius Catulus. Night of 7–8 (or 8–9) November 63 BC.

(i) Sallust, *Bellum Catilinae* 35:

L. Catilina Q. Catulo. Egregia tua fides, re cognita, grata mihi magnis in meis periculis, fiduciam commendationi meae tribuit. quam ob rem defensionem in novo consilio non statui parare: satisfactionem ex nulla conscientia de culpa proponere decrevi, quam me dius fidius veram licet cognoscas.

Iniuriis contumeliisque concitatus, quod fructu laboris industriaeque meae privatus statum dignitatis non obtinebam, publicam miserorum causam pro mea consuetudine suscepi, non quin aes alienum meis nominibus ex possessionibus solvere non possem—et alienis nominibus liberalitas Orestillae suis filiaeque copiis persolveret—sed quod non dignos homines honore honestatos videbam meque falsa suspicione alienatum esse sentiebam. hoc nomine satis honestas pro meo casu spes relicuae dignitatis conservandae sum secutus.

Plura quom scribere vellem, nuntiatum est vim mihi parari. nunc Orestillam commendo tuaeque fidei trado; eam ab iniuria defendas, per liberos tuos rogatus. haveto.

Lucius Catilina to Quintus Catulus. Your exceptional fidelity, known to me by experience and welcome to me in my great dangers, gives confidence to this commission of mine. For that reason I have decided not to prepare a defense of my novel course of action; but I have determined to put forward, though from no consciousness of guilt, an explanation which, as heaven is my witness, you can recognize as true.

Goaded by wrongs and aspersions, and because after being deprived of the fruit of my toil and industry I was unable to keep up the position of my rank, I publicly undertook the cause of the wretched, as is my custom; it was not that I could not pay off the debts against my name from my own possessions (or that the generosity of Orestilla could not pay off those against others' names from her own and her daughter's funds), but because I kept seeing unworthy men honored by the honor of office and I came to realize that I had been disqualified because of a false suspicion. On this account I have followed the hope—quite honorable, given my situation—of preserving what rank I have left.

Though I would like to write more, I am told that force is being prepared against me. As it is, I commit Orestilla to you and entrust her to your fidelity: keep her from harm, asked as you are in the name of your children. Farewell.

APPENDIX 3

Two Bowls Inscribed with the Names of Catiline and Cato

O n pp. 20–25, in a discussion of Catiline's campaign for the consulship in 63 BC, the evidence of two small bowls inscribed with the names of Cassius (the Catilinarian conspirator), Catiline, and Cato (*CIL* 6.40897, 40904) was cited. It was suggested that the close correspondence between the inscriptions and the characters and situations of Catiline and Cato constitutes an argument for the authenticity of the bowls. Some further arguments regarding their authenticity are offered here.

The bowls were published in 1980 by Silvio Panciera (he calls them "coppette").[1] In his paper, Panciera describes them and discusses their provenance, the historical information they convey, the language of their inscriptions, the forms of the names, the letter forms, and the scripts. The paper is accompanied by a technical appendix by Ninina Cuomo di Caprio, Isabella Mainoni, Franco Sacchi, and Giorgio Spinola that presents the results of a thermoluminescence dating of the bowls and an analysis of the calcareous deposits on their outer surface. Panciera and his colleagues concluded that the bowls are ancient, and could indeed date from 63 BC,[2] but they were unable either to prove or to disprove the

---

[1] Panciera 1980.
[2] Panciera 1980: 1643, 1658.

authenticity of the inscriptions.[3] If the calcareous deposits, which have built up over centuries as a result of contact with water, had obscured the inscriptions on the insides of the bowls, that would prove that the inscriptions are not modern.[4] But the insides of both bowls are free of deposits. When Panciera republished his paper in 2006, he added a postscript stating that he felt that he had perhaps been too cautious in 1980, and that since then he had become convinced of the authenticity of the bowls, and he expressed his regret that they had been largely ignored by scholarship.[5]

Unfortunately, the provenance of the bowls is somewhat obscure: they were presented as a gift in 1969 to a resident of Rome by a truck driver who had been transporting soil from an unspecified part of Rome to a public dumping area in the Via Conca d'Oro in the northeast of the city.[6] The obscure provenance does not by itself prove the bowls to be fakes; there are many thousands of genuine Greek, Etruscan, and Roman antiquities that have to come to light in Italy independently of the authorities. It does, however, expose the bowls to greater suspicion, if suspicion is already aroused on other grounds.[7]

If the bowls seem "too good to be true" because they relate to two famous personalities in a well-known year of Roman history,[8] a similar objection would also apply to other ancient artifacts apparently linked to independently attested individuals, such as the stone anchor dedicated by a Sostratos (Hdt. 4.152.3) to Apollo at

---

[3] Panciera 1980: 1661.
[4] Panciera 1980: 1648.
[5] Panciera 2006: 1068: "Molto (forse troppo) cauto nella prima presentazione per le ragioni che ho indicato; mi sono via via andato convincendo della loro autenticità. Gli indizi a favore della stessa mi sembrano infatti preponderanti. Comunque negli studi successivi le coppette sono state per lo più sfortunatamente ignorate."
[6] Panciera 1980: 1637–38. Panciera's knowledge of the provenance of the bowls was limited, and his account of it is imprecise. He was able to interview the man to whom the truck driver gave the bowls, a dealer in agricultural machinery, but not the truck driver himself.
[7] On the importance of provenance, see Jones 2016: 31–32. Jones believes, however, that the Warren cup, which lacks a secure provenance, is not a fake.
[8] Panciera 1980: 1651.

Gravisca (*SEG* 39.1040), or the archaic dedication by the followers of a Poplios Valesios (= P. Valerius Poplicola?),[9] or the papyrus containing verses by the lost elegist Gaius Cornelius Gallus.[10] All three were found in the 1970s. The Pericles cup, discovered in a tomb at Cephisia in Athens in 2014, is inscribed with the names, perhaps autographs, of Pericles, his elder brother Ariphron, and four others (there is also a further name on the base), and is considered an authentic relic of the great Athenian statesman.[11] The Pylos combat agate, a sealstone found in the grave of the Griffin Warrior at Pylos in 2015, does not specifically refer to historical or (so far as is known) mythical individuals but is another recent find that could be considered "too good to be true." In their publication of this artifact, Sharon R. Stocker and Jack L. Davis remark, "Had it not been discovered in proper excavation, the medium, as well as aspects of its style, might have led one to think that it was a forgery."[12] Statistically, out of the millions of objects that have survived from the ancient world, one would expect a few, by the law of averages, to be "too good to be true." But this is another way of saying that such items are exceptionally rare. If the Catiline and Cato bowls are genuine, it would not seem likely that, bearing famous names and originating from different elections, they were discarded in the same place, separately from any similar items. Cristina Rosillo-López has therefore suggested that they were preserved by individuals of the imperial period or later, and she points out that objects of such simple manufacture would hardly have been considered worth keeping if they had not featured the names of such celebrated personages.[13] If the bowls were deliberately collected and preserved, that could also explain why they are unbroken and in good condition (similarly, British commemorative

---

[9] See A. Momigliano in Walbank et al. 1989: 97–98. I owe these two parallels to Peter Wiseman.

[10] See Courtney 1993: 263–68; Hollis 2007: 224–30, 241–52.

[11] Rhodes 2018: 11.

[12] Stocker and Davis 2017: 584 n. 3.

[13] Rosillo-López 2010: 65.

china bearing the names of royalty usually survives in perfect condition as a result of never having been used).

There is one unusual feature in the forms of the names: on the Catiline bowl, the name "Cassius Longinus" appears without the *praenomen* "L." (i.e., "Lucius"). This style of address, although still rare, was "coming into vogue" at the end of the republic.[14] Its appearance on the bowl may be an indication of authenticity—unless a forger deliberately chose the more questionable form.

Regarding the carelessness of the writing, there are three errors. On the Catiline bowl, there is the repeated SV: the word SVFRAGATVR is started where there is no room for it, and then started again on a new line below the first one. On the Cato bowl, the first letter of TRIBVNV is written as C (for CATO, or CONSVLATVM?) and then corrected, and TRIBVNV ("tribune") is written for TRIBVNATV ("tribunate"; cf. *TLL* 10.1.1967.21–23, on this inscription, "personam pro munere"). These errors can easily be explained on the hypothesis that in each case an inattentive slave, perhaps a child, was forced to inscribe the same text many times.

Against the authenticity of the bowls it might be objected that at *Pro Murena* 76–77, where Cicero questions whether Cato's methods of canvassing were consistent with his high moral principles, he does not bring up Cato's distribution of food to the voters. However, this is not the only example of an opportunity to criticize that Cicero passes up. He also forbears to mention Cato's hypocrisy in threatening to prosecute any of the consular candidates for bribery except, specifically, his own brother-in-law Silanus (Plut. *Cat. Min.* 21.2). Michael C. Alexander accounts for Cicero's silence on this point by arguing that such criticism would not have been in keeping with the "live and let live" persona that Cicero adopts in this speech and is integral to his defense.[15] This same consideration can explain Cicero's decision not to mention Cato's distribution of food: he would not have wished either to criticize Cato for distributing food (because it would have

---

[14] Adams 1978: 145 n. 1; cf. Panciera 1980: 1646–47.
[15] Alexander 2002: 126.

made him, Cicero, appear strict) or to condone the practice (because it was illegal).

There is no other evidence for the use of inscribed tableware in the context of Roman elections, and therefore nothing for a forger to have based his forgeries on.[16] A forger might have modeled his inscriptions on the formulae occurring in the Pompeian electoral dipinti;[17] the inscriptions on the bowls, however, provide no parallels with the dipinti. Since the bowls came to light in the 1960s, no individual has claimed to have forged them or been revealed as having forged them, and, as far as is known, the bowls have never been sold. If a forger did forge the inscriptions, he would no doubt have been gratified by seeing the bowls displayed in the Museo Nazionale Romano in Rome but may have been disappointed by the lack of impact that they have had on the world of scholarship.

For all these reasons, in addition to the one given at pp. 23–25, my own view, for what it is worth, is that the bowls are almost certainly genuine. But they cannot be declared genuine beyond question. The main reason for doubt, in my view, is not the obscure provenance of the bowls or the famous names written on them but the lack of any other examples of bowls inscribed in this way. If it was a normal practice to distribute inscribed bowls to the voters at Roman elections, then such bowls must have been produced in considerable quantities, and one would expect more of them to have survived, either intact or in fragments. In the event that further such items appear, inscribed with the names of other candidates for public office (such as Murena, on whose behalf food is known to have been distributed to voters), there would then be no reason to doubt the authenticity of these bowls.

In any case, the bowls deserve to be better known. They were omitted from volume 3 of T. Robert S. Broughton's *The Magistrates*

---

[16] Rosillo-López 2010: 65: "Il faut souligner qu'aucune source, qui aurait pu servir de base aux éventuels faussaires, ne mentionne d'offres à des citoyens de ce genre de coupes, avec des inscriptions à caractère électoral."

[17] For these formulae, see Chiavia 2002: 65–73.

of the Roman Republic in 1986 (as pointed out in the review by Edward Champlin)[18] and, despite being on permanent public display in the Museo Nazionale Romano (Inv. 441423, 441422), have never been mentioned, as far as I can ascertain, in any publication on Catiline, Cato, or Cicero.[19] They are a symbol of many things: the political ambition of which Sallust and other contemporary authors complain, the vitality of Roman democracy at the end of the republic, and the sharing of the wealth derived ultimately from Rome's empire among Rome's poorer citizens. But, most importantly, they bring the world of Cicero and Catiline alive before our eyes.

---

[18] Broughton 1986, reviewed by Champlin 1989: 59 n. 3.

[19] The only other references to the bowls that I have discovered, besides those already mentioned here and in chapter 1, are Ridgway 1981: 502 (a two-sentence summary of Panciera 1980 in a review of the six-volume Festschrift in which Panciera's paper appears); Deniaux 1987: 302 (a brief summary of Panciera 1980); Norbye 2011: 29 (an illustration of the Cato bowl—wrongly dated to 62 BC—in a magazine article); Santangelo 2017: 70–71 (an entry in a sourcebook); Tatum 2018: 42 (a brief description with the comment "Although these finds seem too good to be true, they are not certainly fakes"; the bowls are wrongly said to be in Naples). I also mention the Catiline bowl at Berry 2014–15: 184–85 (a review of Levick 2015).

Maps

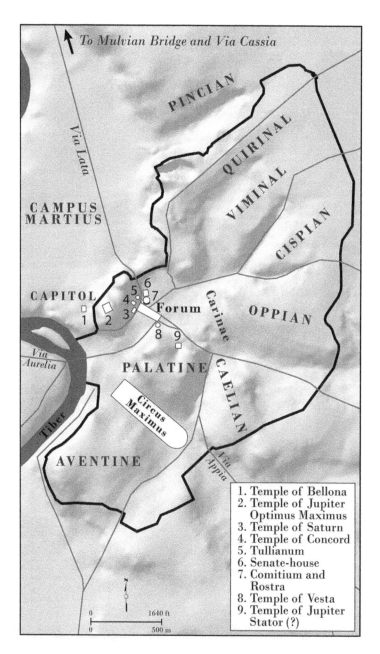

To Mulvian Bridge and Via Cassia

PINCIAN

QUIRINAL

VIMINAL

CISPIAN

Via Lata

CAMPUS
MARTIUS

CAPITOL

Forum

Carinae

OPPIAN

5 6
4 7
3

1 2

8 9

Via
Aurelia

PALATINE

CAELIAN

Tiber

Circus
Maximus

Via
Appia

AVENTINE

N

0   1640 ft
0   500 m

1. Temple of Bellona
2. Temple of Jupiter
   Optimus Maximus
3. Temple of Saturn
4. Temple of Concord
5. Tullianum
6. Senate-house
7. Comitium and
   Rostra
8. Temple of Vesta
9. Temple of Jupiter
   Stator (?)

MAP 1 Rome in 63 BC

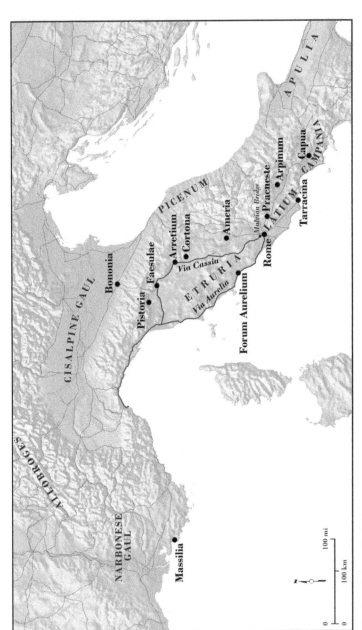

MAP 2 Italy in 63 BC

Bibliography

Aarseth, A. 1994. "Ibsen's Dramatic Apprenticeship." In J. W. McFarlane, ed., *The Cambridge Companion to Ibsen*. Cambridge. 1–11.

Adams, J. N. 1978. "Conventions of Naming in Cicero." *Classical Quarterly* 28: 145–66.

Adkin, N. 1992. "*Hieronymus Ciceronianus*: The Catilinarians in Jerome." *Latomus* 51: 408–20.

Adkin, N. 2003. "*Biblia Catilinaria.*" *Maia* 55: 93–98.

Albrecht, M. von. 2003. *Cicero's Style: A Synopsis*. Mnemosyne Supplement 245. Leiden and Boston.

Alexander, M. C. 1990. *Trials in the Late Roman Republic, 149 BC to 50 BC*. Phoenix Supplement 26. Toronto.

Alexander, M. C. 1999. "The Role of Torquatus the Younger in the *Ambitus* Prosecution of Sulla in 66 BC, and Cicero *De Finibus* 2.62." *Classical Philology* 94: 65–69.

Alexander, M. C. 2002. *The Case for the Prosecution in the Ciceronian Era*. Ann Arbor.

Allély, A. 2012. *La déclaration d'hostis sous la République romaine*. Bordeaux.

Allen, W. 1938. "In Defense of Catiline." *Classical Journal* 34: 70–85.

Allen, W. 1956. "*O fortunatam natam* . . . " *Transactions and Proceedings of the American Philological Association* 87: 130–46.

Altman, W. H. F., ed. 2015. *Brill's Companion to the Reception of Cicero*. Leiden and Boston.

Austin, R. G., ed. 1960. *Cicero: Pro M. Caelio oratio*. 3rd ed. Oxford.

Badian, E. 1959. "Caesar's *Cursus* and the Intervals between Offices." *Journal of Roman Studies* 49: 81–89.

Barlow, J. 1994. "Cicero's Sacrilege in 63 BC." In C. Deroux, ed., *Studies in Latin Literature and Roman History* 7. Brussels. 180–89.

Batstone, W. W. 1994. "Cicero's Construction of Consular *Ethos* in the *First Catilinarian*." *Transactions of the American Philological Association* 124: 211–66.

Batstone, W. W. 2010a. "Catiline's Speeches in Sallust's *Bellum Catilinae*." In Berry and Erskine 2010. 227–46.

Batstone, W. W., trans. 2010b. *Sallust: Catiline's Conspiracy, The Jugurthine War, Histories*. Oxford World's Classics. Oxford.

Beard, M. 2013. *Confronting the Classics: Traditions, Adventures and Innovations*. London.

Beesly, E. S. 1878. "Catiline." In E. S. Beesly, *Catiline, Clodius, and Tiberius*. London. 1–37.

Benson, J. M. 1986. "Catiline and the Date of the Consular Elections of 63 BC." In C. Deroux, ed., *Studies in Latin Literature and Roman History* 4. Brussels. 234–46.

Berry, D. H. 1992. "The Criminals in Virgil's Tartarus: Contemporary Allusions in *Aeneid* 6.621–4." *Classical Quarterly* 42: 416–20.

Berry, D. H., ed. 1996. *Cicero: Pro P. Sulla oratio*. Cambridge Classical Texts and Commentaries 30. Cambridge.

Berry, D. H., trans. 2000. *Cicero: Defence Speeches*. Oxford World's Classics. Oxford.

Berry, D. H. 2003. "*Equester ordo tuus est*: Did Cicero Win His Cases Because of His Support for the *Equites*?" *Classical Quarterly* 53: 222–34.

Berry, D. H. 2004. "The Publication of Cicero's *Pro Roscio Amerino*." *Mnemosyne* 57: 80–87.

Berry, D. H. 2005. "Oratory." In S. J. Harrison, ed., *A Companion to Latin Literature*. Oxford. 257–69.

Berry, D. H., trans. 2006. *Cicero: Political Speeches*. Oxford World's Classics. Oxford.

Berry, D. H. 2014–15. Review of Levick 2015. *Classics Ireland* 21–22: 181–85.

Berry, D. H., and A. Erskine, eds. 2010. *Form and Function in Roman Oratory*. Cambridge.

Berry, D. H., and M. Heath. 1997. "Oratory and Declamation." In S. E. Porter, ed., *Handbook of Classical Rhetoric in the Hellenistic Period 330 BC–AD 400*. Leiden. 393–420.

Blackman, R. 2014. "Did Cicero Swear the Tennis Court Oath?" *French History* 28: 471–97.

Blades, W. 1875. *Some Early Type Specimen Books of England, Holland, France, Italy, and Germany*. London.

Blom, H. van der. 2010. *Cicero's Role Models: The Political Strategy of a Newcomer*. Oxford.

Blom, H. van der. 2016. *Oratory and Political Career in the Late Roman Republic*. Cambridge.

Boissier, G. 1908. *La conjuration de Catilina*. 2nd ed. Paris.

Booth, J., ed. 2007. *Cicero on the Attack: Invective and Subversion in the Orations and Beyond*. Swansea.

Bradley, K. R. 1978. "Slaves and the Conspiracy of Catiline." *Classical Philology* 73: 329–36.

Briscoe, J. 1987. "Sallust, *Cat.* 50.3–5: A Reply to Heyworth and Woodman." *Liverpool Classical Monthly* 12: 50–51.

Briscoe, J. 2008. *A Commentary on Livy Books 38–40*. Oxford.

Brock, R. W. 1995. "Versions, 'Inversions' and Evasions: Classical Historiography and the 'Published' Speech." *Papers of the Leeds International Latin Seminar* 8: 209–24.

Broughton, T. R. S. 1936. "Was Sallust Fair to Cicero?" *Transactions and Proceedings of the American Philological Association* 67: 34–46.

Broughton, T. R. S. 1951–52. *The Magistrates of the Roman Republic*. 2 vols. New York.

Broughton, T. R. S. 1986. *The Magistrates of the Roman Republic*. Vol. 3, Supplement. Atlanta.

Broughton, T. R. S. 1991. "Candidates Defeated in Roman Elections: Some Ancient Roman 'Also-Rans.'" *Transactions of the American Philosophical Society* 81.4: 1–64.

Brown, K. R. 1983. "The Wilczek Bronze Reconsidered." *Pantheon* 41: 3–6.

Brown, T. 2017. *The Vanity Fair Diaries: 1983–1992*. London.

Brunt, P. A. 1963. "The Conspiracy of Catiline." *History Today* 13.1: 14–21.

Brunt, P. A. 1966. "The Roman Mob." *Past and Present* 35: 3–27.

Brunt, P. A. 1971. *Social Conflicts in the Roman Republic*. London.

Brunt, P. A. 1998. *The Fall of the Roman Republic and Related Essays*. Oxford.

Butler, S. 2002. *The Hand of Cicero*. London and New York.

Cadoux, T. J. 1980. "Sallust and Sempronia." In B. A. Marshall, ed., *Vindex humanitatis: Essays in Honour of John Huntly Bishop*. Armidale. 93–122.

Cadoux, T. J. 2005. "Catiline and the Vestal Virgins." *Historia* 54: 162–79.

Cadoux, T. J. 2006. "The Absent Senator of 5 December 63 BC." *Classical Quarterly* 56: 612–18.

Cairns, F. 2012. "Lentulus' Letter: Cicero *In Catilinam* 3.12; Sallust *Bellum Catilinae* 44.3–6." *Historia* 61: 78–82.

Cape, R. W. 1995. "The Rhetoric of Politics in Cicero's *Fourth Catilinarian.*" *American Journal of Philology* 116: 255–77.

Cape, R. W. 2002. "Cicero's Consular Speeches." In May 2002. 113–58.

Casotti, G., ed. 1718. *Prose e rime de' due Buonaccorsi da Montemagno con annotazione ed alcune rime di Niccolò Tinucci.* Florence.

Champlin, E. 1989. "Magisterial Revisions." *Classical Philology* 84: 51–59.

Chiavia, C. 2002. *Programmata: Manifesti elettorali nella colonia romana di Pompei.* Turin.

Clarke, M. L. 1996. *Rhetoric at Rome: A Historical Survey.* Rev. D. H. Berry. 3rd ed. London.

Classen, C. J. 1998. "Romulus in der römischen Republik." In C. J. Classen, *Zur Literatur und Gesellschaft der Römer.* Stuttgart. 21–54.

Clauss, J. J. 1997. "*Domestici hostes*: The Nausicaa in Medea, the Catiline in Hannibal." *Materiali e discussioni per l'analisi dei testi classici* 39: 165–85.

Clift, E. H. 1945. *Latin Pseudepigrapha: A Study in Literary Attributions.* Baltimore.

Cole, S. 2013. *Cicero and the Rise of Deification at Rome.* Cambridge.

Corbeill, A. 1996. *Controlling Laughter: Political Humor in the Late Roman Republic.* Princeton.

Corbeill, A. 2008. "*O singulare prodigium*: Ciceronian Invective as a Religious Expiation." In T. Stevenson and M. Wilson, eds., *Cicero's Philippics: History, Rhetoric and Ideology.* Prudentia 37 and 38. Auckland. 240–54.

Courtney, E., ed. 1993. *The Fragmentary Latin Poets.* Oxford.

Craig, C. P. 1993. "Three Simple Questions for Teaching Cicero's *First Catilinarian.*" *Classical Journal* 88: 255–67.

Craig, C. P. 2007a. "Cicero as Orator." In Dominik and Hall 2007. 264–84.

Craig, C. P. 2007b. "Self-restraint, Invective, and Credibility in Cicero's *First Catilinarian Oration.*" *American Journal of Philology* 128: 335–39.

Crane, T. 1965–66. "Times of the Night in Cicero's *First Catilinarian.*" *Classical Journal* 61: 264–67.

Crawford, J. W. 1984. *M. Tullius Cicero: The Lost and Unpublished Orations.* Hypomnemata 80. Göttingen.

Crawford, J. W., ed. 1994. *M. Tullius Cicero: The Fragmentary Speeches*. 2nd ed. American Philological Association: American Classical Studies 37. Atlanta.

Crawford, M. H. 1974. *Roman Republican Coinage*. 2 vols. Cambridge.

Criniti, N. 1971. *Bibliografia catilinaria*. Milan.

Crook, J. A., A. W. Lintott, and E. D. Rawson, eds. 1994. *The Cambridge Ancient History*. 2nd ed., Vol. 9: *The Last Age of the Roman Republic, 146– 43 BC*. Cambridge.

De Marco, M., trans. 1967. *Cicero: La Consolazione; le orazioni spurie*. Milan.

De Marco, M., ed. 1991. *[M. Tulli Ciceronis] Orationes spuriae. Pars prior. Oratio pridie quam in exilium iret, Quinta Catilinaria, Responsio Catiline*. Milan.

Deniaux, E. 1987. "De l'*ambitio* à l'*ambitus*: Les lieux de la propagande et de la corruption électorale à la fin de la République." In *L'Urbs: Espace urbain et histoire (Ier siècle av. J.-C.–IIIe siècle ap. J.-C.); Actes du colloque international organisé par le Centre national de la recherche scientifique et l'École française de Rome (Rome, 8–12 mai 1985)*. Collection de l'École française de Rome 98. Rome. 279–304.

Diehl, H. 1988. *Sulla und seine Zeit im Urteil Ciceros*. Hildesheim.

Dominik, W. J., and J. Hall, eds. 2007. *A Companion to Roman Rhetoric*. Oxford.

Dorey, T. A., ed. 1964. *Cicero*. Studies in Latin Literature and its Influence. London.

Douglas, A. E. 1979. *Cicero*. 2nd ed. Greece and Rome New Surveys in the Classics 2. Oxford.

Draheim, H. 1917. "Die ursprüngliche Form der katilinarischen Reden Ciceros." *Wochenschrift für klassische Philologie* 34: 1061–71.

Drexler, H. 1976. *Die catilinarische Verschwörung: Ein Quellenheft*. Darmstadt.

Drummond, A. 1995. *Law, Politics and Power: Sallust and the Execution of the Catilinarian Conspirators*. Historia Einzelschriften 93. Stuttgart.

Dubin, N. L. 2016. "The Catiline Conspiracy and the Credibility of Letters in French Revolutionary Art." In Manuwald 2016. 177–98.

Dunkle, J. R. 1971–72. "The Rhetorical Tyrant in Roman Historiography: Sallust, Livy and Tacitus." *Classical World* 65: 12–20.

Dyck, A. R., ed. 2008. *Cicero: Catilinarian Speeches*. Cambridge Greek and Latin Classics. Cambridge.

Dyck, A. R. 2010. "Cicero's Abridgement of His Speeches for Publication." *Palingenesia* 98: 369–74.

Eagle, E. D. 1949. "Catiline and the *Concordia Ordinum*." *Phoenix* 3: 15–30.

Evans, R. J. 1987. "Catiline's Wife." *Acta Classica* 30: 69–72.

Ewbank, I.-S., ed. 2012. "Catiline His Conspiracy." In D. Bevington, M. Butler, and I. Donaldson, eds., *The Cambridge Edition of the Works of Ben Jonson.* Vol. 4. Cambridge. 1–185.

Fantham, E. 1997. "The Contexts and Occasions of Roman Public Rhetoric." In W. J. Dominik, ed., *Roman Eloquence: Rhetoric in Society and Literature.* London and New York. 111–28.

Fini, M. 1996. *Catilina: Ritratto di un uomo in rivolta.* Milan.

Fordyce, C. J., ed. 1961. *Catullus: A Commentary.* Oxford.

Forsythe, G. 1992. "The Municipal *Origo* of the Catilinarian T. Volturcius." *American Journal of Philology* 113: 407–12.

Fox, M. 2013. "Cicero during the Enlightenment." In C. E. W. Steel, ed., *The Cambridge Companion to Cicero.* Cambridge. 318–36.

Frazel, T. D. 2004. "The Composition and Circulation of Cicero's *In Verrem.*" *Classical Quarterly* 54: 128–42.

Frederiksen, M. W. 1966. "Caesar, Cicero and the Problem of Debt." *Journal of Roman Studies* 56: 128–41.

Friggeri, R., M. G. G. Cecere, and G. L. Gregori, eds. 2012. *Terme di Diocleziano: La collezione epigrafica.* Milan.

Fuchs, H. 1959. "Eine Doppelfassung in Ciceros Catilinarischen Reden." *Hermes* 87: 463–69.

Fuhrmann, M. 1992. *Cicero and the Roman Republic.* Trans. W. E. Yuill. Oxford.

Gabba, E. 1976. *Republican Rome, the Army and the Allies.* Trans. P. J. Cuff. Oxford.

Galassi, F. 2014. *Catiline, the Monster of Rome: An Ancient Case of Political Assassination.* Yardley, PA.

Gildenhard, I. 2011. *Creative Eloquence: The Construction of Reality in Cicero's Speeches.* Oxford.

Ginsberg, L. 2016. "Jocasta's Catilinarian Oration (Sen. *Phoen.* 632–43)." *Classical Journal* 111: 483–94.

Giovannini, A. 1995. "Catilina et le problème des dettes." In I. Malkin and Z. W. Rubinsohn, eds., *Leaders and Masses in the Roman World: Studies in Honor of Zvi Yavetz.* Leiden. 15–32.

Glei, R. F. 2002. "Catilinas Rede gegen Cicero: Literarische Fälschung, rhetorische Übung oder politisches Pamphlet?" *Neulateinisches Jahrbuch: Journal of Neo-Latin Language and Literature* 4: 155–72.

Glei, R. F., and M. Köhler, eds. 2002. *Bonacursius de Monte Magno: Oratio L. Catilinae in M. Ciceronem. Neulateinisches Jahrbuch: Journal of Neo-Latin Language and Literature* 4: 173–96.

Goar, R. J. 1972. *Cicero and the State Religion.* Amsterdam.

Grillo, L., ed. 2015. *Cicero's* De provinciis consularibus oratio. New York.

Gruen, E. S. 1968. *Roman Politics and the Criminal Courts, 149–78 BC.* Cambridge, MA.

Gruen, E. S. 1969. "Notes on the 'First Catilinarian Conspiracy.'" *Classical Philology* 64: 20–24.

Gruen, E. S. 1973. "The Trial of C. Antonius." *Latomus* 32: 301–10.

Gruen, E. S. 1974. *The Last Generation of the Roman Republic.* London.

Gurd, S. 2007. "Cicero and Editorial Revision." *Classical Antiquity* 26: 49–80.

Habicht, C. 1990. *Cicero the Politician.* Baltimore and London.

Hagendahl, H. 1958. *Latin Fathers and the Classics: A Study on the Apologists, Jerome and Other Christian Writers.* Studia Graeca et Latina Gothoburgensia 6. Göteborg.

Hagendahl, H. 1967. *Augustine and the Latin Classics.* Studia Graeca et Latina Gothoburgensia 20. 2 vols. Göteborg.

Hardy, E. G. 1924. *The Catilinarian Conspiracy: A Re-Study of the Evidence.* Oxford.

Harlan, M. 1995. *Roman Republican Moneyers and Their Coins 63 BC–49 BC.* Aspects of Ancient Classical Coins. London.

Harries, J. 2006. *Cicero and the Jurists: From Citizens' Law to the Lawful State.* London.

Harris, W. V. 1971. *Rome in Etruria and Umbria.* Oxford.

Harrison, I. 2008. "Catiline, Clodius, and Popular Politics at Rome during the 60s and 50s BCE." *Bulletin of the Institute of Classical Studies* 51: 95–118.

Harrison, S. J. 1997. "The Survival and Supremacy of Rome: The Unity of the Shield of Aeneas." *Journal of Roman Studies* 87: 70–76.

Heibges, U. 1969. "Religion and Rhetoric in Cicero's Speeches." *Latomus* 28: 833–49.

Helm, C. 1979. "Zur Redaktion der ciceronischen Konsulatsreden." PhD diss., University of Göttingen.

Highet, G. 1949. *The Classical Tradition: Greek and Roman Influences on Western Literature.* Oxford.

Hollis, A. S., ed. and trans. 2007. *Fragments of Roman Poetry, c. 60 BC–AD 20.* Oxford.

Holmes, T. R. 1923. *The Roman Republic and the Founder of the Empire*. 3 vols. Oxford.

Horsfall, N., ed. and trans. 2013. *Virgil, Aeneid 6: A Commentary*. 2 vols. Berlin and Boston.

Hunt, M. 2016. "Jonson vs. Shakespeare: The Roman Plays." *Ben Jonson Journal* 23: 75–100.

Hurt, J. 1972. *Catiline's Dream: An Essay on Ibsen's Plays*. Urbana.

Hutchinson, G. O. 1995. "Rhythm, Style, and Meaning in Cicero's Prose." *Classical Quarterly* 45: 485–99.

Hutchinson, G. O. 2010. "Deflected Addresses: Apostrophe and Space (Sophocles, Aeschines, Plautus, Cicero, Virgil and Others)." *Classical Quarterly* 60: 96–109.

Ingram, R. G. 2015. "Conyers Middleton's *Cicero*: Enlightenment, Scholarship, and Polemic." In Altman 2015. 95–123.

Innes, D. C. 1977. "*Quo usque tandem patiemini?*" *Classical Quarterly* 27: 468.

Internullo, D. 2011–12. "Cicerone latinogreco: *Corpus* dei papiri bilingui delle *Catilinarie* di Cicerone." *Papyrologica Lupiensia* 20–21: 25–150.

Internullo, D. 2016. "*P.Vindob.* L 17 identificato: Cicero, *In Catilinam* I, 14–15 + 27." *Zeitschrift für Papyrologie und Epigraphik* 199: 36–40.

John, C. 1876. *Die Entstehungsgeschichte der catilinarischen Verschwörung: Ein Beitrag zur Kritik des Sallustius*. Jahrbücher für classische Philologie Supplement 8. Leipzig. 701–819.

Johnston, B. 1980. *To the Third Empire: Ibsen's Early Drama*. Minneapolis.

Jones, C. P. 2016. "A Syntax of Forgery." *Proceedings of the American Philosophical Society* 160: 26–36.

Kaplan, A. 1968. *Catiline: The Man and His Role in the Roman Revolution*. New York.

Kaster, R. A., trans. 2006. *Marcus Tullius Cicero: Speech on Behalf of Publius Sestius*. Clarendon Ancient History Series. Oxford.

Keeline, T. J. 2018. *The Reception of Cicero in the Early Roman Empire: The Rhetorical Schoolroom and the Creation of a Cultural Legend*. Cambridge.

Kennedy, G. A. 1972. *The Art of Rhetoric in the Roman World, 300 BC–AD 300*. Princeton.

Knox, P. E. 2011. "Cicero as a Hellenistic Poet." *Classical Quarterly* 61: 192–204.

Krebs, C. B. 2008. "Catiline's Ravaged Mind: *Vastus Animus* (Sall. *BC* 5.5)." *Classical Quarterly* 58: 682–86.

Kristoferson, H., ed. 1928. *Declamatio in L. Sergium Catilinam: Text och Tradition*. Göteborg.

Laan, T. F. van, trans. 1992. *Henrik Ibsen: Catiline and The Burial Mound*. World Literature in Translation 11. New York and London.

Levene, D. S. 2010. *Livy on the Hannibalic War*. Oxford.

Levick, B. M. 2015. *Catiline*. Ancients in Action. London.

Lewis, R. G. 2001. "Catilina and the Vestal." *Classical Quarterly* 51: 141–49.

Lintott, A. W. 1990. "Electoral Bribery in the Roman Republic." *Journal of Roman Studies* 80: 1–16.

Lintott, A. W. 1999a. *The Constitution of the Roman Republic*. Oxford.

Lintott, A. W. 1999b. *Violence in Republican Rome*. 2nd ed. Oxford.

Lintott, A. W. 2008. *Cicero as Evidence: A Historian's Companion*. Oxford.

Lintott, A. W., trans. 2013. *Plutarch: Demosthenes and Cicero*. Clarendon Ancient History Series. Oxford.

Liong, K. 2016. "Breathing Crime and Contagion: Catiline as *scelus anhelans* (Cic. *Cat*. 2.1)." *Rheinisches Museum für Philologie* 159: 348–68.

Macdonald, C., ed. and trans. 1977. *Cicero: In Catilinam I–IV, Pro Murena, Pro Sulla, Pro Flacco*. Loeb Classical Library. Cambridge, MA and London.

MacKendrick, P. 1995. *The Speeches of Cicero: Context, Law, Rhetoric*. London.

Madden, J. D. 1977–78. Review of Macdonald 1977. *Classical World* 71: 276–78.

Malcolm, D. A. 1979. "*Quo usque tandem . . . ?*" *Classical Quarterly* 29: 219–20.

Malcovati, E., ed. 1976. *Oratorum Romanorum fragmenta liberae rei publicae*. Vol. 1. 4th ed. Turin.

Manni, E. 1969. *Lucio Sergio Catilina*. 2nd ed. Palermo.

Manuwald, G. 2012. "The Speeches to the People in Cicero's Oratorical Corpora." *Rhetorica* 30: 153–75.

Manuwald, G. 2015. *Cicero*. Understanding Classics. London and New York.

Manuwald, G, ed. 2016. *The Afterlife of Cicero*. Bulletin of the Institute of Classical Studies Supplement 135. London.

Maraniss, D. 1995. *First in His Class: The Biography of Bill Clinton*. New York.

March, D. A. 1988–89. "Cicero and the 'Gang of Five.'" *Classical World* 82: 225–34.

Marshall, B. A. 1976–77. "Catilina: Court Cases and Consular Candidature." *Scripta Classica Israelica* 3: 127–37.

Marshall, B. A. 1977a. "The Date of Catilina's Marriage to Aurelia Orestilla." *Rivista di filologia e di istruzione classica* 105: 151–54.

Marshall, B. A. 1977b. "The Vote of a Bodyguard for the Consuls of 65." *Classical Philology* 72: 318–20.

Marshall, B. A. 1985. "Catilina and the Execution of M. Marius Gratidianus." *Classical Quarterly* 35: 124–33.

Martin, R. H. 1969. "Tacitus and His Predecessors." In T. A. Dorey, ed., *Tacitus*. London. 117–47.

Martin, R. H., and A. J. Woodman, eds. 1989. *Tacitus Annals Book IV*. Cambridge Greek and Latin Classics. Cambridge.

Maslowski, T., ed. 2003. *M. Tullius Cicero: Orationes in L. Catilinam quattuor*. Bibliotheca Teubneriana. Munich and Leipzig.

May, J. M. 1988. *Trials of Character: The Eloquence of Ciceronian Ethos*. Chapel Hill and London.

May, J. M., ed. 2002. *Brill's Companion to Cicero: Oratory and Rhetoric*. Leiden.

McDermott, W. C. 1972. "Cicero's Publication of His Consular Orations." *Philologus* 116: 277–84.

McFarlane, J. W., and G. Orton, eds. 1970. *The Oxford Ibsen*. Vol. 1, *Early Plays*. Oxford.

McLaughlin, M. 2016. "*Renascens ad superos Cicero*: Ciceronian and Anti-Ciceronian Styles in the Italian Renaissance." In Manuwald 2016. 67–81.

McPherson, D. 1974. "Ben Jonson's Library and Marginalia: An Annotated Catalogue." *Studies in Philology* 71.5.

Millar, F. 1998. *The Crowd in Rome in the Late Republic*. Ann Arbor.

Milner, S. J. 2005. "Exile, Rhetoric, and the Limits of Civic Republican Discourse." In S. J. Milner, ed., *At the Margins: Minority Groups in Premodern Italy*. Medieval Cultures 39. Minneapolis. 162–91.

Mitchell, T. N. 1979. *Cicero: The Ascending Years*. New Haven and London.

Moles, J. L., ed. and trans. 1988. *Plutarch: The Life of Cicero*. Warminster.

Morgan, P. 2005. *The Insider: The Private Diaries of a Scandalous Decade*. London.

Morstein-Marx, R. 2004. *Mass Oratory and Political Power in the Late Roman Republic*. Cambridge.

Mouritsen, H. 2001. *Plebs and Politics in the Late Roman Republic*. Cambridge.

Mouritsen, H. 2013. "From Meeting to Text: The *Contio* in the Late Republic." In Steel and Blom 2013. 63–82.

Murray, R. J. 1966. "Cicero and the Gracchi." *Transactions and Proceedings of the American Philological Association* 97: 291–98.

Muse, K. 2007. "Sergestus and Tarchon in the *Aeneid*." *Classical Quarterly* 57: 586–605.

Napoleon III. 1865. *Histoire de Jules César*.Vol. 1. New York.

Nicolet, C. 1960. "*Consul togatus*: Remarques sur le vocabulaire politique de Cicéron et de Tite-Live." *Revue des études latines* 38: 236–63.

Nisbet, R. G. M., ed. 1961. *Cicero: In Calpurnium Pisonem oratio*. Oxford.

Nisbet, R. G. M. 1964. "The Speeches." In Dorey 1964. 47–79.

Norbye, M. 2011. "Latin Epigraphy: How to Read and Understand Roman Inscriptions, Part I." *ARA News* 26: 24–29.

Nousek, D. L. 2010. "Echoes of Cicero in Livy's Bacchanalian Narrative (39.8–19)." *Classical Quarterly* 60: 156–66.

Oakley, S. P. 1997. *A Commentary on Livy Books VI–X*.Vol. 1. Oxford.

Odahl, C. M. 2010. *Cicero and the Catilinarian Conspiracy*. New York and Abingdon.

Offermann, H. 1995. "Überarbeitung oder nicht—Überlegungen zur 1. Catilinarie." *Anregung: Zeitschrift für Gymnasialpädagogik* 41: 227–35.

Ogilvie, R. M. 1978. *The Library of Lactantius*. Oxford.

Osmond, P. J. 1995. "*Princeps historiae Romanae*: Sallust in Renaissance PoliticalThought." *Memoirs of the American Academy in Rome* 40: 101–43.

Osmond, P. J. 2000. "Catiline in Fiesole and Florence: The After-Life of a Roman Conspirator." *International Journal of the Classical Tradition* 7: 3–38.

Osmond, P. J., and R. W. Ulery, Jr. 1995. "Constantius Felicius Durantinus and the Renaissance Origins of Anti-Sallustian Criticism." *International Journal of the Classical Tradition* 1: 29–56.

Osmond, P. J., and R. W. Ulery, Jr. 2003. "Sallustius Crispus, Gaius." In V. Brown, J. Hankins, and R. A. Kaster, eds., *Catalogus translationum et commentariorum: Medieval and Renaissance Latin Translations and Commentaries; Annotated Lists and Guides*. Vol. 8. Washington, DC. 183–326.

Ournac, P., M. Passelac, and G. Rancoule 2009. *Carte archéologique de la Gaule: 11/2 L'Aude*. Paris.

Overy, R. 2001. *Interrogations: The Nazi Elite in Allied Hands, 1945*. London.

Pagán, V. E. 2004. *Conspiracy Narratives in Roman History*. Austin.

Panciera, S. 1980. "Catilina e Catone su due coppette romane," with an "Appendice tecnica" by N. Cuomo di Caprio, I. Mainoni, F. Sacchi, and G. Spinola. In M. J. Fontana, M. T. Piraino, and F. P. Rizzo, eds., ΦΙΛΙΑΣ XAPIN: *Miscellanea di studi classici in onore di Eugenio Manni*.Vol. 5. Rome. 1635–61.

Panciera, S. 2006. *Epigrafi, epigrafia, epigrafisti: Scritti vari editi e inediti (1956–2005) con note complementari e indici.* 3 vols. Rome.

Pareti, L. 1934. *La congiura di Catilina.* Catania.

Passelac, M. 1972. "Le bronze d'applique de Fendeille." *Revue archéologique de Narbonnaise* 5: 185–90.

Pelling, C. B. R. 1985. "Plutarch and Catiline." *Hermes* 113: 311–29.

Pelling, C. B. R., trans. 2011. *Plutarch: Caesar.* Clarendon Ancient History Series. Oxford.

Phillips, E. J. 1970. "Cicero, *Ad Atticum* I.2." *Philologus* 114: 291–94.

Phillips, E. J. 1976. "Catiline's Conspiracy." *Historia* 25: 441–48.

Phillips, J. J. 1985–86. "Atticus and the Publication of Cicero's Works." *Classical World* 79: 227–37.

Potter, F. H. 1925–26. "The Date of Cicero's First Oration against Catiline." *Classical Journal* 21: 164–76.

Powell, J. G. F. 2007. "Invective and the Orator: Ciceronian Theory and Practice." In Booth 2007. 1–23.

Powell, J. G. F., and J. J. Paterson, eds. 2004a. *Cicero the Advocate.* Oxford.

Powell, J. G. F., and J. J. Paterson. 2004b. "Introduction." In Powell and Paterson 2004a. 1–57.

Price, J. J. 1998. "The Failure of Cicero's *First Catilinarian.*" In C. Deroux, ed., *Studies in Latin Literature and Roman History* 9. Brussels. 106–28.

Primmer, A. 1977. "Historisches und Oratorisches zur ersten Catilinaria." *Gymnasium* 84: 18–38.

Quinn, K., ed. 1970. *Catullus: The Poems.* London and Basingstoke.

Ramsey, J. T. 1980. "The Prosecution of C. Manilius in 66 BC and Cicero's *Pro Manilio.*" *Phoenix* 34: 323–36.

Ramsey, J. T. 1982. "Cicero, *Pro Sulla* 68 and Catiline's Candidacy in 66 BC." *Harvard Studies in Classical Philology* 86: 121–31.

Ramsey, J. T. 1985. "Asconius P. 60 (Clark), † *prima pars*: The Trial and Conviction of C. Manilius in 65 BC." *American Journal of Philology* 106: 367–73.

Ramsey, J. T. 2007a. "Roman Senatorial Oratory." In Dominik and Hall 2007. 122–35.

Ramsey, J. T., ed. 2007b. *Sallust's* Bellum Catilinae. 2nd ed. New York.

Ramsey, J. T. 2019. "The Date of the Consular Elections in 63 and the Inception of Catiline's Conspiracy." *Harvard Studies in Classical Philology* 110: 213–69.

Rawson, E. D. 1975. *Cicero: A Portrait.* London.

Reinach, T. 1904. "Catulus ou Catilina?" *Revue des études grecques* 17: 5–11.

Renehan, R. 1976. "A Traditional Pattern of Imitation in Sallust and His Sources." *Classical Philology* 71: 97–105.

Rhodes, P. J. 2018. *Periclean Athens.* London.

Richard, C. J. 2015. "Cicero and the American Founders." In Altman 2015. 124–43.

Ridgway, B. S. 1981. Review of M. J. Fontana, M. T. Piraino, and F. P. Rizzo, eds., *ΦΙΛΙΑΣ ΧΑΡΙΝ: Miscellanea di studi classici in onore di Eugenio Manni. American Journal of Archaeology* 85: 501–2.

Riggsby, A. M. 1999. *Crime and Community in Ciceronian Rome.* Austin.

Riggsby, A. M. 2010. "Form as Global Strategy in Cicero's *Second Catilinarian.*" In Berry and Erskine 2010. 92–104.

Robinson, A. 1994. "Avoiding the Responsibility: Cicero and the Suppression of Catiline's Conspiracy." *Syllecta Classica* 5: 43–51.

Rolfe, J. C., ed. and trans. 2013. *Sallust: The War with Catiline, The War with Jugurtha.* Rev. J. T. Ramsey. Loeb Classical Library. 2nd ed. Cambridge, MA, and London.

Roselaar, S. T. 2012. "Roman State Prisoners in Latin and Italian Cities." *Classical Quarterly* 62: 189–200.

Rosillo-López, C. 2010. *La Corruption à la fin de la République romaine (IIe–Iers. av. J.-C.): Aspects politiques et financiers.* Historia Einzelschriften 200. Stuttgart.

Rosillo-López, C. 2018. "Political Participation and the Identification of Politicians in the Late Roman Republic." In H. van der Blom, C. Gray, and C. Steel, eds., *Institutions and Ideology in Republican Rome: Speech, Audience and Decision.* Cambridge. 69–87.

Rouse, R. H., and M. D. Reeve 1983. "Cicero: Speeches." In L. D. Reynolds, ed., *Texts and Transmission: A Survey of the Latin Classics.* Oxford. 54–98.

Ryan, F. X. 1997. "The Praetorship of L. Roscius Otho." *Hermes* 125: 236–40.

Ryan, F. X. 1998. *Rank and Participation in the Republican Senate.* Stuttgart.

Ryan, F. X. 2006. "Die Apollinarspiele zur Zeit der Republik." *Aevum* 80: 67–104.

Sallmann, K., ed. 1997. *Die Literatur des Umbruchs: Von der römischen zur christlichen Literatur, 117 bis 284 n. Chr.* Vol. 4 of R. Herzog and P. L. Schmidt, eds., *Handbuch der lateinischen Literatur der Antike.* Munich.

Sánchez-Ostiz, Á. 2013. "*Cicero Graecus*: Notes on Ciceronian Papyri from Egypt." *Zeitschrift für Papyrologie und Epigraphik* 187: 144–53.

Santangelo, F. 2013. *Divination, Prediction and the End of the Roman Republic.* Cambridge.

Santangelo, F., ed. 2017. *Late Republican Rome, 88–31 BC.* Trans. J. Murrell and F. Santangelo. LACTOR 7. London.

Scanlon, T. F. 1986. "*Historia quasi fabula*: The Catiline Theme in Sallust and Jonson." In J. Redmond, ed., *Historical Drama.* Themes in Drama 8. Cambridge. 17–29.

Schurgacz, K., ed. and trans. 2004. *Die* Declamatio in L. Sergium Catilinam: *Einleitung, Text, Übersetzung, Kommentar. Bochumer Altertumswissenschaftliches Colloquium 58.* Trier.

Seager, R. J. 1964. "The First Catilinarian Conspiracy." *Historia* 13: 338–47.

Seager, R. J. 1973. "*Iusta Catilinae.*" *Historia* 22: 240–48.

Seager, R. J. 2002. *Pompey the Great: A Political Biography.* 2nd ed. Oxford.

Seider, R. 1979. "Beiträge zur Geschichte und Paläographie der antiken Cicerohandschriften." *Bibliothek und Wissenschaft* 13: 101–49.

Shackleton Bailey, D. R., ed. and trans. 1966–70. *Cicero's Letters to Atticus.* 7 vols. Cambridge Classical Texts and Commentaries 3–9. Cambridge.

Shackleton Bailey, D. R. 1992. *Onomasticon to Cicero's Speeches.* Stuttgart and Leipzig.

Sharpe, M. 2015. "Cicero, Voltaire, and the *Philosophes* in the French Enlightenment." In Altman 2015. 329–56.

Sherman, N. 2012. "The Dunlap Broadside." Contributed on July 5, 2012. *Fonts in Use.* https://fontsinuse.com/uses/1666/the-dunlap-broadside (accessed 11 October 2018).

Smith, C., and R. Covino, eds. 2011. *Praise and Blame in Roman Republican Rhetoric.* Swansea.

Speck, H. B. G. 1906. *Katilina im Drama der Weltliteratur: Ein Beitrag zur vergleichenden Stoffgeschichte des Römerdramas, 1597–1905.* Leipzig.

Steel, C. E. W. 2005. *Reading Cicero: Genre and Performance in Late Republican Rome.* London.

Steel, C. E. W. 2006a. "Consul and *Consilium*: Suppressing the Catilinarian Conspiracy." In D. Spencer and E. Theodorakopoulos, eds., *Advice and its Rhetoric in Greece and Rome.* Bari. 63–78.

Steel, C. E. W. 2006b. *Roman Oratory.* Greece and Rome New Surveys in the Classics 36. Cambridge.

Steel, C. E. W. 2007. "Name and Shame? Invective against Clodius and Others in the Post-Exile Speeches." In Booth 2007. 105–28.

Steel, C. E. W., and H. van der Blom, eds. 2013. *Community and Communication: Oratory and Politics in Republican Rome*. Oxford.

Stewart, R. 1995. "Catiline and the Crisis of 63–60 BC: The Italian Perspective." *Latomus* 54: 62–78.

Stinchcomb, J. 1934. "Catiline on the Stage." *Classical Weekly* 28: 49–52.

Stocker, S. R., and J. L. Davis 2017. "The Combat Agate from the Grave of the Griffin Warrior at Pylos." *Hesperia* 86: 583–605.

Stockton, D. L. 1971. *Cicero: A Political Biography*. Oxford.

Stroh, W. 1975. *Taxis und Taktik: Die advokatische Dispositionskunst in Ciceros Gerichtsreden*. Stuttgart.

Stroh, W. 2000. "Ciceros erste Rede gegen Catilina." In J. Leonhardt and G. Ott, eds., *Apocrypha: Entlegene Schriften*. Stuttgart. 64–78.

Sumner, G. V. 1963. "The Last Journey of L. Sergius Catilina." *Classical Philology* 58: 215–19.

Sumner, G. V. 1965. "The Consular Elections of 66 BC." *Phoenix* 19: 226–31.

Syme, R. 1939. *The Roman Revolution*. Oxford.

Syme, R. 1964. *Sallust*. Berkeley.

Syme, R. 2016. *Approaching the Roman Revolution: Papers on Republican History*. Ed. F. Santangelo. Oxford.

Tannenbaum, R. F. 2005. "What Caesar Said: Rhetoric and History in Sallust's *Coniuratio Catilinae* 51." In K. Welch and T. W. Hillard, *Roman Crossings: Theory and Practice in the Roman Republic*. Swansea. 209–23.

Tatum, W. J., ed. and trans. 2018. *Quintus Cicero: A Brief Handbook on Canvassing for Office*, Commentariolum Petitionis. Clarendon Ancient History Series. Oxford.

Taylor, L. R. 1949. *Party Politics in the Age of Caesar*. Berkeley.

Taylor, L. R. 1966. *Roman Voting Assemblies from the Hannibalic War to the Dictatorship of Caesar*. Ann Arbor.

Taylor, L. R., and R. T. Scott. 1969. "Seating Space in the Roman Senate and the *Senatores pedarii*." *Transactions and Proceedings of the American Philological Association* 100: 529–82.

Thein, A. 2010. "Sulla's Veteran Settlement Policy." In F. Daubner, ed., *Militärsiedlungen und Territorialherrschaft in der Antike*. Topoi: Berlin Studies of the Ancient World 3. Berlin. 79–99.

Todd, O. J. 1952. "Dates in the Autumn of 63 BC." In M. White, ed., *Studies in Honour of Gilbert Norwood*. Toronto. 156–62.

Treggiari, S. 2007. *Terentia, Tullia and Publilia: The Women of Cicero's Family*. Abingdon and New York.

Tzounakas, S. C. 2006. "The Personified *Patria* in Cicero's *First Catilinarian*: Significance and Inconsistencies." *Philologus* 150: 222–31.

Tzounakas, S. C. 2015. "Catiline as Atreus in Cicero's *First Catilinarian*." In G. A. Xenis, ed., *Literature, Scholarship, Philosophy, and History: Classical Studies in Memory of Ioannis Taifacos*. Stuttgart. 53–71.

Ungern-Sternberg, J. von. 1971. "Ciceros erste Catilinarische Rede und Diodor XL 5a." *Gymnasium* 78: 47–54.

Usher, S. 1965. "*Occultatio* in Cicero's Speeches." *American Journal of Philology* 86: 175–92.

Usher, S. 2008. *Cicero's Speeches: The Critic in Action*. Warminster.

Vasaly, A. 1993. *Representations: Images of the World in Ciceronian Oratory*. Berkeley.

Volk, K., and J. E. G. Zetzel. 2015. "Laurel, Tongue and Glory (Cicero, *De consulatu suo* Fr. 6 Soubiran)." *Classical Quarterly* 65: 204–23.

Walbank, F. W., A. E. Astin, M. W. Frederiksen, R. M. Ogilvie, and A. Drummond, eds. 1989. *The Cambridge Ancient History*. 2nd ed., Volume 7, Part 2: *The Rise of Rome to 220 BC*. Cambridge.

Ward, A. M. 1977. *Marcus Crassus and the Late Roman Republic*. Columbia, MO, and London.

Waters, K. H. 1970. "Cicero, Sallust and Catiline." *Historia* 19: 195–215.

Wiedemann, T. 1979. "The Figure of Catiline in the *Historia Augusta*." *Classical Quarterly* 29: 479–84.

Wilkins, A. T. 1994. *Villain or Hero: Sallust's Portrayal of Catiline*. American University Studies Series 17; Classical Languages and Literature 15. New York.

Winterbottom, M. 1982. "Schoolroom and Courtroom." In B. Vickers, ed., *Rhetoric Revalued*. Medieval and Renaissance Texts and Studies 19. New York. 59–70.

Wiseman, T. P. 1974. "Legendary Genealogies in Late-Republican Rome." *Greece and Rome* 21: 153–64.

Wiseman, T. P. 1994. "The Peasants' Revolt and the Bankrupts' Plot." In Crook, Lintott, and Rawson 1994. 346–58.

Wiseman, T. P. 1998. "E. S. Beesly and the Roman Revolution." In T. P. Wiseman, *Roman Drama and Roman History*. Exeter. 121–34.

Wiseman, T. P. 2013. "The Palatine, from Evander to Elagabalus." *Journal of Roman Studies* 103: 234–68.

Wood, N. 1988. *Cicero's Social and Political Thought*. Berkeley.

Woodman, A. J., trans. 2007. *Sallust: Catiline's War, The Jugurthine War, Histories*. Penguin Classics. London.

Woodman, A. J., ed. 2018. *The Annals of Tacitus Book 4*. Cambridge Classical Texts and Commentaries 58. Cambridge.

Yavetz, Z. 1958. "The Living Conditions of the Urban Plebs in Republican Rome." *Latomus* 17: 500–17.

Yavetz, Z. 1963. "The Failure of Catiline's Conspiracy." *Historia* 12: 485–99.

Zielinski, T. 1929. *Cicero im Wandel der Jahrhunderte*. 4th ed. Leipzig.

Zimmerer, H., ed. 1888. *Declamatio in Lucium Sergium Catilinam: Eine Schuldeklamation aus der römischen Kaiserzeit*. Munich.

Index

Roman authors (including Cicero, but not Caesar) and Roman emperors are listed under their most familiar name (e.g., Catullus, not Valerius). Other Romans are listed under their *nomen* or "clan name" (thus Catiline appears as "Sergius Catilina, Lucius"). Dates of magistracies are given only where necessary to differentiate between persons of the same name; if an individual held a magistracy more than once, only the first date is given.

For the benefit of digital users, indexed terms that span two or more pages (e.g., 52–54) may, on occasion, appear on only one of those pages.

Accius, 96n.18
Adams, John, 213
Adams, John Quincy, 213
Aelius Sejanus, Lucius, 199–200
Aemilius Lepidus, Manius, 33
Aemilius Lepidus, Marcus, xxiv–xxv
Aemilius Paullus, Lucius (consul 182), 52–54, 185–86
Aemilius Paullus, Lucius (consul 50), 33, 52–54
Allobroges, 42–44, 45–46, 47–48, 52, 122–23, 126–27, 139–47, 148, 155, 156–58, 160–61, 165–66, 197–99, 207–8, 211–12
    number of envoys of, 42–44, 220
Ampelius, 166n.8, 172–73
Annius Chilo, Quintus, 46–47, 166

Annius Milo, Titus, xix–xx, 37–38n.64, 57–58, 138–39
Antonius, Marcus (consul 99), 19–20
Antonius, Marcus (consul 44), xix–xx, xxiv, 4–5n.6, 19–20, 57–58, 195
Antonius Hybrida, Gaius, xx–xxiv, 19–20, 25–26, 42–44, 46–47, 51–52, 54–55, 100–1, 122–23, 130–31, 148–49, 207–8
Appian, 9n.12, 19–20, 28–29n.50, 35–36, 42, 166–69, 170–72, 232, 238
Approaches A and B, 87–89
Appuleius Saturninus, Lucius, 165–66
Apuleius, 92–93
Apulia, 33, 44–45, 141–42
Arnobius, 155n.51
Arpinum, 1, 11–12, 35–36

Arretium, 13, 27–28, 37–38, 42–44
Arrius, Quintus, 31–32
Asconius, 14, 15–17, 18–23, 35, 37–
    38n.64, 57–59, 128n.16, 130–32,
    138–39, 208, 209–10, 232
atque + a consonant, 181n.28
Aufidius Orestes, Gnaeus, 42–44n.72
Augustine, 62–63, 200–1
Augustus, 30n.53, 196–97
Aurelia Orestilla, 18–19, 38–41, 195,
    196, 211–12
    daughter of, 18–19, 38–39
Aurelius Cotta, Lucius, 15–17, 155
Autronius Paetus, Publius, 15–17, 25–
    26, 45–46, 131–32, 143–44

Bacchanalian conspiracy, 199–200
Beesly, Edward Spencer, 2–3
Bellienus, Lucius, 20
Bellona, Temple of, 119–20
Bononia, 52
Bonus Eventus, 52–54
bowls bearing names of Catiline and
    Cato, 20–25, 42–44, 240–45
Brown, Tina, 84–85n.2
Bruni, Leonardo, 203–4, 205–6

Caecilius Metellus, Marcus, 33
Caecilius Metellus Celer, Quintus, 20,
    33, 52
Caecilius Metellus Creticus, Quintus,
    33, 44–45
Caecilius Metellus Nepos, Quintus,
    67–69, 71, 75–76, 124–25, 167–
    69, 180–81
Caecilius Metellus Pius Scipio Nasica,
    Quintus, 31–32
Caelius Rufus, Marcus, xxi–xxiii, 5–6,
    7, 18, 54–55
Caeparius, Marcus, 44–47, 48–49,
    141–42, 143–44, 164–65
Calliope, 161–62

Calpurnius Bestia, Lucius, 67–69, 71,
    75–76, 124–25, 167–69, 180–81
Calpurnius Piso, Gaius, 47–48
Campania, 28–29, 118–19
Cappellini, Federico, 217
Capua, 33, 100–1
Carinae, 31–32
Carthage, 185–86
Caslon, William, 213
Cassius Dio, 15n.23, 42, 51n.91, 58–59,
    66–67, 101–2, 132–34, 155n.51,
    156–58, 162, 166–69, 235–36
Cassius Longinus, Lucius, 3–4,
    19–25, 42–44, 45–47, 126–27,
    131–32, 140–41, 144–45, 166,
    240, 243
Casti, Giovanni Battista, 217
Catilinarian conspiracy, 31–52 and *passim*
    Cicero's dissuasion of audience from
        joining, 127–36
    "first Catilinarian conspiracy," 15–17,
        96–97
    importance in history, xxiii–xxiv
    importance in literature, xxiv–xxv
Catullus, 101–2, 159–60n.59, 195–96
Caucilius, Quintus, 12–13
cedant arma togae, 161–62
Charles II, 211–12
Chettle, Henry, 206
Chronica de origine civitatis, 203–4
Cicero, *passim*
    Academica, 73–75n.40
    account of his consulship in Greek,
        xxi, 35–36n.61, 50–51n.89,
        66–67, 81–82, 197–99
    account of his consulship in Latin,
        66–67
    Ad Atticum, xxiv, 17–18, 48–49, 56–57,
        59–62, 66–67, 69, 76–77, 80,
        81–82n.46, 89–90, 101–3, 113–
        14, 124–25, 138, 158–59, 165–69,
        171–72, 182–83, 190–91, 201–2

Ad Brutum, 101–2
Ad familiares, 67–68, 124–25
Ad Quintum fratrem, 61–62
Brutus, 101–2, 128n.16
career, 11–55
civic crown for, 46–47
commentarii, 57
consular corpus, xxi, 69, 80, 101–3,
    117–18, 120–21, 158–59
Consulatus suus, xxi, 45–46, 66–67,
    81–82, 129–30n.20, 155n.51,
    156–62
Contra contionem Q. Metelli, 67–68,
    73–75n.40
cut-and-paste composition, 73–75
De divinatione, 12, 45–46, 66–67,
    156–58, 160–61
De domo sua, 50–51, 61–62, 140n.33
De gloria, 73–75n.40
De imperio Cn. Pompei, 15–17, 61–62,
    117–18
De lege agraria 1, 60
De lege agraria 2, 60, 117–19, 120–21,
    125–26, 162
De lege agraria 3, 60, 117–18
De lege agraria 4, 60, 117–18
De officiis, 29–30, 79–80, 127–28,
    186–87
De Othone, 60, 117–18, 119–21,
    125–26, 162
exile, xxi, 69, 103, 163
In Catilinam 1, xx–xxiii, 25–26, 31–
    32, 35–36, 40–41, 59–60, 62–63,
    65–66n.27, 69–72, 83, 121–22,
    124–25, 131–32, 138, 149, 150,
    152, 153–54, 169–70, 176, 191–
    92, 207–8, 235, 236–37
    date of delivery, 35–36n.61,
        210–11n.49
    a denunciation, not an invective,
        90–91
    influence, 196–97, 210, 213

    purposes, 90–91, 103–4, 113–15
    structure, 91–92
    success, 115–16, 190–92
In Catilinam 2, xx–xxi, 35–36, 41–42,
    60, 69–72, 81, 89–91, 97, 105–6,
    107–8, 113–14, 120–21, 124–25,
    127–38, 149, 151–52, 154–55,
    159–60, 175, 180–81
    influence, 199–200, 220–21
    purposes, 125–26
    structure, 121–22
    success, 162–63, 190–92
In Catilinam 3, xx–xxi, 3–5, 9, 47,
    48–49, 60, 69–71, 72, 75–76,
    80, 90–91, 108, 113–14, 120–21,
    127, 129, 131–34, 137, 138–50,
    153–58, 159–60, 161–62, 175
    purposes, 126–27
    structure, 122–24
    success, 162–63, 190–92
In Catilinam 4, xx–xxi, 48–50, 52–54,
    60, 69–72, 73–80, 81–82, 90–91,
    146–47, 150–51, 152, 164–70,
    171–92
    influence, 200–1, 210–11
    purposes, 189–90
    structure, 176–77
    success, 163, 190–92
In Pisonem, 46–47, 58–59, 61–62,
    65–66, 188–89
In toga candida, 12–13, 14, 15–17,
    18–20, 35–36, 61–62, 128n.16,
    130–31n.21, 142–43, 195, 197–
    99, 208, 209–10
In Vatinium, 56–57n.1
In Verrem, 57–58, 59, 81–82n.46, 137,
    200–2
Orator, 37
other Catilinarian speeches besides
    Catilinarians, 30, 66–67
parent/father of his country, 1, 2,
    46–47, 67–68, 205

Cicero, *passim* (*cont.*)
  Philippics, 4–5n.6, 57–58, 59, 81, 178,
    188–89, 200–1
  Post reditum ad Quirites, 57–58n.6,
    103, 129–30n.18
  Post reditum in senatu, 56–57, 101–2,
    103
  powers of prophecy, 71–72n.34,
    72–75
  Pro Archia, 59
  Pro Caelio, xxi–xxiii, 5–7, 9, 12,
    17–18, 40–41, 98–99, 197–200,
    209–10
  Pro Flacco, 42, 44n.78, 55, 56–57n.1,
    160n.62, 190–91
  Pro Fonteio, 56–57
  Pro Ligario, 73–75n.40
  Pro Marcello, 100–2, 200–1
  Pro Milone, 58–59, 65–66, 103, 137,
    138–39, 173–75n.22
  Pro Murena, xxi–xxiii, 20–23, 25–28, 30,
    40–41, 56–57, 61–62n.14, 66–67,
    67–68n.32, 121–22n.14, 130–31,
    158, 197–99, 233–35, 243–44
  Pro Plancio, 56–57n.1
  Pro Rabirio perduellionis reo, 60
  Pro Roscio Amerino, 58–59, 65–66, 97,
    132–34, 137
  Pro Sestio, 46–47, 59, 67–68, 71–72,
    100–1, 124–25, 188–89
  Pro Sulla, xxi–xxiii, 15–17, 35–36n.61,
    60–61n.12, 68–72, 75–76, 101–
    2n.26, 126–27, 131–32, 161–62,
    182–83, 188–89, 197–99, 215–16,
    235–36
  revision and publication of
    Catilinarians, xxi, 59–82, 86,
    101–3, 124–25, 188–89
  revision and publication of his other
    speeches, 56–59
  thanksgiving to gods for, 46–47,
    122–23, 148–50, 154, 156

  trickery of the conspirators, 42–44,
    138–49, 197–99, 207–8
  Tusculan Disputations, 11–12
  young admirers of, 60–62, 81–82,
    101–3, 114–15
Cimbri, 27–28
Civil War (49–45 BC), xxi–xxiii,
  xxiv–xxv
Claudii Marcelli, 101–2n.26
Claudius, 196–97
Claudius Caecus, Appius, 98–99
Claudius Marcellus, Marcus, 31–32, 100–3
Claudius Nero, Tiberius, 170–71
clausulae, 111–12
clemens, 69–71
Clinton, Bill, 223–24
Clodius Pulcher, Publius, xxi, 9–10,
  17–18, 37–38n.64, 66–68, 69,
  72–76, 124–25, 127, 138–39, 158,
  180–81, 184–85
Concord, Temple of, 45–46, 48–49,
  155, 178
Concordia, 52–54
Constantius Felicius Durantinus, 207–8,
  209–11
consular elections of 63, date of,
  25–26n.46
Cornelius, Gaius, 34, 35, 46–47
Cornelius Cethegus, Gaius, 1, 3–4, 33,
  42–48, 52–54, 122–23, 140–41,
  142, 144–45, 146–47, 164–65,
  170–71, 172, 182, 196–97, 200–1,
  207–8
  brother of, 172–73
Cornelius Chrysogonus, Lucius, 13
Cornelius Cinna, Lucius, 11–12, 131–
  32, 144–45
Cornelius Dolabella, Publius, 9–10
Cornelius Gallus, Gaius, 241–43
Cornelius Lentulus, Publius, 146–47
Cornelius Lentulus Spinther, Publius,
  46–47

Cornelius Lentulus Sura, Publius, 3–4, 9, 38, 42–44, 45–48, 50–51, 72–73, 80, 122–23, 124–25, 128, 131–32, 139–42, 143–45, 146–47, 148–49, 150–51, 164–66, 167–71, 172, 178–79, 180–81, 182–83, 209–10, 211–12
 letter to Catiline, 38, 42–44, 141, 142–45, 146–47
Cornelius Scipio Aemilianus Africanus, Publius, 185–86
Cornelius Scipio Africanus, Publius, 79, 185–86
Cornelius Severus, 196–97
Cornelius Sulla, Lucius, xxiii–xxiv, 8–9, 12–13, 19–20, 27–29, 58–59, 118–19n.3, 128n.16, 131–34, 136, 144–45
 ghost of, 206–8, 217, 220–21
 veterans/colonists of, xxiii–xxiv, 20–23, 27–29, 33, 46–47, 132–34, 136
Cornelius Sulla, Publius, xxi–xxiii, 15–17, 25–26, 68–69
Cornelius Sulla, Servius, 45–46, 143–44
Cornificius, Quintus, 46–47
Cortona, 42–44
Crébillon, Prosper Joliot de, 213–15
crudelis, crudelitas, 68–72, 78, 110–11, 124
Curius, Quintus, 35, 42–44, 131–32, 207–8

Dante Alighieri, 204
Danton, 215–16
debate of 5 December 63
 reconstructed, 165–73
debt, xxiii–xxiv, 19–20, 26, 27–30, 32, 38–39, 40–41, 42–44, 44n.78, 47–48, 52–54n.92, 106, 127–29, 130–35, 136, 150–51, 199–200

Declamatio in L. Sergium Catilinam, 201–2, 209–10
Declaration of Independence, 213
Demosthenes, 60
Diodorus, 89–90, 100–1n.23
disease imagery, 111–12, 121–22n.14
Dumas, Alexandre (the elder), 217–18
Dunlap, John, 213
Dynamius, 62–63

Egypt, 201–2
emergency decree; see senatus consultum ultimum
Ennius, 96n.18
equestrians, xxi–xxiii, 1, 11–12, 19–20, 23, 29–30, 35–36, 47–48, 120, 132–34, 169–70, 172–73, 183, 186–87
Etruria, xx–xxi, xxiii–xxiv, 20–23, 27–28, 31–32, 33–34, 100–1, 124–25, 128
expulsions from senate, 15, 19–20, 34, 35, 42–44, 46–47, 131–32

Fabia (Vestal virgin), 14, 144–45
Fabius Sanga, Quintus, 42–44, 139–40, 207–8
Faesulae (Fiesole), 27–28, 32–33, 37–38, 42–44, 46–47, 51–52, 203–5
Fendeille bronze, 62–63, 201–2
Ferrari, Serafino Amedeo De, 217
Fifth Catilinarian (Quinta Catilinaria), speeches called, 201–3, 209–10
Florence, 202–6
Florus, 233
Forum Aurelium, 37–38, 105–6
Francesconi, Pietro Emilio, 217
French Revolution, 215–16
Freud, Sigmund, 222
Fulvia (mistress of Curius), 35, 207–8, 211–12

Fulvius, 41–42, 135
Furius, Publius, 46–47, 132–34, 166

Gabinius Capito, Publius, 42–47,
    122–23, 139–42, 143–44, 146–47,
    164–65, 182
Gellius, Aulus, 46–47
Gellius Poplicola, Lucius, 46–47
Gosson, Stephen, 206
Gratidia (grandmother of Cicero), 11–12
Gratidius, Marcus, 11–12
Guthrie, William, 212

Hamilton, Alexander, 216
Hamilton, Iain, 217
Hannibal, 10–11, 185–86, 199–200
Harris, Robert, 211–12
Helvia (mother of Cicero), 11–12
Herodotus, 241–43
Historia Augusta, 199–200
Hitler, Adolf, 7–8
Hortensius Hortalus, Quintus, 14–15,
    42, 201–2
Hybreas, 61–62

Ibsen, Henrik, 218–23
invective, 5–6, 7, 18–19, 90–91, 96–97,
    106, 108n.31, 121–22, 134–35,
    172, 201–2, 232
Isaeus, 57

Jefferson, Thomas, 216
Jerome, 200–1
Jonson, Ben, xix–xx, 206–12, 217–18, 220–21
Judges, Book of, 200–1
Julius Caesar, Gaius, xxi–xxiii, xxiv–xxv,
    19–20, 29–30, 46–48, 49–50, 71,
    76–77, 101–2, 110–11, 150–51,
    166–69, 170–75, 176, 179–81, 189–
    92, 194, 197–99, 204–5, 210–11
Julius Caesar, Lucius, xix–xx, 45–46
Junius Brutus, Decimus, 42–44, 139–40

Junius Brutus, Marcus, 8, 57–58, 76–77,
    182–83
Junius Brutus Albinus, Decimus, 141n.34
Junius Silanus, Decimus, xix–xx, 1–2,
    20–23, 25–26, 30–31, 76–77,
    166–72, 173–75, 176, 179–80,
    210–11, 243–44
Jupiter, statue of, 45–46, 123–24, 155–
    58, 160–61, 162
Jupiter Stator, Temple of, 35–36, 56, 95,
    112, 150, 210
Juvenal, xxi–xxiii, 1, 2, 8, 196–97

King James Bible, 206
Kürnberger, Ferdinand, 218, 222

Lactantius, 200–1
Latini, Brunetto, 204
Leech, John, 35–36
lenitas theme, 69–72, 95, 124–25, 135–36, 181
lex Calpurnia, 25–26
lex Manilia, 15–17
lex Sempronia, 167–70
lex Tullia, 25–26, 31, 42, 128
Libro fiesolano, 203–4, 205
Licinia (Vestal virgin), 144–45
Licinius Archias, Aulus, xix–xx
Licinius Crassus, Marcus, 19–20, 29–30,
    31–32, 33, 42, 46–48, 100–1,
    167–69n.13, 180–81, 197–99
Licinius Murena, Lucius, xix–xx, xxi–xxiii,
    1–2, 20–23, 30–31, 40–41, 42–44,
    50–51, 121–22n.14, 166–67, 244
Livy, 92–93, 129–30n.18, 199–200
Louvet, 215–16
Lucan, 196–97, 206–7
Lucceius, Lucius, 20, 195
Ludi Apollinares, 119–20
Lutatius Catulus, Quintus, 12–13, 14,
    37–41, 47–48, 100–1n.23, 167–
    69, 171–72, 173–75
    children of, 39–41

Maccari, Cesare, 35–36
Malispini, Ricordano, 205
Manilius, Gaius, 15–17
Manlius, Gaius, 20–23, 27–28, 31–34,
    37–38, 42, 52, 81, 93–96, 103–6,
    107, 109–11, 113–14, 121–22,
    132–34, 205n.39, 207–8
  connection with Catiline, 20–23,
    27–28, 32, 33–34
Manlius Capitolinus, Marcus,
    199–200
Manlius Torquatus, Lucius (consul 65),
    15–18, 20, 68–69, 96–97, 155
Manlius Torquatus, Lucius (praetor 49),
    15, 68–69
Maquet, Auguste, 217–18
Marcius Figulus, Gaius, xix–xx
Marcius Rex, Quintus, 33–34
Marcus Aurelius, 199–200
Maria (sister of Marius), 11–12
Marius, Gaius, xxiii–xxiv, 11–12, 27–28,
    105–6, 185–86
Marius, Marcus, 11–12
Marius Gratidianus, Marcus, 11–13
Massilia, 37–38
Middleton, Conyers, 212, 215
Minucius, 37–38, 117–18
Mirabeau, 215–16
misericors, misericordia, 69–71, 78, 96–97
Mithradates VI Eupator, xxiii–xxv,
    15–17
Mithradatic War, Third, 28–29
Mons Albanus, 160–61
Montemagno, Buonaccorso da, 202–3,
    205–6, 209–10
Morgan, Piers, 83–87
Mulvian Bridge, 42–45, 122–23,
    141–42

Nanneius, 12–13
Napoleon III, 40–41
narration, use of, 137–49

Nero, 25–26, 196–97
Nerva, 52–54
novus homo/new man, 1, 2, 11–12, 13–14,
    19–20, 40–41, 118–19, 196–97, 232
Numantia, 185–86

Obsequens, 155n.51
occultatio, 96, 154–55
o fortunatam natam, 159–60
o tempora, o mores, xix–xx, 210–11, 213

Palazzo Madama, 35–36
papyri, 81–82n.46, 201–2, 241–43
patria, 98–99, 109–11, 150–51, 160–61,
    169–70, 181, 183, 210–11
patricians, 9–10, 20–23, 35–37, 40–41,
    129, 136, 141, 199–200
Pellegrin, Simon-Joseph, 213–15
Pepys, Samuel, 211–12
Pericles cup, 241–43
Perseus of Macedon, 52–54, 185–86
Petreius, Marcus, 52, 205n.39, 206–8, 210–11
Picenum, 33
Pinarius Natta, Lucius, 23
Pistoria (Pistoia), 52, 202–5, 206–7
Pliny the Elder, 10–11, 46–47, 61–62n.15,
    118–19
Pliny the Younger, 57
Plutarch
  Life of Brutus, 171–72
  Life of Caesar, 57–169, 171–73
  Life of Cato the Younger, 23–26, 34,
    60–61, 166–67, 170–73,
    243–44
  Life of Cicero, xxiii–xxiv, 9n.11,
    11–12, 18–19n.34, 20–23,
    30–32, 34, 35–36n.61, 37–
    38n.64, 42, 42–44n.71, 44–45,
    50–51, 76–77, 101–2, 118–20,
    150–51, 160n.62, 166–69,
    170–75, 190–91, 208, 209–10,
    215–16, 235

Poggio Bracciolini, 201–2
Pompeian dipinti, 244
Pompeius Magnus, Gnaeus, xxiii–xxv,
    67–68, 79–81, 118–19, 123–25,
    148–49, 161–62, 185–87
  children of, xxiii–xxiv, 209–10
Pompeius Magnus (Pius), Sextus, 195,
    196–97
Pompeius Rufus, Quintus, 33
Pompeius Strabo, Gnaeus, 12
Pomponius Atticus, Titus, 17–18, 59–62,
    65–67, 69, 73–75, 76–77, 80,
    81–82n.46, 113–14, 138, 158,
    182–83, 190–91
Pomptinus, Gaius, 44, 46–47, 122–23,
    141–42, 148–49
Porcius Cato, Marcus, xxi–xxiii, xxv,
    8, 23–25, 31, 42, 49–50, 60–61,
    76–77, 87–88, 166–67n.10,
    167–69, 171–75, 188–89,
    190–91, 194, 195, 197–99, 204,
    206–7, 210–11
  bowl bearing name of; see bowls
    bearing names of Catiline and
    Cato
Porcius Laeca, Marcus, 34, 35, 92–93,
    94, 137–38, 201–2
Porcius Latro, Marcus, 209–10
Poulton, Mike, 211–12
Praeneste, 33
Prescott, John, 134–35n.31
proscriptions, 12–13, 19–20, 28–30,
    47–48, 60, 117–19, 132–34
prosopopoeia, 98–99, 109–10,
    210–11
prudentia, 151–52n.44, 154–55
Publicius, 37–38, 117–18
Publilia (second wife of Cicero),
    18–19n.34
Punic War, Second, 10–11
Puteal Scribonianum, 52–54
Pylos combat agate, 241–43

Quinctius, Publius, xix–xx
Quintilian, 57–59, 115–16n.38, 155n.51,
    155–56n.53, 201–2
Quo usque tandem ...? (Cat. 1.1),
    xix–xx, 35–36, 56, 61–63, 92–93,
    197–200, 210, 213

relegatio, 95–96
religion, exploitation of, 139, 149–62
Responsio Catiline, 202–3, 209–10
reticentia, 103–4
rex, regnum, 68–72, 110–11, 177, 182–83, 190
Robespierre, 215–16
Romulus, 150, 153–54, 155, 156–58,
    159–61
Roscius, Sextus, 13
Roscius Otho, Lucius, 119–20

Salieri, 217
Sallust, Bellum Catilinae, passim
  characterization of Catiline, 8–9,
    108, 197–99
  monograph, xxi–xxiii
  narrative compared with Cicero's,
    138–49
  not hostile to Cicero, xxi–xxiii,
    35–36, 92–93, 163, 197–99
  relationship to Catilinarians, 197–99
  sources, 197–99
  speech of Caesar, 49–50, 166–67
  speech of Cato, 49–50, 172
Sallust, Histories, 12–13
Sanzanome, 203–4
Saturnalia, 144–45
Saylor, Steven, 211–12
Scribonius Libo, 52–54
Sempronia (wife of Decimus Junius
    Brutus), 42–44, 139–40, 141,
    211–12
Sempronii Gracchi, 118–19
Sempronius Gracchus, Gaius, 31–32,
    146–47, 165–66

Sempronius Gracchus, Tiberius, 165–66
senatus consultum ultimum, 31–32, 50,
    67–68, 93–94, 166, 199–200,
    207–8
Seneca the Elder, 61–62
Seneca the Younger, 196–97, 206–7
Septimius Severus, 199–200
Sergestus, 10–11, 196
Sergii, 9–11, 196
Sergius Catilina, Lucius, *passim*
    ancestry, 10–11
    birth year, 9–10
    bowl bearing name of; *see* bowls
        bearing names of Catiline and
        Cato
    career, 12–52
    character, xxi–xxiii, xxv, 2–9, 40–41,
        106–8, 197–99
    coins commemorating defeat of,
        52–54
    companions on departure from
        Rome, 37–38, 94–95, 113–14
    death, 52
    declared a public enemy, 42, 109–10
    funeral, 55
    letter to Catulus, 37–41, 130–31,
        238–39
    murders allegedly committed by,
        12–13, 18–19, 96
    not a *popularis*, 128n.16
    "obituary" of, 5–6, 7, 108, 124–25,
        127
    omission of *praenomen*, 93–94
    plan to burn Rome, xxiii–xxiv, 1, 34,
        47, 94, 126–27, 143–44, 165–66,
        196–97
    prosecution of, threatened by Cato,
        25–26
    prosecution of, threatened by
        Paullus, 33
    surviving words of, 232–39
    trial for extortion, 14, 17–18, 96–97

trial for murders under Sulla, 20
trial for sexual misconduct, 14,
    40–41
Sergius Silus, Marcus (praetor 197),
    10–12
Sergius Silus, Marcus (quaestor 116 or
    115), 10–11n.16
Sertorius, Quintus, xxiv–xxv
Servilia (half-sister of Cato), 171–72
Servilius Rullus, Publius, 28–29, 118–
    19, 127, 128, 131–32
Sestius, Publius, 100–3
Sibyl, 195
Sibylline prophecies, 144–45, 146–47,
    150–51, 154, 182
Silius Italicus, 196–97
Simplicius, 62–63
slaves, 28–29, 33, 42–45, 47–48, 51, 69–
    71, 129, 130–31, 141–42, 143–44,
    146–47, 165–66, 169–70, 183,
    243
Social War, 12
soothsayers, 45–46, 144–45, 150–51,
    154, 155
Sostratos, 241–43
Spartacus, 28–29
Speer, Albert, 8
Statilius, Lucius, 42–47, 122–23, 140–41,
    144–45, 146–47, 164–65
Suetonius, 30n.53, 51n.91, 166–67,
    170–71, 172–73
Sulpicius, Gaius, 44–45, 142
Sulpicius Rufus, Servius, 20–23, 25–26,
    31, 42

Tacitus, xix–xx, 25–26, 199–200
Tanusius, Lucius, 12–13
Tarquinius, Lucius, 47–48
Tartarus, 194, 195, 196–97, 221–22
Terentia (first wife of Cicero), 13–14
Terentius, Gaius, 46–47
Tiberius, 170–71, 196–97, 199–200

Titinius, 12–13
Tongilius, 37–38, 117–18
Torre di Catilina, 203–4
Tullia (daughter of Cicero), 13–14
Tullius, Attius, 11–12
Tullius, Servius, 11–12
Tullius Cicero, Marcus (son of Cicero),
    17–18, 61–62, 77–78, 175,
    187–88
Tullius Cicero, Quintus, 20, 23, 156–58,
    170–71, 175
Tullius Tiro, Marcus, 18–19n.34, 57,
    60–61

Umbrenus, Publius, 42–44, 46–47,
    139–40, 141, 166
underworld, 132–34, 172, 194, 195,
    206–7, 219–21
Urania, 160–61

Valerius Flaccus, Lucius, 44–46, 122–23,
    141–42, 148–49, 190–91
Valerius Maximus, 233

Valesios, Poplios, 241–43
Vargunteius, Lucius, 34, 35, 45–47,
    131–32
Velleius, 166n.8, 171–72
Verres, Gaius, xix–xx, 14–15, 57–58
Vespasian, 52–54
Via Aurelia, 37–38
Via Cassia, 37–38, 42–44
Via Lata, 42–44
Villani, Giovanni, 203–5
Virgil, xxv, 10–11, 62–63, 194–95,
    196–97
Vitellius, 52–54
Volcacius Tullus, Lucius, 15
Voltaire, 213–15
Volturcius, Titus, 42–44, 45–46, 47–48,
    122–23, 126–27, 139, 141–47, 155
Volumnius, Marcus, 12–13

Warren cup, 241n.7
Watergate scandal, 217
Wilczek bronze, 62–63
Wilson, Robert, 206